Why Haven't You Left?

The Dinka Cross. In the late 1980s and early 1990s a great revival took place in the Diocese of Bor, Sudan. Thousands of Dinka people became Christians. Many sought a symbol of this new salvation, hope, and trust in God. Using the roots of ebony trees, they fashioned crosses like the one shown above. Often the crosses are decorated with brass rings created from the spent bullet cartridges scattered across the landscape because of the civil war in Sudan. Most Dinka Christians carry at least a simple wooden cross with them at all times. (Artwork used by permission of Trinity Church, New York.)

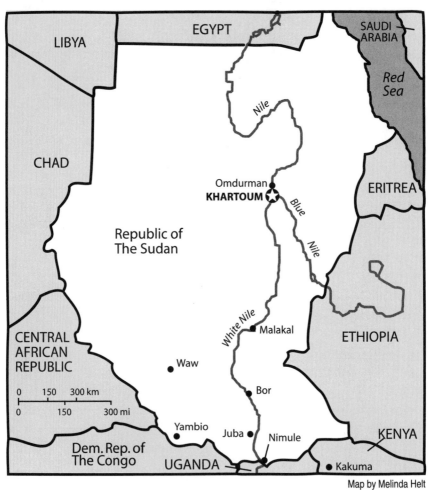

Map by Melinda Helt

Why Haven't You Left?

LETTERS FROM THE SUDAN

MARC NIKKEL

EDITED BY
GRANT LEMARQUAND

CHURCH PUBLISHING
an imprint of
Church Publishing Incorporated, New York

Library of Congress Cataloging-in-Publication Data

Nikkel, Marc R., d. 2000.
    Why haven't you left? : letters from the Sudan / by Marc Nikkel ;
edited by Grant LeMarquand.
      p. cm.
    Includes bibliographical references.
    ISBN 0-89869-472-8
    1. Missions – Sudan – Correspondence. 2. Nikkel, Marc R.,
d. 2000 – Correspondence. 3. Missionaries – Sudan – Correspondence.
I. LeMarquand, Grant, 1954- II. Title.
BV2121.S73N55 2005
266.009624 – dc22

                                    2006000467

Church Publishing Incorporated
445 Fifth Avenue
New York, NY 10016
www.churchpublishing.org

5 4 3 2 1

For the Martyrs of the Sudan

Contents

Abbreviations

ACROSS	Association of Christian Resource Organizations Serving Sudan
BBC	British Broadcasting Corporation
BGC	Bishop Gwynne College (located in Mundri until 1987 and in Juba since that time)
CMS	Church Missionary (now "Mission") Society
ECS	The Episcopal Church of the Sudan
ECUSA	The Episcopal Church of the United States of America
LWF	The Lutheran World Federation
NGO	Non-Governmental Organization
NSCC	New Sudan Council of Churches
OXFAM	Oxford Committee for Famine Relief
RC	Roman Catholic
RPG	Rocket-propelled grenade
SCF	Sudanese Christian Fellowship
SPLA	Sudanese People's Liberation Army
SPLM	Sudanese People's Liberation Movement
SRRA	Sudan Relief and Rehabilitation Association
UNHCR	United Nations High Commissioner for Refugees
UNICEF	United Nations Children's Emergency Fund
USAID	United States Agency for International Development
WCC	World Council of Churches
WFP	United Nations World Food Programme

Preface

It is a risky business tampering with someone else's mail, let alone editing a whole corpus of letters. In this volume I have attempted to add background material in footnotes and in short introductions that will enable the reader to understand the political, religious, and cultural contexts of Marc Nikkel's words a bit more fully. It should be noted that Marc had already begun this process of annotation himself. The letter of December 1994 is essentially an exegetical exercise in seeking to understand and explain the wonderful prayer of a Sudanese widow, Rebekah Lueth. Marc wrote most of the footnotes as a part of the original letter. The letter of October 1987 was annotated by Marc at my request and published in the journal *Anglican and Episcopal History* in a special issue devoted to the Sudan.[1] I have added some footnotes to that letter and changed some of Marc's first-person references to third-person references to avoid confusion. I have tried to keep references to secondary literature short in the footnotes — just using the author's name and a short version of the title. Those who desire to read further (and I hope that they are many) can consult the bibliography.

I have tried my best not to do damage to Marc's wonderful prose, which is so poignant, so staggeringly beautiful, and so moving that I am still brought to tears when I read the letters, although I have now read them all many, many times. I have taken the liberty of removing some of the redundancies that appear in the original typescripts. I have made the spelling consistent. Marc was a person of three continents who *tended* to use British rather than American spelling. With great regret and with apologies to my "home and native land" of Canada I have changed all of the spelling to American usage.

One of the most important editorial changes was the decision to use the term "Jieng" rather than "Dinka." In most of Marc's early letters he speaks of the largest ethnic group in southern Sudan as the "Dinka," the term by which they are commonly known outside of the Sudan. Later in his life, however, Marc began to speak of them by their preferred name, Jieng. In a paper published in 1997 he wrote, "Throughout this paper the name 'Jieng' has been used in place of the

---

1. "Essays on the Anglican Church in the Sudan," *Anglican and Episcopal History* 71, no. 2 (June 2002); many thanks to Prof. John Woolverton, the editor, for allowing that letter to be republished as a part of this book.

more familiar 'Dinka.' This is in deference to the term by which all Jieng know and refer to themselves, and by which many would prefer to be known in the outside world. The name 'Dinka' appears to be an early corruption of 'Jieng.' "[2] When Marc edited his October 1987 letter for publication, he changed "Dinka" to "Jieng" throughout. I have little doubt that had he lived to edit these letters himself he would have made the same change.

Many people deserve thanks for helping this project come to fruition. Among these are Allison Dokolo, Samuel Kayanga, Allison Abe Enosa, James Baak, Joseph Acuil, Abraham Nhial, Bishop Nathaniel Garang, Archdeacon John Kelei, Archdeacon Zechariah Kuol, and Andrew Wheeler for conversations about the Sudan, Bishop Gwynne College and Marc; Nancy Frank for sending artwork; Dr. Eleanor Johnson for finding something in an archive; Maxine Moore, Kristi Cobb, Lauren Ellis for computer help; Melinda Helt for producing the map; Dr. Ian Douglas for his enthusiasm for this project; Frank Tedeschi and Kenneth Arnold at Church Publishing in New York for their patience; Vina Sweetman and the Isaiah 40 Foundation in Montreal for providing a quiet and prayerful place to write; and especially Marvis and Sam Bergen for their desire to have this story told.

This is not a book about Marc Nikkel, although the reader will discover many things about him in these pages. This book is primarily the story of a suffering and faithful people as seen through the eyes of one who loved them. It is dedicated to all those who have given their lives for the sake of the gospel of Jesus in that land.

They shall hunger no more, neither thirst anymore; the sun shall not strike them, nor any scorching heat. For the Lamb in the midst of the throne will be their Shepherd, and he will guide them to the springs of living water, and God will wipe away every tear from their eyes. (Revelation 7:16–17)

Grant LeMarquand
The Feast of the Martyrs of Uganda 2005

2. " 'Children of our Fathers' Divinities' or 'Children of the Red Foreigners'?"

Why Haven't You Left?

Introduction

This book is a volume of letters written by one person. Since they are letters, and since they were penned over a twenty-year period, they are necessarily uneven in tone: some are joyful, some anxious; some are filled with faith, others express profound doubt. Because these words are written by one person, they manifest an intensely personal vision. In his correspondence with his friends and family Marc Nikkel presents his own perspective on a world, a world that in many ways is very different from his own.

Marc was an American, raised in a Mennonite home in California. He trained as an artist. As a young man he spent two periods of nine months in Africa — in Zaïre (now the Democratic Republic of the Congo) with his sister and brother-in-law who were missionaries there, and in Nigeria. He studied theology and mission at Fuller Seminary in Pasadena. During his time at Fuller he became attracted to Anglicanism and joined the Episcopal Church. He went to the Sudan in 1981 as a new and happy "convert" to Anglicanism, but his Anabaptist background, and especially the Mennonite commitment to peace and reconciliation, never left him.

After a term in Sudan Marc returned to the United States to study for ordination at General Theological Seminary in New York. It was during this year that we met. My wife, Wendy, and I had been considering a vocation as cross-cultural missionaries. In 1985 we traveled from Montreal to Toronto to meet with the staff of the World Mission office of the Anglican Church of Canada. Canada had had a commitment to a relationship with the Sudan, and especially with Bishop Gwynne College in Mundri.[1] Marc showed us slides of the college and spoke passionately about the students and the faculty. We were hooked. We looked forward to going to Sudan and to working in such a place. But since we had a baby in tow the staff of Church House in Toronto thought it unwise for us to go to the Sudan in the late 1980s. We were diverted to Kenya and told, "Wait until Sudan gets better." We lived in Kenya in 1987, 1988, and 1989.

---

1. The Rev. Fred Crabb (later archbishop) had become the first principal of the college in 1945. He and his wife, Marjory, stayed until 1951. The Rev. Ross and Mrs. Muriel Kreager represented the Anglican Church of Canada at Bishop Gwynne during the 1970s and 1980s.

In the meantime, Marc was ordained as a deacon in the United States and then returned to Sudan. He was ordained a priest in the chapel of Bishop Gwynne College in 1987. Later that year Marc was abducted from Mundri by the Sudanese Liberation Army.[2] After his release he was not able to return to Sudan immediately, but he did return to Africa — and lived next door to us for most of a year in Kenya. Our friendship was renewed as we shared life together for a time.

These letters are written, therefore, by an outsider, attempting, often with amazing fervor, to attempt to understand an "Other." Although loved by the people of the Sudan, and especially by the Jieng,[3] whose language and culture he knew possibly as well as any Westerner, Marc was always aware of a gap, a difference. Although he was known by Jieng names, he was not a Jieng. Even when he was called a "Dinka" he was a "white Dinka." This book, therefore, contains the views and opinions and judgments of one white, male, American "missionary."[4]

But this book is also about Sudan. Geographically Africa's largest nation, the Sudan has a painful history of civil conflict. It could be said that there have been, since the opening of the Nile basin in the mid-nineteenth century, over 140 years of civil war. During the twentieth century the Anglo-Egyptian Condominium (1898–1955) brought a period of relative calm, in part by isolating the largely black, African south of the country from the Arabized and Islamized north. But civil conflict erupted again in 1955, just prior to national independence, and continued until the Addis Ababa Peace Agreement of 1972, with the loss of at least half a million lives. The recent phase of Sudan's civil conflict, more devastating than any previous period, emerged in the territory of the Jieng on the east side of the Nile in 1983. By the year 2004, the twenty-one-year conflict was both the longest war in the world and probably the most costly in terms of human life, with over two million people dead due to war-related causes.[5] The Sudanese People's Liberation Army (the SPLA) and its political movement

---

2. See the letter of October 1987 (p. 57) for that story.

3. The "Jieng," widely known as "Dinka," are the largest ethnic group in Sudan. Alongside the Nuer, Shilluk, and Anuak, they are one of the great Nilotic pastoral peoples of Sudan, their traditional homelands spreading from Bahr el Ghazal in the west of southern Sudan, across to Upper Nile Province in the east.

4. Marc was well aware that his view was limited. Just before his death in September 2000 he wrote this: "When my friend Grant LeMarquand asked if he might copy and distribute my 'missionary letters' to his mission students for reflection, I had no problem. When, some months later, he asked if they might not be edited and published for the benefit of a wider audience, I said I wondered if they gave the full picture. Don't these letters in actuality represent but one very narrow and quite idiosyncratic perspective on my life and work abroad? Weren't they the 'set pieces' prepared by one Westerner in a foreign context putting his own life and work on display for folk in his land of origin?"

5. It is crucial to recognize that although many of the deaths that have occurred in the Sudan since the 1980s have been due to starvation and disease, these plagues have largely been of human origin. Not only has the war cut off southern Sudan from food and medical aid from the outside, but the troops of the government of Sudan have often targeted civilian infrastructures. Schools, hospitals,

(the SPLM) emerged as the main military and political faction opposing the government of Sudan.

What kind of "liberation" has the SPLA sought? At first the SPLA claimed to be fighting on behalf of all oppressed Sudanese peoples, north and south, who suffer under the domination of the "elite ruling clique in Khartoum," referring to several powerful northern Arab families who have monopolized political power since national independence in 1955. During the 1990s the territory claimed by the SPLA encompassed southern Sudan and the Nuba Mountains. Since a coup in 1989 the government of Sudan has been under the control of the National Islamic Front, whose stated objective has been to make of Sudan an Islamic state, and to that end has imposed *shari'a* (Islamic law) on the entire country. The economic objectives of the government encompass control of Sudan's significant oil wealth, all located in the ancestral lands of southern peoples; the waters of the Nile River, which control the development of northeast Africa, especially the Sudan, Ethiopia, and Egypt; and the fertile agricultural lands of the south. Literally for millennia the encounter between north and south has been marked by racial, economic, educational, and political inequality. In all of these spheres southern Sudanese have demanded liberation with full self-determination.

But a desire for a new form of liberation has sprouted up in recent years. Transcending, but certainly not excluding, the political, economic, social, and racial issues of this war, the people of southern Sudan have en masse begun to embrace a quest for a religious and spiritual revolution. As their traditional ways of life as pastoral and agricultural peoples have been shattered, the many and varied African ethnic groups of southern Sudan have turned from their ancient deities, who have been exposed as powerless and impotent in the face of war, disease, starvation, and slavery. In place of, or in addition to, their old traditions, hundreds of thousands, perhaps millions of Sudanese have turned to a God who suffers with them, a God seen in the anguish and abandonment of the cross.

Marc's letters bear witness to the agony and torment of a people — but they are also eloquent testimony of a profound transformation taking place in the midst of misery. Although the witness and perspective of these letters is Marc's very personal description, it is also a sympathetic account, an angle of vision that seeks to understand what God is doing in a situation of pain. And so this is also a book about hope and joy and new life. Marc agreed to allow these letters to be published, not because he wanted his own story told, but because he wanted the story of the people and the church of southern Sudan to be known.

---

and churches were the targets of bombing, crops were burned and cattle were slaughtered, and fields were sewn with land mines.

These letters do also contain the story of Marc's own suffering, his own joy, his own faith and his struggle to know God's ways. Marc was diagnosed with stomach cancer in 1998. Amazingly, he was granted two years, two very full years, in which he continued to write and work (when he could) for the benefit of the people of Sudan. Those who knew Marc could not often read his letters without tears. But we also read them with great thankfulness for Marc, for his life, for his work, and for his love for the Sudan.

Part One

Life in "the Village of God"

Pre-War Letters, 1981–83

On the night of July 20, 1964, soldiers of the government of Sudan surrounded the compound of Bishop Gwynne College, where Bishop (later archbishop) Elinana Ngalamu had stopped for the night on his way to Jerusalem for church meetings.[1] The government had expelled all of the missionaries from the country in February and March of that year, suddenly leaving the young Episcopal Church in charge of its own affairs for the first time. At about 3:00 a.m. the soldiers attempted to arrest the bishop and the staff and students of the college. In the confusion all but one person escaped, the bishop himself hiding in a ditch. When morning came the bishop and the whole college community evacuated and began a three-month journey to the Congo and from there on to Uganda, where many southern Sudanese spent the rest of this, independent Sudan's first civil war, in exile.

Bishop Gwynne College, named after Llewellyn Gwynne, the first Church Missionary Society (CMS) missionary to Sudan as well as the first Anglican bishop in the Sudan,[2] was for many years the sole Protestant theological college in the Sudan. The Yei Divinity School, founded in 1945, was moved to what became the town of Mundri[3] in 1947, Mundri being considered a much more central location for Anglican mission work at the time. The third principal, David Brown, called BGC "The Village of God," and throughout its history it has lived up to that designation as a place where Christian character was formed in the context of a Christian community of work and worship and study. In 1975, three years after Sudan's first civil war had ended, the Rev. Eluzai Munda returned from Nigeria, where he had been studying theology, and brought a group of students from Juba to Mundri to refound Bishop Gwynne College.

Before Marc Nikkel arrived in Mundri, just a few months shy of his thirty-first birthday, he was told that one could find the place by going to the end of the world, and then going on from there for another hundred miles or so. In 1981, BGC was still

---

1. I am dependent for this story on the article "Life in the Village of God" by Andrew Wheeler.
2. See H. C. Jackson, *Pastor on the Nile: A Memoir of Bishop Ll. H. Gwynne.*
3. "Mundri did not exist at the time — it was an empty area of bush" (Wheeler, "Life in the Village of God," 105).

rebuilding. At the time Marc was still a layperson. He taught anthropology, psychology, and worship. Most importantly he spent weekends and extended college vacation times in Jieng cattle camps learning the language, absorbing traditional culture, and learning to love the Jieng people.

Marc's first public letters, sent to friends who had agreed to pray for and give Marc moral support, are full of hope. He was evidently delighted by the sounds and sights and smells of Africa around him and most obviously engrossed in the work of helping to shape the lives and ministries of the students of the college. And yet already in this pre-war period there is a shadow of death in these letters, a strong hint of anxiety about the future. A student returns to campus after the two-month vacation having lost seven nieces and nephews to diseases that would have been curable in the West. Several of the letters look back at the seventeen years of conflict that had ended and look forward wondering if more fighting, more war, is to come. Indeed, shortly before Marc's letter of July 1983 events that were set in motion would lead Sudan into a further and even more destructive civil war.

The picture of "life in the village of God" presented in these letters is not a portrait of an insulated "institution of higher learning" divorced from the realities of sickness, political instability, and social unrest, but a place where the issues and questions of human reality could be brought into God's presence in serious reflection in the context of a caring and praying Christian community.

Bishop Gwynne College
1981

Dear Ones at St. Luke's and other branches of the Family,

It is Sunday, March 21. This morning I awoke to my first Sudanese sunrise from my own back porch. Overhead the full moon still floated. 5:30 a.m. is not too early, for the natural glow of the sun is easier to work in than late hours by kerosene lantern. Within half an hour I spotted at least ten kinds of birds: herons, a crane, a stork; songs of unseen birds weave through the air. There is a gnarled "bo-bo" tree[4] out back that serves as shade when its leaves are full. Beyond that, dry grass and trees that will become a garden; still further, the seemingly limitless savannah disappears eastward in deciduous trees and underbrush. Now, as I write, the rains come, in that even tut-tut-tut on the tin roof; now hard, now soft, veiling the Bishop Gwynne campus in cool gray. I look from my study window through mosquito screen and a metal grill, no glass. This is a good, solid house remaining from before the war:[5] cement floor and walls of beige, locally made brick. The

---

4. A substantial tree that produces a sweet fruit.

5. The Anglo-Egyptian agreement of 1953 called for Sudanese independence from the British colonial administration within three years. This plan, however, was not acceptable to many people in

doors, their frames, and the window frames (sadly, they are all painted aqua blue) are made of hard African teak and mahogany to fend off the termites. There is a living room, a study, a bedroom, with a washroom attached (a cement area with a drain; two buckets, and a cup); a kitchen with its door from the porch; and the outhouse lingering at forest's edge. That's home: I am delighted.

The Bishop Gwynne College campus is a large sprawl of land alongside a river with scattered buildings set perhaps a half mile outside the sleepy Moru[6] village town of Mundri. "BGC" must have been one colonial mission showpiece prior to the war: several massive stone and thatch houses for the European staff; a great half circle of perhaps twenty-five sizable student dwellings, each of stone or brick, thatched in grass, looking for all the world like a transplanted English village, circa 1550. But idyllic thatch takes easily to flame and most buildings were razed with the heat of civil war.

But now is the resurrection. Each building, built anew or reconstructed, is sought for, brick by brick, by pipe and piece of tin in this rural place. Tin replaces thatch for practicality. There are three substantial houses for instructors, one block of three classrooms, a sprinkling of smaller dwellings for students and staff. Finally, central to all, there is the skeleton of the old stone chapel witnessing both to the heritage of worship and of war. The grounds are hardly manicured, with footpaths and roads of dirt, and dry grasses that will spring to green in this new season of rain. There are many trees and much space.

In my travels I have met all the staff now. Benniah Poggo, the principal, and David Kamandalah are bright and committed men, holding a vision for their church. Robin and Mary Ann Anker-Peterson (theology, Oxford, Cambridge)

---

the south and so, even before Sudanese independence became official on January 1, 1956, there were several riots and military mutinies that soon degenerated into civil war, known widely as the "Anya-nya Revolt." All missionaries were expelled in 1964. There were massacres of Christians and other southerners in 1965. Bishop Gwynne College itself was overrun and destroyed, the college community going into exile in Uganda. Partly through the mediation of the World Council of Churches, peace was achieved in 1972 with the signing of the Addis Ababa Agreement (for details see Werner et al., *Day of Devastation*, 364–442). The college was refounded in Mundri in 1975 (see Wheeler, "Life in the Village of God," 109). Marc's mention of the "war" here in the first paragraph of his letters is an ominous sign of the events to come.

6. The Moru are one of the smallest of Sudan's 114 language groups. Their homeland is north of Juba in Western Equatoria at the heart of southern Sudan. They are an agricultural people who proved remarkably receptive to formal education and to the Christian message, both brought to their region since the 1920s by emissaries of the Church Missionary Society under the leadership of Kenneth Fraser. (On the history of the church among the Moru see Peter Obadayo Tingwa, *The History of the Moru Church in Sudan*; on Fraser see the article by Roger Sharland, "Kenneth Grant Fraser: Mission, Evangelism and Development among the Moru," and the book by Eileen Fraser, *The Doctor Comes to Lui*.) Given the Moru prominence in the early history of the Episcopal Church as well as the easy accessibility of the territory by road for other southern ethnic groups, the small rural village of Mundri was selected as the home of Bishop Gwynne College, intended to be the theological training center for leadership from across the country.

are Danish. Andy and Sue Wheeler are English (history, Cambridge). All are energetic, easy, and relaxed folk about my age. The teaching schedule may be quite
a challenge, this being the first year in BGC's post-war life that all three seminary
years are being taught simultaneously: each of four full-time tutors may be responsible for eight courses, sixteen teaching hours per week! My lot will include liturgy
and worship (how's that for a new Anglican!), and four potential-laden courses
on doctrine: Creation; Salvation; God and Incarnation; Christian Initiation and
Growth. In part, it means using the perceptions, values, and visions of a people
and with these probing the meanings of these great theological foundations. The
new term begins on April 27. It is a little breathtaking.

I would like to write on, describing individuals I have met, forms of worship, the
Nile, even a theology of orange drink for holy communion . . . but these will wait.
I am finding a new home that is far more than I had been led to anticipate — in
warm enthusiastic coworkers, in intellectual/spiritual stimulation, even overload,
in a lovely rural habitation, and even in accommodations and provisions.

The negatives? Oh, well apart from a walk to the pit latrine in the downpour,
there is the ubiquitous weevil who scrambles to a refuge atop your cereal when the
milk flood comes. There is the myriad of lizards — foot-long orange/white/black
ones, streamlined iridescent blue ones, and the fat black ones who wriggle beneath
the ceiling mats when you enter the room. There are snakes beneath the house
that keep the rodent population down and termites that surreptitiously devour
your books without asking. Yes, the place is alive, at times startlingly so. But that
life too is perhaps a good thing. *I am very, very glad to be here.* I live sparsely at
present: my goods should be received in Khartoum this week. I am not now able
to travel to meet them because my passport and travel permit have not been
released, a process not to be hurried. But hopefully they will come.

For your assistance, your support, your prayers, and your letters I am very
grateful. As I told a large congregation yesterday, there is much I would like to
communicate from my people back home to the community of faith here, and just
as much, or more, I would like to transmit back to you. I am here both as teacher
and as learner, hopefully for the enriching of this diverse Body of our Lord.

My affection,
Marc Nikkel

Bishop Gwynne College
December 26, 1981

To the Folk at Home,
'Twas the day before Christmas, 5:00 a.m., just before the sky begins to glow
in the cool morning of early dry season. By star and torch light I walk the dirt

road out of the college, the winding pot-holed road through the drying millet gardens, and down the grass path shortcut, past the defunct grinding mill into our village of Mundri. The helter-skelter tin roofs cut the darkness, offering a cool, gentle light. The mango trees that will shade the morning market are black billows on pedestals that sink their tentacles into the hard-pounded earth where four dozen mamas will later squat to sell their produce. Only two industrious folk, black bent shapes, whisk their brooms of branches, cleaning the turf for the day ahead. Apart from them, an aggressively crowing cluster of roosters, and a couple of fumbling goats, the place is silent, even the Jieng butcher's shed of teak poles and tin which will be the site of Christmas morning's greatest scratch, claw, and shuffle (everyone wants fresh meat for Christmas Day but without refrigeration the same slaughtered bull will be battled over to serve five hundred communal Christmas bowls).

One sharp light slashes the night down the road beyond the market's edge. As I walk nearer it appears that half a dozen school desks are clustered tightly to share the white umbrella of one kerosene pressure lamp. What possible motivation gets people working before dawn in southern Sudan? It is boom season for the tailors on these last days before Christmas. The men pump their cast iron wheels and keep the needles flying to meet the unending imperatives of Christmas Day. Everyone in every village needs his new shirt or trousers, her new dress. This is the one time of the year when the often lethargic tailor who sits with head cupped in hands over his machine is called on to sew at breakneck speed and make his mint. A shower of night greetings exchanged, and I move on to the police post at the far end of town.

Three *suuk* lorries (market trucks) are randomly parked on both sides of the teak pole barricade. Dark, man-sized cocoons are scattered over the ground around them like corpses after a great battle. These are last night's travelers, for by law in southern Sudan all transport must stop after 6:00 p.m. to spend the night at the next police post. And so you take a sheet, a blanket, an extra *jalabiyya*[7] and curl up with your compadres on the open ground until the morning breaks. The cocoons squirm and moan as the sky begins to warm behind the small, squared building. With its one-room office, three cluttered desks, and simple veranda (the shady talk spot at this end of town), its barred jail door, and angular tin cap, it seems for all the world like a Dodge City sheriff's office, circa 1850, with a dash of North Africa thrown in. The green suited policemen emerge in the slow light going about absent-minded routines. Six or eight prisoners are released from the tiny urine-smelling cell to fetch water and assist in sweeping the grounds.

---

7. A loose, full-length robe common in Arabic cultures.

After asking, in my broken Arabic, every possible lorry driver if there be any transport for Rumbek, I lay my pack on the veranda and begin the wait . . . hoping, that since there are no overnighters, a vehicle will be leaving Juba early to course through Mundri within three hours. There is never any knowing, but as the hours pass numerous encouragers assure me one will be coming. Nine hours, three *Time* magazines, two books, and a dozen conversations later . . . not one vehicle has passed heading for the regional headquarters on this day before Christmas.

Thankfully boisterous, buoyant Adam offers me a boost of thick sweet coffee as I trudge my way back to Bishop Gwynne College. Hopes for the holidays with my Jieng friend Abraham Mayom Athian Deng are clouded in the warm afternoon dust of the lorry that never came. Christmas in the land of the Jieng would have meant a bustling compound with Mayom's father, his three wives, and the plethora of extended family. In part, it would have meant the feast of the slaughtered goat or ox, leaping Jieng dancing in the town square, and cattle songs[8] galore.

But such are the limitations of transport in Sudan. Plans must always allow a couple of extra days for getting there or getting out, and then for the possible failure of getting there at all. In ten months of footing it or mounting the sporadic set of wheels, I have learned much of the limitations of my friends in Sudan . . . and gained an enormous anticipation for a soon-to-arrive little Suzuki four-wheel drive.

This was the prelude to Christmas Day 1981, which turned out mostly to be a day of much-needed rest after the past hard-driving months. During the last term of our academic year at this tiny rural college, I attempted to cover a mountain of material, guide our students toward the ten final examinations each would take, write the exams, grade them, offer re-sits, and try, in three days, with our skeletal staff to pull off graduation, complete with government dignitaries and a very indigenous nativity play worthy of the occasion. A day after graduation I lorried my way to Juba on top of a load of oranges to test and interview applicants for next academic year, and then lumbered on overcrowded, overheating buses to other archdeaconry centers for further testing. I am responsible for testing in two of Sudan's four dioceses.[9] A year is ended, one calendar year away from the United States, and a first academic year at the seminary of the Episcopal Church in the Province of the Sudan. It is a time for rites of passage, both for me and for my students. For the present, I am thankful the year is over, and I am feeling just

---

8. On the importance of cattle in Jieng culture see Marc's letter of June 9, 1994 (p. 113). The writing and singing of songs in honor and praise of their cows is an essential feature of the traditional life of the Jieng.

9. At the foundation of the Episcopal Church of the Sudan in 1976 there were four dioceses: Juba, Yambio, Rumbek, and Khartoum. By 1999, when the centenary of the coming of Anglicanism to the Sudan was celebrated, there were twenty-four dioceses.

a bit triumphant. On January 4 I will travel with the archbishop of Sudan, Elinana Ngalamu[10] and Bishop Benjamina to the east-side-of-the-Nile Jieng city of Bor with missions and confirmations along the way. These two wizened, patriarchal leaders of the church are men who have buoyantly survived the civil war and retained the vision to hold the Christians of this huge, fragmented land together. I am privileged to go with them (thankfully in the archbishop's Land Rover). Beyond this trip I will continue to Rumbek with a small library, a notebook, and a sketchpad to participate in the life of the cattle camps and villages of the Jieng for six weeks.

My thoughts are often with the friends back home. I realize there has been some concern as Sudan's threats and scuffles have been in the news. You are likely to know more than any of us here, for Sudan is a vast land with poor communications and poorer roads. A skirmish in one region seldom affects life in another, except of course for an all-encompassing civil war. We expatriates are well cared for and could be whisked out if there were any sizable threat. Most of us feel quite well nested and safe. My lack of letters has been simply due to the drive of work.

My thanks for the *Time* and *National Geographic* magazines and the smatter of other volumes. The newsmags particularly are a great gift in keeping the mind linked to the larger world, are read cover to cover on those long rides, and are often perused by a dozen other eyes as they get handed around. I am grateful for that caring enrichment in this faraway place.

My thanks and my love to you in this New Year,
Marc Nikkel

Bishop Gwynne College
December 31, 1981

To My Friends and Family

A sorghum harvest gathered, a rite of passage passed, a grade of age transcended, one academic year is cast: graduation day at Bishop Gwynne College. Seven men and one woman, hopefully deepened for their efforts, move on to assault the potholed roads beyond the college. A year is done for me as well,

---

10. Born in 1917 near Mundri, Elinana Ngalamu, a Moru, was the first archbishop of the Sudan. He studied at Bishop Gwynne College, was made deacon in 1953 and priest in 1955, although it appears that his real conversion seems to have taken place in a revival movement that swept through Moru land in the early 1960s. He was imprisoned in 1962 because of his preaching. He served as assistant bishop to Oliver Allison and was made the first archbishop of the Episcopal Church of the Sudan in 1976. Elinana became a controversial figure late in his life when he was involved on one side of a schism in the ECS, a division that was healed in 1992, shortly before his death (see Samuel Kayanga, "Archbishop Elinana J. Ngalamu," 181–82).

one year away from the United States, one academic year "tutoring" in Sudan. With my students I look back over a period at BGC and then to the peculiar importance of this nestled institution.

In contrast to many of my expatriate comrades, whether their work is agriculture, education, or medicine, in what is everywhere called a "developing nation," my attitudes seem relentlessly (naïvely?) hopeful and laden with anticipation. I feel privileged to be in this land at a forest-shrouded college campus still resurrecting from the devastation of a seventeen-year civil war: a place where I perceive the life-breathing Spirit of God very much at work.

I admit I sometimes look around and think what a motley, ill-formed, haphazardly administrated conglomerate it is. Our students often have no more than intermediate school (junior high equivalent) and some have attained the pinnacle of secondary (high) school. While all pass an English entrance exam, many struggle painfully to grasp a textbook and must look up words through the night to keep pace. Through six months of the year students are in their gardens by sunrise at 5:00 a.m. (and back in the afternoon) in order to support their families . . . and the college. They study into the night by flickering kerosene lantern and cannot study at all after dark when the kerosene supply runs out, as happened twice last year.

The teaching load is carried by three full-time and two part-time tutors who also shoulder the counseling, pastoral, and many administrative responsibilities (to say nothing of the time for maintenance of equipment or obtaining and preparing food in a secluded rural place). Each full-time person tries to carry seven separate courses through the year along with a diocesan chaplaincy. There is but one overloaded secretary whose varied responsibilities keep me typing most of my own mimeograph stencils. Our acting principal, Benaiah Poggo, is a valiantly hard-working man who labors six days a week and spends the seventh in his field for twelve hours. Along with the college administration, teaching, and overseeing construction of buildings, he is head of religious education at the local secondary school, where he also teaches. (Add to this a battery of high-level church meetings and you have good reason for coming down with a ten-week bout of malaria.)

We have a weekly staff meeting that rambles on for three to five hours, covering an array of items including house repair, student counseling, curriculum, and the sale of a school bull. (African administrative technique is not quite what some individuals of other cultures might desire.)

Because few students have any sort of raincoat and tropical rains come in thick wet walls, school generally closes for its entire 7:00 a.m. to 1:00 p.m. day if the morning starts off with hard rain. School may also be spontaneously canceled for a passing dignitary or an unanticipated new holiday.

At year's beginning I had no textbooks for any course, no course outline, nor even a bibliography of our library's mostly out-of-date volumes. There were shelves of books, maybe twenty feet, which had been devoured by termites whose tunnels laced volumes together during a month-long period when the staff was absent.

We have but one rickety mimeograph machine that now leaves a crease of white through each copy, and, naturally, plush carbon paper substitutes for a photocopy machine. We have one lethargic Land Rover, which should have been interred years ago and which demands no end of creative new stopgap repairs.

Graduation two weeks ago was a wish and a promise with me lettering certificates through the last staff meeting the night before and typing the program until twenty minutes prior to take off.

With these tattered edges we call it a "college"? A vital place of education for the forming of church leaders? Observe our southern Sudanese environment, and through it glimpse our little college. Most schools of the south are in a bleak and impaired condition. Whether due to north/south prejudice and resulting inadequate funding, or tribal finagling, or misappropriation of funds by men of power, or the instability in these decades of cultural transition, it is a fact that many secondary schools are in session less than half of the scheduled academic year. (One American teacher taught only forty teaching days out of a nine-month year; an Englishman at a Teacher Training Institute taught forty-four days out of two academic years!) School supplies — books, notebooks, desks, blackboards, maintenance supplies — simply do not exist in many institutions. Classrooms are overcrowded, as with one local primary teacher who labors to channel the energies of 150 children who sit on logs or on the mud floor under a grass roof. Teachers' salaries (as with those of medical personnel and low-level government posts) are often delinquent by four to six months and longer and often never compensated for. Lethargy is rampant among the shapers of the nation's young minds. Student cheating on exams is found at all levels and allowed, sometimes even encouraged. Angry, unqualified, and inept students blur with those gifted and would-be disciplined students, and all of them know they are somehow not being truly educated. In recent years secondary school riots seem on the rise as in the case of our local school where the principal was bludgeoned by students over a food shortage he could not control: another good reason for truncating the academic year. With such conditions good teachers leave their work, and quality declines yet further.

It is in this unsteady, turbulent educational environment that we find ourselves at Bishop Gwynne College. Therefore the significance of our efforts, the importance of the institution, and the standards we manage to attain are all amplified. This motley spot, whether dusty in the dry season or overgrown in the wet, is perceived by many as the Olympus of Theological Education in Sudan. BGC lost only ten days of the last academic year, quite a phenomenal record! Most of its students arrived on time and departed after graduation (in contrast to institutions which have a month or two slack period at both ends of the school year). Each of our tutors, whether expatriate or national, has an authentic sense of vocation and inner spiritual commitment to teaching and to forming the lives of our students. Whether we are infinitely skilled communicators or not, our commitment offers a very special and powerful facet not so easily found. When teachers are barely keeping their own bellies from shriveling, vocation and commitment are rather elusive ideas.

It is difficult to write of our students. Words like "brilliant" and "ingenious" come to mind for some... words that perhaps should never be used and which naturally take on quite a different meaning here. They arise with all the "givens" that must be linked to any description... given the limitations, the impediments to creative thought, to vision, to breadth of knowledge, given the dearth of books... given these, we have a number of exceptional students. It is partly that we and the church select only a few of those dozens who pass our examinations and who are proven in their communities. I could write a dozen biographies on these folk who have survived the civil war and give them honors for the creative ways many have established their lives since... and pay tribute to others simply for the ability to maintain an enormous garden, feed a family with hardly any funds, and maintain a considerable academic load to boot!

Perhaps the greatest wonder and pleasure is that most of these men and women, average age about thirty-two, are hungry, even desperate, to learn. It is both a great privilege and responsibility to attempt to meet the expectations and aspirations of such people who realize this is likely their only opportunity for "higher" education. Course content and teaching style in such a setting provoke questions I could not pretend to answer after one year. However, I would say that each of the staff is concerned about the "formation" of people, ourselves included, more than the didactic relay of blackboard notes, which is the persisting tradition. One belief I have, contrary to many expatriate teachers, is that Sudanese students can handle a good measure of abstract thought and synthesis if ideas are somehow made relevant to their own lives. The further I trust and challenge these people, the more I see them coming to their own living solutions to the deepest problems of their societies. Given that I am responsible for doctrine courses, along with liturgy and worship, anthropology, spiritual formation, and counseling (yes, impossible)... there are endless questions as to how each facet of theology and spirituality or each principle of human psychology may find its expression in the diverse collection of peoples that is Sudan. For this unlikely task I see the only answer in having a working partnership with students. I supply some raw material and attempt to provoke their living questions. They supply the case studies. From our differing sides we seek solutions, whether in the light of biblical revelation or the social sciences. Students remark that this way of study is not to be found elsewhere in the land. For me it is an immeasurable pleasure to challenge these potential-laden people.

Along with these notations on the progress and potential of the college goes the physical resurrection that is as real as all others. In my ten months not fewer than five larger and smaller buildings have arisen from the bushy tombs of pre-war foundations. In part aided by the gifts of partner churches, concrete, wood, and corrugated zinc combine to house the inner life that is ever more astir. Likewise, the library is making acquisitions for a broader academic foundation, and we instructors share the hope that we will have student texts for most courses next year.

The fumbling first moments of this raising up, this death to life, this post-baptismal rite, contain more hope, more possibility, than appearances betray. Four post-war graduating classes exhibit an ever-rising standard and a slowly refining influence in Sudan. Despite ourselves, I hear some students speak of changes from inside themselves. They have grown in maturity and become more thinking people. And still further, deeper, the metamorphosis continues ever more clearly bearing the image of the Risen Christ. Students and staff, alone, together, are asking questions of the inner life with God. This is the place of the true rite of passage; here real rebirthing moves unseen for the life of Bishop Gwynne College, and the hope of southern Sudan.

Marc Nikkel

Bishop Gwynne College
October 16, 1982

Dear Friends at St. Luke's,

It seems an eternity since we've talked. I have begun plodding off my words to you — and stopped midway, unsure just what hits your spots. Is it that our worlds are so different or my words too distant? It has been eight months since I have received any letters from you, except for one. I peck my words into an uncertain space and hope for some response. I am still Marc, just in Sudan now, two years later.

Mundri, Bishop Gwynne College, is more than ever home: at last, as of yesterday, I have running water in my kitchen. We open our third and last term the day after tomorrow to end just before Christmas. Students climb off the overloaded market lorries, bringing bundles and stories from home. I listen as they speak and sometimes wonder how uncertain, even unjust, this land can be.

Lado, dear Lado, has become such a different man in these two years. His thin, scarred body, often bowed head and quiet, meditative manner seemed flickering, uncertain two years ago. He now has an articulate, intent perception of himself, his people. In two months away from home seven children had died, seven children of his brothers and sisters: dead. The simple things — malaria, worms — the illnesses a couple of pills can treat. These younger children would have grown to support Lado in his ministry ahead. His people cannot cry. No tears remain, only sadness.

I remember Shaderaka's return after first-term break. In three months ten family members died. His twelve-year-old son was comatose, laden with fever. Sue gave him drugs and he flew for the next lorry to rumble him the two days home. The boy lived. The *dawa*, the drugs come in — all free — from UNICEF and a myriad of agencies. Last month two tons "disappeared" from the tiny Juba airport. Sometimes you can buy them in the dark shops along the road if you know the proprietor. Several tons of medicine await shipment from Khartoum, but funds have been so haplessly shifted that not even money for road transport remains. Today there are no drugs in much of the southern region.

Forcing Arab administration in government schools is not well received by black peoples of Sudan's south. It was seventeen years of civil war, but it shakes me how often you hear it said: there will be another. Skirmishes continue. Ibrahim came by: two churches were destroyed last week by Muslims in the north. This is where our students, future pastors, will work.

I am only a thick-headed white foreigner. I hear of death. I sense the numb and stolid determination of my friends. But I am shielded from taking it in. My five hundred lavish dollars a month in an American account protect me from starvation; my plush library of three hundred volumes feeds my mind from worlds beyond; my doctor friends provide any cure for the body; and an airplane whisks me out at a moment's disruption. And most of all I am privileged to feel hope.

I look at our little college and my soul seems full to the brim with love and awe. How I respect these thirty-six students. What integrity in this searching after faith. Last term twenty-two sat around my living room two times a week for a class called "Christian Spirituality." How they sought for the God who invites us to know him. And in knowing calls us to truth, and justice, to understanding of another human life. In the middle of our meetings with the desert fathers[11] or with Thomas Merton,[12] came visits from African elders and holy men. The

---

11. "Desert fathers" is a term widely used to refer to the third- and fourth-century monks of Syria, Asia Minor (modern Turkey), and especially Egypt, who sought a life with God by withdrawing into the desert. The best known of these figures is St. Anthony (c. A.D. 251–356).

12. Thomas Merton (1915–68) was a Roman Catholic Trappist monk and author, known both for his dedication to the spiritual life and for his commitment to political transformation and justice.

sorcerers and diviners, the magicians and oracle readers were interrogated as well: "Who is the Spirit of God?" the students asked. And how well have our ancestors known him? I had few answers but was so moved in the presence of our hours together.

This term I will "teach" (lead a meandering dialogue) in three courses. There will be "Creation," a potpourri of theology, anthropological theology, and theological anthropology including sexism, racism, and questions like: "Where is the Garden?" "What kind of fruit?" and "Was the first sin sex?" Then "Psychology 1," a first attempt to invoke Freud or Rogers around the campfire or in mud huts. Regardless, students have pleaded for it since I came. And, finally, "Liturgy and Worship": threads of Anglicanism with the pulse of African souls (my own psychic battle is more often with "Onward Christian Soldiers" and "Fairest Lord Jesus" than with my students' wobbly theology or their malformed leading of Morning Prayer).

In it all there is a sense of becoming which is beyond any of us staff. Shaffer's frightening words in *Equus* come to mind: "In an ultimate sense I cannot know what I do in this place — yet I do ultimate things. Essentially I cannot know what I do — yet I do essential things."[13] Across this vast and lovely land blow disheartening winds. I am so much a part, and yet hardly part at all. From my small place I feel hope and am supremely thankful for this time and place to work. Please write soon.

With love,

Marc Nikkel

Mundri, Sudan
July 14, 1983

The past three months have been rather tenuous times for many of us in southern Sudan. Rumors of armed conflict and possible war fill the air. Some weeks have been particularly tense, and during these times Christians have been drawn together closely in prayer. The following intercessions were made by a young woman, perhaps twenty-five years of age, who is the mother of three small children. As believers have often done during these uncertain times, she recalls the lessons which were learned during the seventeen years of civil war, lessons which often are too easily forgotten.

Marc Nikkel

---

13. Peter Shaffer's *Equus*, a play which won a Tony award in 1974, centers around the story of the mental anguish of an adolescent boy who blinds a stable of horses.

1. Lord Our God, we your children have accepted your punishment because we have sin against you many times and we have forgotten your ways. When you have driven us out from the Country to the countryside for seventeen-year wandering in the bush, you have done this to us that we may learn more of your ways and your truths because you love us.

   Lord in your mercy!

2. In the bush you have kept us save from been kill from Arabs and Anyanya, we were in between those armies.

   Lord in your mercy!

3. From the rain and from the sickness. No houses for your people to live in, no medicine for the sick people. We were leaning under big trees. But you have kept us safe from all the difficult situation.

   Lord in your mercy!

4. You have protected us from the wild animals and snakes and all different kind of dangerous things in the bush. Even you have sent animals to know that there is something wrong going on in the country. That is why people become refugees in their home in the forest!

   Lord hear our cry!

5. You have shut the mouths of small children not to cry when the armies are near to the place where their parents are hiding, because you are the God who take care of little babies.

   Lord in your mercy!

6. People in the bush were expecting death when will they die! These seventeen years are the years of thanksgiving to you, O God, because people were very close to you in prayers day and night. You have made us to learn a great deal about you.

   Lord in your mercy!

7. With our own eyes, with our own ears, we have seen your power, and you have open our ears to hear your voice.

   Lord in your mercy!

8. Every morning we offer you prayer of thanksgiving because you have protected us during the night. Every evening we offer you prayers of thanksgiving because you have protected us during the daytime.

   Lord in your mercy!

9. No division at all, people were united as one body under your umbrella that we are one, we called ourselves Southerners, and we have one color. You have united those who took refugees in the neighboring countries. They called themselves Sudanese. No division at all!

    Lord in your mercy!

10. You ended the war in this country and you brought the peace to us by your mercy O Lord. Only by your power we were defeated not at all. But you have made the Addis Ababa agreement to us, by your mighty hand you brought us together as the Father of many children does when there is any misunderstanding between them.

    Lord in your mercy!

11. Through our repentance and by your mercy you brought us back home from different places where we hid.

    Lord in your mercy!

12. We are now forgetting the past, and we are now claiming our weak power by bringing many confusions and many misunderstandings among us.

    Lord in your mercy!

13. No unity among us, we begin to divide now O Lord! We pray you Oh! Father to not let it happen at all. We are one, make us not divide lest we will come weak.

    Lord in your mercy!

14. Bring peace among us and let us not forget your ways and let us not forget the Addis Ababa Agreement.

    Lord in your mercy!

15. We remember our brothers in Bor and protect them from the war in that area and bring peace among us Lord!

    Lord in your mercy!

Part Two

"Is This My Pain?"

Letters in the Midst of Conflict, 1985–87

During the academic year of 1983–84 as part of his preparation for ordination Marc lived in New York City studying for a master's degree in moral and ascetical theology at General Theological Seminary. The work of completing the thesis for the degree would be delayed by events of the next few years, but would eventually be finished in Kenya in 1988.

The letters from 1981 to 1983 were written during a time of relative peace. The Anya-nya rebellion and the resultant seventeen years of civil war ended in 1972 with the signing of the Addis Ababa Agreement. Bishop Gwynne College was being rebuilt — but Marc's letters of the early 1980s are tinted by the concern that war would come again. Already in 1982 raiders on the border between the north and the south were being armed by the government and carrying out destructive incursions into villages in the western Upper Nile. In June 1983 the government of Sudan under President Jaafer Numeiri abolished the Addis Ababa Agreement. A few months later the government passed the "September Laws," a revision of Sudanese criminal law which brought it into line with shari'a, Islamic law; the code included hudud regulations, punishment of violent crimes and theft by such means as the amputation of limbs. Numeiri began to appear in public in Arabized dress rather than military uniform, signaling a shift toward a more Islamizing policy. In a pastoral letter to the Roman Catholic faithful of the Archdiocese of Khartoum after the passing of the "September Laws," Archbishop Gabriel Zubeir Wako wrote,

> We oppose . . . methods of punishment (which are) degrading, e.g. the lashing of women. Others, like the death penalty, are in some cases not proportionate to the offense. . . . If corporal punishments are executed in public, they will also dull the moral and human feelings of the nation. The citizens should never be trained to enjoy the sufferings of others, no matter how much the suffering is deserved.[1]

---

1. "On the New Penal Code," September 23, 1983, quoted in Werner et al., *Day of Devastation*, 517.

Already in May 1983 a rebellion had taken place at the headquarters of the Sudanese army battalion at Bor. The Jieng soldiers of that battalion relocated to Ethiopia, followed by other deserters from Pibor and Pachalla. These rebellions led to the creation of a new movement, the Sudanese People's Liberation Army (SPLA), formed around Colonel John Garang de Mabior, a U.S.-educated leader of the Jieng people. At first the SPLA campaign was a small-scale guerrilla conflict. The SPLA attacked government facilities more or less at random. Since the SPLA was primarily a Jieng movement, the government responded by attacking Jieng villages and travelers. According to Andrew Wheeler, "During 1984 and 1985 . . . in Mundri, Dinka travelers were commonly being taken off vehicles passing through by the police and the army, and summarily executed a few miles outside of town."[2]

Changes were occurring at a quick pace. Numeiri was overthrown on April 6, 1985. His regime was replaced by a temporary government known as the Transitional Military Council under General Suwar al-Dahab. Elections in April 1986 brought Sadiq al-Mahdi to power.

From the end of 1985, when he returned to Sudan, Marc's letters become more frequent and also more somber in their tone as the events of the new civil war overtake the cities and the countryside of southern Sudan, and as news from the most devastated regions begins to filter out. In the midst of the wreckage of hatred and the destruction of war, Marc's letters give us a glimpse of another reality at work, the reality of faith in a God who is still present with those who suffer.

In the midst of a country sinking into civil war, the Episcopal Church of the Sudan itself slipped into schism. The constitution of the church stated that the archbishop should retire after ten years in office, unless the House of Bishops decided to extend his tenure. In spite of Archbishop Elinana's desire to remain in office, the House de-cided not to renew his term. A declaration was issued that the archbishop's retirement would be effective as of October 12, 1986. Benjamin Yukusuk was elected to be the new primate in February 1988. But Elinana did not go quietly. He consecrated new bishops and the church suddenly found itself with parallel dioceses. A story is told that one of the newly consecrated bishops was walking down a road where some chil-dren were playing. Seeing him, one of the children cried out, "Hello, wrong bishop." But the situation was far from amusing. Elinana's group was refused access to the Lambeth Conference of 1988. There were ethnic dimensions to the division as well, with most Equatorians backing Elinana and most Nilotes backing Yukusuk. Letters of termination and notices of excommunication were exchanged. There were court cases over property. Attempts at reconciliation in 1987 and 1988 failed. Then, in 1989, Eli-nana gave a speech in which he publicly took responsibility for the crisis. This turning

---

2. Werner et al., *Day of Devastation*, 524.

point led to a process of forgiveness and reconciliation which some have described as "miraculous."[3]

The work of Bishop Gwynne College continued in this context of an expanding civil war and a church in confusion.

Bishop Gwynne College
December 27, 1985

Greetings,

Christmastime in Mundri found us last evening around a fire under a perfect full moon. Violet, our college secretary, cooked a couple of hens in savory peanut butter sauce, and some wild pig. We ate with our hands, using the paper-thin *kissera*, rather like crepes made of sorghum flour. Elisama, the college driver and mechanic, told stories in "koinio-koinio Arabic," the homespun pigeon Arabic of the south that kept us laughing. One plump, spirited Moru woman told, giggling, how the sun and the moon were once close friends and worked together. Then the moon became proud because she was so beautiful and refused to work. The sun became angry and threw *madida* (sorghum porridge) in her face. Though the moon moved away, she still has the porridge splattered across her once lovely countenance. Our new tutor, Oxford-bred Richard,[4] even told a sixteenth-century story about Queen Elizabeth, who was in truth (according to this tale at least) a man.

It is that strange, full-empty time at Bishop Gwynne College when the dry season dust blows in the afternoon heat and our students have left us to a barren ghost town of a campus. At every year's end there are those frantic final weeks of teaching, of exams, and marking, amid the preparations for the year's biggest celebration: graduation. In the last month we try to get in all the special times of worship we must share one last time: harvest thanksgiving, baptism, blessing of marriage, a last healing service, a special eucharist for our marching, singing children to share in. One of the most moving of any year is our commissioning service for those graduates who are about to leave us. They kneel around the Table at the center of our round stone chapel,[5] and students and staff lay hands on them and pray, sending them out in the love of Christ from this diverse, intense community they've lived in for three years.

---

3. See Samuel Kayanga and Abe Enosa, "The Miracle of Reconciliation in the ECS."

4. Richard Morgan was appointed by the CMS to teach at Bishop Gwynne.

5. Vivid descriptions of the worship life of the chapel at Bishop Gwynne College can be found in Marc's letters of August and November 1986 and June 1987 (pp. 44, 48, and 51). Former students at Bishop Gwynne such as Allison Dokolo, Allison Abe Enosa, and Samuel Kayanga have mentioned to me that worship at BGC during this period was among the richest experiences of their Christian lives.

Graduation was a pompous, processing, almost dignified affair. Amid some fine addresses from Principal Benaiah and two bishops came an embarrassing blather by the drunken local commissioner. The ceremony was paired with the college Christmas celebration, including Christmas music in no fewer than nine vernacular languages, a delightful, disjointed nativity drama by students, and a grand finale of Nuba[6] and Jieng drumming, singing, and dancing in which the audience joined in raising billows of exultant dust. Four and a half hours it was, topped by the annual feast for graduates and guests.

In these recent weeks at Bishop Gwynne College we have experienced a new eruption of spontaneous, uninhibited, deep down, God-glorifying Sudanese cele-bration. It has been the toughest year since the college's resurrection after the war ended nine years ago. There have been constant rumors of impending rebel invasion. At one point in February all expatriates were evacuated on a heart-wrenching, tearful day. At other times the entire community ran for cover in the forest. With shortage of staff, the severe illness of our principal, and lack of food it was asked if the college would be forced to close. Through these distressing times local pastors supported the meager staff, and with their help the students made it through. This third term has been a sort of renaissance with students working harder, writing better, and holding more vision of Christ in the tumult of Sudan than I recall in any other year.

Still, this third term has been far from easy. I arrived in Juba during the first days of October to find that one of our students had just died two days before. Those were rough, soul-searching days for the college and for church leaders who wondered how they might better have cared for a young northern convert from Islam whose illness seems to have been as much emotional as physical. Three days later I rattled down the dagga-dagga washboard roads to the joyful reception of the college. Within three hours of my arrival our cook of eight years died of a viper bite and again the community was drawn into the grief and wailing that accompanies death. It seemed in those weeks that death was with us daily. Students literally heard several times a week of deaths in their families at this time when health care is at a low ebb throughout the south. Amid memorial services and funerals I found myself wondering what I had come back to. "Is this

---

6. The people of the Nuba Mountains in Kordofan, a province in central Sudan, are collectively called Nuba although they are members of several different religious, cultural, and ethnic groups. The mountains cover an area of approximately forty by ninety miles. There are almost no roads, most of the villages being accessible by footpaths. This area, technically outside of the south, has been one of the most devastated during the civil war. The moderate Sufi traditions of the Muslims there make them as much a target as the Christian population. In 1997 Andrew Wheeler reported that there were "three times as many congregations now as ten years ago, with significant numbers of converts from Islam" (see Wheeler, "Church Growth in Southern Sudan 1983–1996," 35).

my pain?" I asked myself, still recalling the smooth, sleek, affluent narcissism of a year in New York City.

Security for our students has been a particular concern with the edginess of civil war in neighboring regions and the substantial army unit now established in Mundri. In my four years in Sudan I have been closest to the Jieng peoples. It is they, the predominant group behind the rebel movement, who are everywhere suspect in our region. For a time civilians, even students, were taken from the lorries, buses, and private cars that passed through town. They were jailed and without recourse disposed of. Our once-quiet village felt tension in the air and heard whispers of killings. There were shots in the night. Even the lives of our own students were threatened and, while church and college leaders tried to confront local authorities, we kept our students within the campus.

It was in late October that I walked in the *suuk* with my friend Akurdit. He helped me as I struggled with speaking Jieng and in the shops interpreted my requests to the Arab traders. As we returned there was shouting from behind us. We walked on. A drunken soldier strode after us and demanded that Akurdit, a Jieng, go with him, at rifle point. Without Arabic I felt helpless, my eyes darting around the *suuk*. A local trader implored a second soldier to rescue our student. He was released. In those few heart-racing moments I reconnected in Sudan. The pain here became *my* pain as a friend I love was taken away at gunpoint. The suffering and confusion is not simply something I observe. I share it and wrestle with it alongside my Sudanese kinfolk. It is mine.

As public knowledge of such events has increased they seem to have diminished. Regardless, we have done everything possible to ensure the safety of our threatened students. I accompanied those fourteen who needed to fly to Khartoum to Juba, stayed with them through three postponements of their flight, and saw them at last onto the plane. It was a sad kind of relief standing at last in the empty airport.

Amid the tension this term of teaching has had a new vitality for me. Class discussion has often been impassioned and creative as we've struggled with such diverse issues as the baptism of polygamists, the meanings of traditional rituals for physical healing, the values implied in remembering the ancestors, and the spiritual and psychological sides of witchcraft. These are hard issues which are not easily or often discussed openly, but which are of profound importance to Christians here. I find a new maturity in our students to look honestly at their own traditions as well as the inadequacies of the church in dealing with these issues in their tribal areas. Why do so many Zande[7] Christians resort to the

---

7. The Azande, or Zande, people live in southwestern Sudan, the Congo, and Central African Republic. In the eighteenth century the Zande kingdom ruled over a great diversity of people in a tribute state in which conquered peoples were assimilated, although a few retained their own language.

ancient healing rituals when they are sick? Why does the church take no role in seeking the physical healing of its people, but condemns their best efforts? We have tried to look at the often neglected felt needs of people within an often authoritarian church, as well as the frequently valid criticisms leveled at the church by those "pagans" who look on from outside. In it all I think we're coming to know ourselves better and to stand in love and awe before the redemptive work of the Christ who became man and lives among us. He enters and embraces the deepest recesses of our (Sudanese or American) humanity, and even of our distinctive histories and ancestors.

It is good to be back, very good. For now the pain and the joy are mine, along with the people here. In a few hours I will sit with friends under the *madida*-splattered full moon around a fire. I hope we in war-torn Sudan can learn to love and respect each other more than the sun and moon, and learn that any light we have, all light comes from one Creator.

"For God was pleased to have all his fullness dwell in Christ, and through him to reconcile to himself all things whether things on earth or things in heaven, by making peace through his blood, shed on the cross" (Colossians 1:19–20).

A Joyful New Year in our Lord,
Marc Nikkel

Bishop Gwynne College
March 1986

As our 1986 academic year at Bishop Gwynne College nears its opening on April 2, I have just returned from the town of Wau, three hundred miles north-west of Mundri. These two dry season months as a guest of Bishop John Malou offered a stark encounter with one town of southern Sudan during wartime.

Old Makal recites a Jieng proverb in his wizened voice, "The earth has ears. The earth knows those who belong to it. The earth will come back to its own." I sat with him by the hour gleaning his rugged cattle camp philosophy as I laid the groundwork for a paper on Jieng attitudes toward the sick, the stranger, and

---

They are fiercely proud of their culture, of which in recent years the church (both Anglican and Roman Catholic) has become an important custodian: "[In the face of] the perceived disintegration of Zande culture ... in a striking decision, the Episcopal Church made itself the guardian of traditional Zande culture, dedicated to rescuing it from further decay. The synod [of the Diocese of Yambio in 1994] established a committee whose responsibility included gathering traditional artifacts in danger of being lost, ... promoting manufacturing skills such as iron-making, reviving traditional dancing, gathering and spreading knowledge of medicinal herbs and promoting the telling of traditional wisdom by the elders" (Werner et al., *Day of Devastation*, 571–72). For a thorough ethnographic description of the Azande see the works of E. E. Evans-Pritchard, especially *Witchcraft, Oracles and Magic among the Azande*.

the outcast.[8] Makal's confidence in the will of the earth is far from passive. His determination and that of his people pours tens of thousands of men into the rebel movement that holds territories all the way from Ethiopia up to the lands surrounding this town moated by a kink in the Juur River.

Each day in Wau I felt the sorrow and anguish behind the war and the determination that keeps it growing. Daily I wondered what Christ's presence means here, now. What is the work of a small and seemingly negligible church in wartime?

Wau, the provincial capital of Bahr el Ghazal, is set along the river on gentle hills that drift off to the scrub forests and grazing lands. Most striking of its buildings is the enormous domed Roman Catholic cathedral, complete with rose window, set on a hill surrounded by expanses of red brick buildings with long verandas and open compounds that seem akin both to the American West and to nineteenth-century Italian villages. Despite the burgeoning refugee population that floods Wau's markets and private homes, these rambling old complexes seem sparsely peopled, sheltering little of the activity their Italian builders seem to have envisioned.

Official buildings like the governor's office retain the English colonial air with long, shuttered windows, mock battlements, and bric-a-brac. Strange, the layers of races and cultures that merge here — Jieng, Balanda, Arab, Juur, English, Italian — superimposed one over the other. The old style remains as the walls crumble, doors sag, and the paint peels.

The hearts of most of the men who work in these buildings, reflects one Jieng man, are not here. They possess the degrees, hold the titles, and pile up the papers, but their vision is toward the *Toich* areas, the grazing lands rich with cattle. Wealth and prestige are in the herds you possess, the wives you've married, the children you've fathered, the village you return to. But now, in wartime, the cattle are depleted, serving as food for rebel armies.[9] The hearts of the people are tied to the land, but they follow the progress of the Sudanese People's Liberation Army. Daily, folk huddle around every available radio tuned to the 3:00 p.m. SPLA news. Who has joined the movement? How many army casualties? What towns have fallen?

---

8. This paper became the basis for Marc's master's thesis ("The Outcast, the Stranger and the Enemy in Dinka Tradition contrasted with Attitudes of Contemporary Dinka Christians") from General Theological Seminary in New York, accepted in 1988.

9. The rebels who fought the civil war in the Sudan were far from well equipped. They lived in the bush and lived hand to mouth. The result for the civilian population was widespread mistreatment at the hands of SPLA soldiers, who frequently slaughtered local cattle and stole people's crops. Although there was sympathy for the rebel cause, abuses were rampant. See the report by Human Rights Watch/Africa: Jemera Rone, et al., *Civilian Devastation: Abuses by All Parties in the War in Southern Sudan*.

Wau is bursting with people. Weekly, hundreds come in from the "liberated areas" where battle has leveled homes and decimated herds. With the planting season still two months away they come to the town to search for food and family. Townspeople with houses may have twenty or thirty souls gathered for a once-daily meal, and each compound is strewn with sleeping bodies through the night.

Most tragic are the Gogrial people — estimates one hears in Wau run from 150,000 to half a million — who are fleeing from the Baggara Arabs during recent months.[10] Jieng living in the two-hundred-mile stretch of northern Bahr el Ghazal have struggled for generations with their Arab, cattle-herding neighbors, but never before have the neighbors been well supplied with automatic weapons. They flow in on horse and camel looting and killing, raiding cattle in the tens of thousands. Young men and women, it is reported, are taken as slaves. The Baggara are given free reign apparently because this land holds within its womb oil deposits which are more easily exploited if the earth is rid of its age-old inhabitants.[11] For most displaced people the SPLA provides the only hope of salvation. "The earth has ears," promised Makal.

The educated have likewise fled to Wau. Men with degrees from Khartoum, London, and Alexandria, engineers and technicians gather in the tea shops to brood over the politics of inequality. They are frustrated, like one aspiring medical technician who said, "We are the unlucky ones. When I was a child there was civil war and our schools were destroyed. Now I am a man and the way is again closed by war. Those with guns on the war front, they are the lucky ones! At least they can express how they feel!" The litany of injustices from the earliest Arab slave traders right through the seventeen-year civil war and Numeiri's recent disregard for the Addis Ababa Agreement is recited continually both by "townese" and

---

10. The Baggara are one of the largest groups of western Sudan. Although African pastoralists, their skin is somewhat lighter than the Jieng and their religion is Sunni Muslim. They have long been known to groups in the south as "the raiders," often invading the territories of the Jieng and other peoples to steal cattle and slaves. In recent years, however, they have been armed by the government in Khartoum and their raiding has become far more devastating.

11. The dispute concerning the ownership of petroleum resources was one of the major economic issues in the civil war. The oil is found in the south and the only port is in the north. Multinational oil companies have been involved in exploration and drilling and the proceeds from this oil production enabled the Sudanese government to fund the war against the south. "Sudan has ... built new business partnerships with several of the world's major oil companies: Malaysia's Petronas, China's National Petroleum Company, Sweden's Lundin Oil, Austria's OMV, France's TotalFinaElf, and, perhaps most controversially, Canada's Talisman Energy.... Because the oil fields lie almost exclusively in the south, the government has redoubled its efforts to wipe out resistance in the area and consolidate control.... Khartoum is now working hard to displace populations from the oil concession areas" (Randolf Martin, "Sudan's Perfect War," 119; see also Abel Alier, *Southern Sudan: Too Many Agreements Dishonoured* and the vivid description of life along the route of the pipeline during the civil war in Paul Salopek's *National Geographic* article "Shattered Sudan: Drilling for Oil, Hoping for Peace").

village illiterate. One engineer has plans for his European education if Egypt
assists Khartoum with military arms: "I'll be the first to join the SPLA as an
engineer and design a canal to divert the Nile. They don't think we can do it?
We *will!"*[12] Such is the determination that "the earth will come back to its own."

Most of the town dwellers of Wau bear Christian names, but to what extent
does Christianity serve simply as one more barrier against Islam and the northern
foe? One Jieng was asked by an Arab what would have to be done for him to
become a Muslim. The retort: "When you become Christian, we will all become
Muslim!" Defiance is in the bones. On the day of my arrival in Wau another
guest, a representative of the Muslim Brotherhood and the organization known
as "Dawa Islamia," or Islamic Aid, secretly arrived in Wau. Suddenly the youth
were running through the streets chanting the war songs of the SPLA. A crowd
gathered with knives and sticks and the big house of Islamic Aid, filled with
money and supplies, was gutted by fire. The visitor fled onto a waiting plane, and
Wau's people still delight at his speedy ousting.

With aggressive Muslims proclaiming an Islamic state from the north and a
civil war fueled by weapons and training from Marxist lands to the east,[13] what
does a small Christian church have to say in wartime? What does Christ look like
when he walks in a *suuk* full of refugees with sounds of mortar shells and land
mines exploding in the distance? Does the Lord of the earth have ears?

One response comes as I watch the passionate life of Bishop John Malou,
consecrated to work in Wau just a year ago. He is a native of Rumbek, a large Jieng
town which fell to the rebels three weeks ago and last week received a barrage
of Libyan bombs. Providentially, perhaps, he studied theology in Lebanon.[14] He
writes letters by kerosene lantern each night until midnight. With creativity and
care he urges on a dozen pastors-in-training across the world and nurtures the
bonds of compassion with people on every continent. His wife, Rachel, is up by
5:00 in the darkness at the hand pump filling every tin and plastic container in
the house with water. With thirty or so guests to cook for daily and a dry season

---

12. Egypt has been reluctant to encourage an independent southern Sudan precisely because of
the fear of having the people of the South gaining control of the White Nile.

13. The rule of Emperor Haile Selassie I of Ethiopia was overthrown in 1974. Until 1991 the "Provi-
sional Military Administrative Council," under Mengistu Haile Mariam, ruled Ethiopia, increasingly
according to Marxist-Leninist principles. From 1987 until 1991 Ethiopia was officially named the
"People's Democratic Republic of Ethiopia." For a time, the Soviet Union supplied arms to the SPLA
through Ethiopia.

14. On the life of John Malou Ater see Wheeler in Werner et al., *Day of Devastation*, 461, 603;
Nikkel, *Dinka Christianity* 232; Malou himself published the testimony of his coming to faith in Christ
in *Out of Confusion*; Nikkel hoped that Malou would one day revise and publish his master's thesis
from the Near East School of Theology, entitled "The Dinka Priesthood." The high respect which
Nikkel held for Malou is revealed in the dedication of *Dinka Christianity:* "In memory of John Malou
Ater, former bishop of the Episcopal Diocese of Wau: a respected *Ran Nhialic* ["person of God"],
exemplary Dinka priest and beloved friend."

pump that's empty by 7:00 a.m. she uses every drop. By 7:30, after prayers, John strides out of the house on a slightly lame leg or throws his six foot, four inch frame in the saddle of a dilapidated bicycle to make visits to the governor's office and a dozen other places. The big people and the children, everyone, it seems knows Bishop John as he peddles around town. With his unswerving hope in a God who hears even in wartime John has brought representatives from OXFAM, World Vision, Band Aid, and other agencies to assist in feeding and sheltering the newcomers to Wau. Even when the weekly UNICEF airplane was grazed by a rebel missile for flying too low and flights were terminated, when three roads were mined and lorries destroyed, John anticipated the arrival of World Vision representatives to sign a contract with the governor. They came and the grain is coming! Bishop John has had land allocated and bulldozed, wells dug, and building materials hauled in for two large refugee camps. Whether he is teaching a Bible study class with wisdom and receptivity, or designing three new development projects for the diocese, I am most amazed by John's unswerving confidence that God will care for his own. The Lord of the earth has ears.

May 1, 1986

It is over a month since the above was written. In that time American planes bombed Libya, our neighbor to the north.[15] I have asked myself why I have delayed in sending this letter. I think it was, first, because it revealed a part of the horrible prejudice and hostility that seethes across this land. From this side it seemed too vulnerable to expose. You don't say it openly here.

More important, this letter seemed too smooth and objective a description. I tried to say truthfully what I saw and heard ... and yet those questions reverberate: Am I only an observer? Am I the beneficent Christian who tries to provide my feeble-minded answers in chaos I cannot understand? How tidily I have observed the violence and recounted the drama!

With the bombing of Libya this Sudanese war becomes my own. Our own. Around me, on every side I see the prejudice that keeps one person blind to the soul of another, the mindless fear that fires on civilians, slaughtering dozens every day. I hear the sound of munitions made in America or Russia, cold and dead to their human targets. All that I find most evil and incomprehensible around me in this war ... is mine too. As Americans it is ours and we help fan the fires. I carry in my own heart the prejudice and chaos I see around me.

---

15. On April 14, 1986, U.S. president Ronald Reagan ordered bombing raids against targets in Tripoli and Benghazi in apparent retaliation for a terrorist attack on a German nightclub frequented by American military personnel which killed three people. Some sixty people were killed in the American bombings, including a daughter of Libyan leader Muammar Al Qadhafi.

In the past month Wau has been flooded with thousands of army reinforce-ments and fresh arms from the Arab world. Nearly all civilian flights are halted. World Vision was able to get some nine trucks of grain into Wau, a pittance con-sidering the needs to come. In the aftermath of the Libyan bombing, I am told, all World Vision personnel have been evacuated. Food for civilians decreases quickly, and people turn back to rural areas for refuge. Those families with means seek ways to send their dependents to Khartoum. A three-mile military sweep around Wau left unknown numbers of civilians dead. The city of Rumbek is now under siege and reports suggest that high numbers are being killed daily.

Makal's determined words still rise saltily in my mind. A rejoinder comes from the Lord's words in Chronicles:

> . . . if my people, who are called by my name, will humble themselves and pray and seek my face and turn from their wicked ways, then will I hear from heaven and will forgive their sin and will heal their land. (2 Chronicles 7:14)

Those words are feeble as the wind-swept broken wells of Wau if I try telling them to old Makal, if I publish them for the tribes of Sudan or before the northern military. They are fiery and purging and healing if I apply them to myself and to my own American brethren. We, each one, share in this broken land. We, each one — American, Arab, English, Jieng, and Balanda[16] — must somehow humble ourselves and seek and pray and turn. Makal, may the Lord of heaven and earth heal your broken land.

Love,
Marc Nikkel

Bishop Gwynne College
August 19, 1986

With frequent rains the nights are often cool as we gather in the compound behind our house to practice new Jieng songs.[17] Kongoor and I stuff the dry husks from Akurdit's just-harvested maize underneath three big logs. With lots of fanning the old wood flames up midway through our hours of singing. The coals become a glowing bed for roasting fresh ears of maize. Each time we hone a song to satisfaction we nibble off the singed corn and sip cups of hot tea. These are

---

16. A group of Sudanese people who live in western Bahr al Ghazal and the western part of Equatoria.

17. The Christian hymns of the Jieng people written during the war became a special focus of Marc's doctoral research. See especially chapter 7 of *Dinka Christianity* entitled "Who Are Those Marching Once Again?" and the appendix, which contains the Jieng text and English translation of several of the most important of these songs. The recently published book of Jieng hymns (*Dinka-Bor Hymnal*) is dedicated to Marc Nikkel.

the new songs of worship, the ones that rise from the struggling Christian groups in Khartoum, in Bor, in Juba. The beat often reaches the soul and clasps more tightly with each verse. The haunting tone transfixes even those who cannot understand the language. So perfectly do these songs meld the sorrow and the trauma of these years together with the rhythm and word. As we sing "Father of our Lord in Heaven" it is the last, hard beating line of each verse that leaves a chill:

1. Father of our Lord in Heaven
   Visit us for we are worried in our hearts
   We are without faith, O Lord; try to visit us all.
   We are all worried; the hardships of this world are upon us.
   The sin of the world has cut us away from your path.
   We are left alone, we are left, we are left, we are left.

2. The Father of our Lord, who has power,
   Help us for we are all worried.
   Don't allow the evil spirit to crush us.
   Help us, we are mourning, we are mourning, all of us are mourning.
   The sin of the world is preventing us from taking your path.
   We are left alone, we are left, we are left, we are left.

3. The Father of our Lord, who has Love,
   Follow us with your heavenly power.
   We are scattered like the sheep who have no shepherd.
   The world is scattering us; we are all being scattered.
   The sin of this world has cut us off from our Lord.
   We are left alone, we are left, we are left, we are left.

4. Father of our Lord, who is able to help,
   Allow us to sit at your right hand.
   Your Truth I have heard, O Lord.
   Release us from sin for we are falling in the fire.
   The sin of this world has divided us and thrown us into the fire, O Lord.
   We are burning, we are dying, we are burning, we are burning, we are burning.[18]

---

18. The reference to "fire" in the verse is most probably related to the biblical image of the three young men in the book of Daniel, Shadrach, Meshach, and Abednego, who were thrown into the fiery furnace by King Nebuchadnezzar for refusing to bow down to an idol. That story from Daniel 3 has been one of the most important biblical stories for Sudanese Christians. The chapel at Bishop Gwynne College had a mural of this story, designed by Marc Nikkel in 1986, covering much of the wall space. A photograph of a part of the mural can be found in Werner et al., *Day of Devastation*, in the photographs following page 528.

Each time that last verse throbs to an abrupt end I find a knot in my throat. "Like sheep who have no shepherd." In my last letter I wrote of my dry season and the months spent in the city of Wau as the guest of John Malou. In wartime it was John who was the most hopeful vision of Christ in a fearful town, among a warring people. Just days after I mailed that letter we learned that he had been killed. He was on a mission to his besieged hometown of Rumbek, one of the first to go in when the army claimed it had regained control. After a three-hour visit to a virtually leveled mass of rubble, at the start of the return journey, a rebel missile shot down the helicopter in which he was traveling. It was about noon on Pentecost Day. For the Jieng John was the only church leader chosen *by* them *for* them. He was a man of integrity, great skill, and compassion. Among the two or three million Jieng the church is often perceived as a pathetic, weak, poorly educated, and negligible community amid a proud and determined people. John was one churchman who challenged the stereotype and graciously received the respect and gave council to Khartoum "intellectuals" as much as to village chiefs or prophets. I expect the image of his wizened and determined manner, full of hope, comes to many Jieng Christians as it does to me almost every day. I hear friends ask, "Where is there anyone to replace him? There is not another educated man with the spirit of Malou. May God somehow raise up another." And the song goes on, "We are left alone, we are left, we are left, we are left."

"It is the most difficult time the church in Sudan has ever known," said our principal, Benaiah, as we sat together in my study yesterday. Indeed, our archbishop has been out of the country for six months, recuperating from illness in Nairobi. The Diocese of Khartoum has been left without a bishop for over a year, and divisions and power struggles shred the church there. The chaos and danger of the war leaves some leaders numb to act, while a few use the opportunity for gain. Some try with paltry resources to build the Kingdom of God in this desolation. From behind the battle lines in rebel territory sketchy bits of news tell us the church strains on amid near starvation. Small preaching centers of mud and grass are assembled in the bush. Bishop Nathaniel Garang, our former student, a Jieng, has only shreds of cloth to wear as he moves about baptizing, preaching, and building. This we hear secondhand from his wife, who walked 120 miles to buy a bit of grain and soap to carry back.[19]

---

19. Bishop Garang is the bishop of Bor. He was consecrated in 1984. From 1985 to 1990 he ministered in SPLA territory, cut off from the outside world, and became known as "the lost bishop." In 1988 Marc received a letter from the bishop, mailed from a refugee camp in Ethiopia. The bishop informed Marc that the work was going well, the gospel was being preached, and churches were being established. His purple shirt, however, had worn out. Marc and I went to Nairobi and bought a purple clergy shirt and we sent it to Ethiopia with a spare collar of mine. See the brief essay "The Diocese of Bor," in Kayanga and Wheeler, *But God Is Not Defeated!*

At BGC we continue on with a mystifying balance between the routine of classes along with harvesting our gardens and daily news of the threat around us. After a two-hour staff meeting last week in which we discussed a five-year plan to build a preschool nursery and the beginning of our three-year diploma program, I met with a cluster of expatriates to consider war developments and possible evacuation from the college. My colleague Steve[20] found himself working on Moru language study with his tutor as he busily packed up his emergency travel bag. Are we staying? Are we leaving? Somehow painting murals and working out color combinations in our chapel is desperately incongruous with the thirty-five hundred "displaced persons" who have nearly doubled the size of our village of Mundri. Now they come daily to receive relief food doled out from one of our sleek, new staff houses which serves as a warehouse. Your sermons sometimes leave a bad taste in the mouth when you emerge from chapel to find a desperate mother, hand outstretched, with three naked children, one attached to a dry and wrinkled breast.

The madness and blind injustice on both sides that fan the flames of this blazing war seem to make a mockery of our tender human values. What worth is the life of a hungry child before you when two million people are now dying of starvation? Amid the tensions I expand my course in "Contextual Theology." We debate the church's role in the face of this injustice. What is the prophetic voice of church leaders to be, whether under the domination of another religion, or in the tumult of a Marxist revolution? We chew on the pros and cons of liberation theology and read the writings of Desmond Tutu. Today we hear the harsh, incisive words of the Sudanese Roman Catholic archbishop Subair. In the fury of the war truth is hard to come by. How desperately we need people who are perceptive to discern it and courageous to proclaim it.

Among our students, alongside our learning, questions percolate more steadily each day. Will we evacuate? How? Where to? On August 13, SPLA radio announces a major offensive on towns throughout the south, the capital of Juba included. Soon we learn that their promise to shoot all airplanes traveling in the "war zone" is no bluff. Sixty civilians are killed as their Sudan Air flight falls in flames from the sky near Malakal. The rebels warn that civilians must evacuate four major towns as they plan attacks on military garrisons. At 3:00 we hear that the city of Wau was attacked, resulting in heavy damage. Akurdit and I look at each other wondering about close friends, three of our graduates among them, scattered across the town we know so well. "I wonder how many civilians were killed among the 160 deaths reported," says Akurdit. I recall the relentless hope

---

20. Stephen Anderson, an American.

of John Malou just four months ago. How the church would thrive, Wau would stand. Together we would work . . . even behind the battle lines. And the song drums on, "We are burning, we are dying, we are burning, we are burning, we are burning."

It is hard to describe how it feels just now for us expats. In a few years we have found our homes here in the midst of people's lives. Our hearts are bonded. We sing in harmony the painful words of lamentation and of hope. We roast maize and pray around the glowing coals. To leave in rough times like these feels like deserting your own family. It is almost unthinkable. In this unsteady time there is something very true, very firm, about the gospel of Christ. We are not alone. We have not left. We are here.

Please stand by us. Hold us in your prayer.

Love,

Marc Nikkel

Bishop Gwynne College
November 3, 1986

"Mabrok Kwari, I baptize you in the name of the Father, and of the Son, and of the Holy Spirit." These words I spoke just two days ago as I held the tiny bronze-brown body of the seven-week-old baby of Peter and Susanne. We welcomed him into the worldwide Family of the Lord: "We are members together of the body of Christ; we are children of the same heavenly Father; we are inheritors together of the Kingdom of God. We welcome you," said the people gathered in our round, tin-roofed chapel. I think of my own Anabaptist Mennonite forebears — also part of that universal family — and wonder how they would respond as their episcopally ordained son performs an infant baptism. Certainly the words I spoke to the parents and godparents at the heart of our chapel, with many witnesses, stated bluntly the challenge they take upon themselves. They confess their own faith and then their commitment to teach and nurture Mabrok (meaning "congratulations" in Arabic) in the faith of Christ. It is a solemn vow before God to the tiny, sleepy-eyed boy. His future will not be easy. When his father graduates in six weeks the family, with their three young sons, will return to the Nuba Mountains. There persecution of the struggling Christian church burns on. As Mabrok grows it will never be easy as the son of a Christian minister. How he needs the persistent prayer and encouragement to "fight valiantly under the banner of Christ against sin, the world, and the devil." What a privilege, now as a priest, to blend these awesome realities in hope and wonder at Bishop Gwynne College.

It was earlier in the same service that Mabrok's parents received God's blessing upon their marriage. Peter Alprs and Susanna Kany had been married some years ago in the Nuba tradition with the exchange of bride price between their families, but like many young Christian couples they had not experienced the blessing of God amid the Christian Family. In a service accented by rumbling, joyful music in four languages, they committed themselves as I joined their hands before God. We could not, however, leave out some sign of God's grace in the Nuba tradition. Our elder, the Rev. Canon Benaiah, sprinkled cooling water, a sign of refreshment, cleansing, and purity, on the couple, and on all of us gathered. In Nuba fashion, we reached out to "catch" the blessing. Benaiah then laid hands on them each and blew upon them — reminiscent of the Old Testament imagery of breath and spirit — and asked that God grant them the coolness of temper that enlivens love and peace in their home and relationships.

With a heavy downpour of rains before and after the festivities, the sprinkling blessing, and the waters of baptism, it was a service full of the strongest images of God's encompassing, cleansing love. To the beat of Bari[21] music we processed out of the chapel and over to the compound of Peter and Susanna with its mud-and-thatch *tukhls* (huts). There was a Nuba naming ceremony for little Mabrok with the college children endowing him with symbols of his future courage and strength. At last we shared a feast, eating from common bowls in clusters of six or seven around each small table. When the last downpour came the stragglers huddled together in the grass-roofed cooking *tukhl* or sprinted to their own homes: no better sign of God's blessing on a parched land!

That was Saturday night. Sunday found me celebrating an All Souls' service of holy communion in which we struggled with our memories of the dead, those who died in the faith of Christ and those who died apart. This is a profound pastoral question in a land where the ancestors play such a central role among the living. How do we release them? How to find forgiveness? How to release the fear? How do we come to know the one Mediator, the one True Ancestor in Jesus Christ? The repression so common in the church is not satisfactory, nor is the desperate syncretism. And so we asked yesterday, how all that we are, our memories, our history, the hope and fear, and joy and pain, can be offered into the hands of God. My friend Akurdit asked, "How can I name them? It may drive me mad. They are in my dreams and my quiet moments, and there are so many. Certainly three-quarters of all the people I have known from my home, my youth...they are dead, all dead. The sadness is too great." And yet he treasured yesterday's

---

21. "Bari" is an inclusive term describing a large cluster of Bari-speaking language groups of Nilotic peoples in the eastern parts of southern Sudan in what is known as the Equatoria region. These groups include the Bari proper, the Pajulu, Nyepo, the Kuku, Kakwa, Ligi, Nyangwara, Mundari (or Shir), and Acholi.

silent intercessions, recalling his own agemates,[22] many killed and left to rot on the battlefields of the present war.

The afternoon found perhaps two hundred people gathered at the home of our college secretary, Violet, whose father died two months ago. For her it has been a tragic and difficult year, sustaining two families as a single parent and encountering the deaths of three close family members. I preached at this memorial service yesterday, seeking with the community to embrace and encourage a mourning friend.

The newly born, the revitalizing of married love, the memory of the dead, God's blessing on our struggling efforts, and those all enfolded into the sacrament of the death and resurrection in Jesus Christ. This is the new stage begun for me, also in our college chapel, on October 5. I was ordained a priest under the hands of three bishops and perhaps twenty clergy of the Episcopal Church in the Province of the Sudan.[23] Happily, it was my own bishop, Benjamina, of the Diocese of Rumbek[24] (for which I am college chaplain) who officiated, now serving as acting archbishop. He traveled with Bishop Manasseh[25] the grueling two-day journey from Juba. Our own area bishop, Eluzai,[26] joined them. My only sorrow is that the late Bishop John Malou, with whom I had envisioned the ordination seven months ago, was not here. It was the Jieng community, with soul-bursting song, that brought together the best of past and future hopes as my eyes filled with tears just before the prayer of consecration. My colleague and former student, Christopher Jumma, was ordained deacon as we together passed to a new stage in our lives.

With each of these events our college chapel takes on, in my thoughts, an added resonance. Made of local materials, the eight-sided structure stands at the heart of our college with the foundations of the pre-war chapel just beneath its octagonal floor tiles. In my last letter I mentioned the incongruity I feel of mixing up pots of paint to work out color combinations for the chapel and painting angels in the midst of famine and civil war. Yet I spent our last two-week holiday submerged in doing just that, assisted by a Ugandan refugee. Four gospel figures, the man, the lion, the ox, and the eagle of Revelation 4, are set into our crosswork balcony. The south door has a blue and green river flowing down its center and the words

---

22. The term "agemates" refers to a group of young boys or girls of approximately the same age who are put together for a period around the time of puberty to learn about adult life and to prepare for initiation. Initiation rites themselves vary widely between different ethnic groups.

23. Marc had been ordained deacon in the Diocese of Southwestern Virginia in 1985.

24. Benjamin Wani Yukusuk was consecrated in 1971 and became bishop of Rumbek in 1976. He became the second archbishop of the Episcopal Church of the Sudan in 1988 (see the article by Paul Yukusuk "Archbishop Benjamin Wani Yukusuk").

25. Manasseh Dawidi Binyi was ordained bishop in 1984 to serve as assistant in the Diocese of Juba. In 1989 he was elected bishop of Kajo-Keji.

26. Eluzai Munda was elected to be the first bishop of the Diocese of Mundri in 1984.

"Gifts will be brought from a people tall and smooth skinned . . . whose land is divided by rivers" (Isaiah 18:7).[27] The north door, which is first met when entering the college campus, ablaze with orange, red, pink, blue, and purple, and bearing dark hands upstretched, proclaims, "The Sudanese will raise their hands in prayer to God" (Psalm 68:31, GNB). Incongruous, yes! Three days ago I received a letter from our great supporters, folk in the Diocese of Salisbury in England. There the Salisbury cathedral glassworks have just finished stained-glass windows to fit into the twenty-some odd shapes that make a grand crossburst splashed across the twenty-foot-high east wall. Bright colors will radiate, marked with the crests of our churches, and even a fragment of thirteenth-century cathedral glass embedded in the finely crafted array. In the letter from Salisbury I sense the awkwardness of such a magnificent — and so impractical — gift in the midst of starvation and battle. Strangely, this is the glorious ambiguity of our faith, the wonder of fellowship, beauty, and the vision of the Spirit in the most unlikely places. This is our worship. We lift our hands in prayer along with little Mabrok, with Violet and her dear father, old Nyerakisa, and Akurdit, and Peter and Susanna, with Benaiah, and ten thousand soldiers, and starving children. We at Bishop Gwynne College lift our hands with you in England and America and other far-flung corners. We lift our hands in prayer to God.

Love,

"Abuna" Marc Nikkel

Bishop Gwynne College
June 19, 1987

Those centuries-old Ethiopian cherubs fascinate me with their large, black, serious eyes, their brilliant, spiky wings, feathers all in rows of deep blue, yellow and red, polka dot with white. Are they children's toys or messengers from God? Wing tips mesh like cog wheels or flirt between the beams on the ceiling of an old church like the one in Debra Berhan, Ethiopia. During our dry season holiday in February I had the delight of a five-day stopover in Addis Ababa as the guest of our sister seminary, Mekana Yesus.[28] I wanted to know more about the church's survival through these twelve years of the Marxist revolution. I hoped for some glimpse into the hearts of Sudan's suppressed Christian neighbors, and I wanted to know more of the ancient Orthodox Church and, yes, to see the icons and murals

---

27. On this text and several other biblical texts important for the Christian community in Sudan see the two articles by LeMarquand: "Bibles, Crosses, Songs, Guns and Oil" and "Appropriations of the Cross among the Jieng People of Southern Sudan."

28. This seminary is for the Ethiopian Protestant church Mekana Yesus, which means "House of Jesus" in Amharic.

swashed in primary colors across church walls and collected in the museums of Addis.

One small Abyssinian painting, "The Beheading of St. George," has particularly stayed with me this year in Sudan. The grimacing executioner thrusts his sword to heaven having just slashed off the head of the kneeling saint. Above them seven of those bodiless cherubs hover tightly, together, their somber eyes trained below. They have no bodies, just red and green wings with a head circled by dark hair suspended between them. They are static, but they are all-seeing, all-present. At the right the only angel with a body, wearing plush flowered robes, her wingtips like spears pointing upward, receives the saint's severed head into a dark red cloth.

What do they see, these angels? How do they respond, these messengers from the court of the Most High? Are they only onlookers, perhaps voyeurs, hovering over our tormented, quivering world? They make me ask, Where is God? How near is God in the midst of this suffering?

It is eight months since I have written one of these duplicated letters which seem always to try to catch hold of some glimmer of hope amid the severed heads. But the glimmer seems elusive in this difficult year. I sometimes wonder if friends across the miles really want to hear more of this dark, distant stuff, of our Sudanese St. Georges and their kin. This year as I look at the chaos in our church, as I thrash with students over Christian responses to violence and Marxist ideology, or feel the tribal prejudice bristle among our staff or students, as rebel recruitment advances and near neighbors are killed, the question echoes, where is God? Here, now? What messages do those cherubs take of what they see? And what response do we await? For all the wings, heaven often seems all too quiet.

In February I wrote a long, personal letter about my close Jieng friend and former student Akurdit. My letter was not posted.[29] It was the tumultuous story of his love for Nyaluak, the daughter of a crusty old patriarch who refused to allow her to marry, and of her flight for refuge to my house...the house of her "father in law." That night, December 15, our graduation day, the father and his two sons, spear and clubs in hand, came, broke down the door of our house, and left Akurdit bloodied and bruised as they retrieved their daughter. Then came the long, oppressive "negotiations" as I tried to carry the unlikely role of Akurdit's deceased father, Ngong, and ultimately made a payment to cover fifteen overpriced Jieng cows.[30] Thankfully, several expatriate friends stood in as

---

29. Although a revised version of this letter is in my possession, it is the opinion of several Jieng friends that it should not be published at this time.

30. The "bride-price" or "bride-wealth" or "dowry" is a custom practiced all over Africa, although its importance varies from place to place. The gift may take the form of money or food, although cattle are most commonly used. "It is a token of gratitude on the part of the bridegroom's people to

Marc's sketches of Ethiopian cherubs, included on his letter of June 19, 1987.

our "kinfolk" carrying nearly a third of the dowry payment. A baby was born to Akurdit and Nyaluak last month, a small but genuine joy. Now, after these three years of forced separation from his war-torn homeland, after the death of his father, his brothers, and nearly every one of his agemates, Akurdit wrote me a short radio message from Juba last week: "Inform Nyaluak and her father that our daughter's name is to be Agum." The word means "suffering." I find myself referred to as the grandfather of a tiny baby girl whose name means "suffering."

Holy Week found the cherubs hovering close over our college chapel. We had what I expect was Sudan's first tenebrae (Latin for "darkness" or "shadow") service in which fifteen candles are extinguished one by one interspersed with Psalms and prayers, leaving the congregation finally in total darkness. How thoroughly did the darkness and the silence witness to what was to come we could not know. Maundy Thursday, as has become our tradition, the faculty, men and women, knelt to wash the feet of our students and their families, always a silent proclamation of the gospel's great reversal among the stratified, hierarchical societies from which we come. "Then if I, your Lord and Master, have washed your feet, you also ought to wash one another's feet. I have set you an example: you are to do as I have done for you" (John 13:14–15).

It was Good Friday, however, that burst forth with the Sudanese genius for the Passion. The three-hour service, meditating on Christ's words from the cross, began with a violent, heartrending drama. It was as if every sinew of Sudan's sorrow, ridicule, injustice, and death were flung out as our students became mocking crowds, cruel soldiers, arrogant authorities, and fearful disciples. They lived it as they live the violence of the civil war, a Sudanese Passion. A short homily, each by one of our students, accompanied Christ's words from the cross. These were the most finely honed and expressed meditations I have heard from our young theologians. We were all there at the cross, observers, with the angels.

---

those of the bride, for their care for her and for allowing her to become his wife.... The two families are involved in a relationship which, among other things, demands an exchange of material and other gifts" (John Mbiti, *African Religions and Philosophy*, 140). Although there are many positive dimensions to this custom, it is also true that it may be abused, as seems to have been the case in the instance Marc relates here about Akurdit and his wife, Nyaluak.

It was not until Holy Saturday morning that we began to learn of the tragedy which had taken place on Good Friday in our neighboring town of Maridi. This was not drama. Rebel troops had made several raids near the town. Police commandeered a relief truck and driver to carry policemen to the area. Three miles from town a land mine blew the truck to pieces killing all eighteen men, policemen and civilians. When the body parts were hauled into the already unnerved town several policemen went wild. They took arms to shoot down any person of the Jieng tribe they could find (Jieng being the original prime movers behind the SPLA rebels and so targets for revenge). By day's end houses were burned, properties stolen, and seven Jieng civilians lay dead. Many people had run to the forest and 150 took refuge under the protection of the Roman Catholic bishop.

It was in Maridi that three of our college students worked during our February and March college break, and within this Jieng community a small new church had been planted. Twenty-three had been baptized. One of these was now dead. All had run for their lives. The fear of these senseless killings cut deeply into our own Jieng students at the college.

It was less than a year ago that thirteen Jieng civilians were similarly slaughtered in Juba. Could this same madness break out in our small town? In our chapel we celebrated the Easter Vigil with the Service of Light. "Christ has risen, Alleluia!" The darkness is conquered, and yet the news filtered in, confirming that twenty-five people died on Good Friday. Where are the angels?

In the war people throughout southern Sudan run for their lives. In Mundri our population increased by thirty-five hundred of the Juur[31] tribe, who fill hungry camps two miles away. During March in Khartoum I saw some of the estimated five hundred thousand displaced persons and refugees who came in recent months flooding the capital city. Thousands of dark-skinned southern children, having recently survived the long trek from southern Sudan war zones, now beg on the streets. This was hardly known in Khartoum only a year ago. Daily I saw the northern police arrest and lead off southerners who are often forcibly taken far away to work settlement camps. And yet relief aid representatives told me that many efforts to care for those in the burgeoning shantytowns are thwarted. The setting up of feeding programs, provision of temporary housing and water supply, or the creation of jobs is blocked in bold and subtle ways. Their presence is not

---

31. The homeland of the Juur (or Jur) people is between that of the Jieng and the region known as Equatoria. When the rumors of war began in 1983, the Juur were some of the first people to become displaced by fighting. Settlements of Juur were established in the Mundri area by 1985, although they at first suffered discrimination from the local people. Evangelists like lay reader Frederick Amba persisted in preaching Christ among the Juur in spite of opposition from both government soldiers and the SPLA. A revival among the Juur in 1989 led to the planting of churches in many Juur communities, and at present most Juur consider themselves to be Christians (see Werner et al., *Day of Devastation*, 573–75, and Sapana Abuyi, "From the Margins to the Centre").

wanted. Khartoum becomes progressively more tense for all its varied groups, and the angels are silent.

In times of such fear and prejudice, with land mines beneath banana leaves, where do we turn for the presence of God? Certainly to the church. Last November our Episcopal and Roman Catholic bishops journeyed to Khartoum and Addis to call for peace negotiations between the leaders in Sudan's civil war. Hope blossomed with the public pleas for reconciliation. But this year marks the darkest hour for leadership in both churches as bishops and clergy seem to have taken the grotesque mirror image of the nation's warring parties. The ten-year term of our Archbishop Elinana Ngalamu came to an end in November 1986. Only a vote of the House of Bishops would constitutionally see him continue in office. The province's dean, Bishop Benjamina Yukusuk, set out with the seven diocesan and assistant bishops to call meetings, which unanimously voted for Elinana's retirement. The provincial chancellor, however, supports Elinana claiming that the meetings were illegal. Hostilities rose with guilt and fear among our once revered elders. The church's bank accounts were frozen. Threats have been made. The bishops have been reprimanded by the regional governor. Murmurs of "tribalism" grow in the struggle for power. Communicants refuse to receive the eucharist from the hands of bishops until there is reconciliation. The church seems severed, body and soul, with two administrative offices defying one another. Would-be reconcilers have turned away in disgust and even letters from England's Archbishop Runcie and Sudan's former bishop Allison have brought no sign of resolve.[32] Do the angels weep or laugh? The demons seem to have full reign among us. Where is God for the simple lay people who turn away in disillusionment?

When will the cherubs sing songs of joy and God's redeeming presence burst through the darkness? There are the simpler times, the soothing times, around the bonfire among our college family. Last week agemate Richard (ten days my junior) and I planned a dual birthday party, a Sudanese feast, in my back yard. We called twenty-five or so students from the Dioceses of Khartoum and Rumbek for which we are chaplains. Four savory chickens were cooked with beef *mulai*, sorghum *asida*, and mountains of fresh bread. There was singing in four languages, and after dinner we settled into storytelling. Oxford-bred Richard, renowned for whimsical fables, related how King Stork ate all his subjects, the frogs. Abraham Noon unfolded the Jieng cattle camp myth of Chief Lion, who tried to deceive his fellows into believing that his bull had given birth. More music, and Bismark Avokaya prepared us for a game that would find us all making sounds of goats, dogs, or chickens. In the din Principal Benaiah emerged out of the darkness to

---

32. Thankfully, a reconciliation was achieved, but not until late in 1992. See Kayanga and Enosa, "The Miracle of Reconciliation in the ECS."

call me aside. He explained that the police had passed information that a troop of three hundred SPLA rebels was eight miles away advancing for an attack on Mundri. They would likely approach on our side of town by morning. So much for festivities. With the coming of a light drizzle we pulled our party into the house and, nerves on end, settled into prayer. Some students were already frantically packing their belongings for a trek through the forests. Others bustled children into our stone-walled chapel to spend a fitful night knowing that mud-walled *tukhls* serve no protection against bullets. Armed soldiers glided through the darkness, and guns pointed our direction from the bridge leading to town.

Clearer thinking, however, helped our fears subside. This band of rebels must be the one which has been recruiting young men in our district for the past several weeks. They would not be preparing for an attack. Rather, they came our way seeking a place to cross the brimming Yei river. So it proved to be. The tremor, however, showed how unprepared the college would be in time of an assault. Our staff met to decide that we will "encourage" wives and children to be moved to their home areas. In the event of an attack these would find it most difficult to trek miles through the forests. By now, a week later, many have left. While rebel recruitment is intensive this season it seems that real confrontations will not begin until next year. For the present we, with our students, hope to continue at our college campus through our December 4 graduation. Was God in our moments of throbbing fear? How do we discern his presence there, or in the death of innocent people, or within the ruptured church? Are his angels silent, or do they gather protectively around our bonfire? These are questions I have asked this year.

There is another ancient picture that speaks to my soul and provides a response. This radiant mural, displayed in the Khartoum Museum, bears witness to the faith of our Nubian Christian forebears of a thousand years ago. In the center of a burnt-red background surrounded by spikes of flame stands a radiant white and gold angel, wings stretching out on either side. Under those peacock-feathered wings stand three men with their hands upheld in worship. These are Shadrach, Meshach, and Abednego in the fiery furnace: "... four men walking around in the fire unbound, and the fourth looks like a son of the gods" (Daniel 3:25). This ancient picture, my colleague Andy Wheeler tells me, was commonly painted above the men's entrance to the Nubian churches. There are no cherubs hovering overhead. No, here is the angel — the Christ figure — in the very heart of the flames carrying the cross-crowned scepter. Our belief with the ancient Nubians is in a God that enters the flames with us. To this day some Eastern Orthodox Churches read Daniel 3 at the Easter Vigil as a vision of Christ's descent to the place of the dead to retrieve humankind. This is the God who takes upon himself the full force of the land mine, the tragedy of meaningless death, and the alienation of brother from brother. He is the God who enters the heart of the furnace and perseveres amid fear and who will not depart, will not leave until this evil is redeemed, until this brokenness is healed. That one "like a son of the gods" at the heart of the furnace with three faithful men is a vision of the resurrection, of final triumph as death is turned to life.

Was it all my hours before Ethiopian icons, or the last chance to work with my skilled Ugandan friend Mokili before he was off to university, or my own spiritual need that got us painting our version of the fiery furnace in the college chapel? No masterpiece, this; no fine icon. It took many hours daubing away with enamel paint, covering a wall and two doors. What a peculiar waste of time, decorating, when evacuation seems eminent. And yet it is that image, the emissary of God in the furnace, that helps sustain us here. This God enters into the flames and fear and explosion of this hour in Sudan. That picture is my prayer.

Love,
Marc Nikkel

October 1987[33]

"Why did you stay in Mundri? Why didn't you leave when you were ordered?" The words sometimes came between clenched teeth. "Why did you remain when you were repeatedly warned to get out?" The questions, whether framed in refined or broken Sudanese English, were those most frequently asked in the early days of our captivity. The four of us, Stephen,[34] Katie,[35] Heather,[36] and myself — three Americans, one Briton — were awakened by the chaotic advance of armed men at about 1:00 a.m. on Tuesday, July 7, and marched from our homes in tense confusion. Why indeed, had we hung on despite the rampant rumors of impending attacks, despite the evacuation of three police posts within twenty miles of the college and word of mounting numbers of rebel troops, now in their thousands, in our region of southern Sudan? How could we have dreamed of seeing graduation day, December 5, 1987, still five months away? No, we hadn't heard any *explicit* warnings on SPLA Radio directed specifically at Mundri district; general warnings to all expatriates in southern Sudan, yes, but those had been broadcast for three years. Why indeed had we stayed?

---

33. Although this letter was first written and circulated in October of 1987, Marc revised it thirteen years after these events occurred. This draft includes the addition of names and elements of the story that could not be included in the original. I received this version from Marc by mail the week before his death. Marc wrote most, but not all, of the footnotes for this letter. A version was previously published as " 'Hostages of the Situation in Sudan,' 1987: Christian Missionaries in Wartime."

34. Stephen Anderson.

35. Katharine Taylor was an American teaching at BGC. At the time of her abduction she had been in Africa only for a few weeks.

36. Heather Sinclair was a missionary nurse and midwife from Northern Ireland on the staff of BGC.

Could our captors — or "armed escorts" on our "evacuation," if you will — understand our desperation to hold together our fragile communal life at Bishop Gwynne College? Could they sense the order and familiarity that held us in place...or much more the intense caring, the desperate commitment to one another that increased in proportion to our shared vulnerability? Could they grasp my desire to "defend" or "protect" clusters of endangered students, I who must seem more like a soft white, plump and vulnerable ant larva than an aggressive, dark, lean army ant among them?[37] Was it so naïve to think of ourselves as a unique community in warring and fragmented Sudan that perhaps, because of God's peculiar grace, we might be allowed to continue? Or would they understand the terror that disruption meant to the local people, not least the Moru church and community leaders from whom we took our lead? To see the college evacuate would be the final sign of dissolution: the war had shattered our serene world. Denial was the easier course for many. For any of us it was painful to give up the work that had become our purpose. None wanted to abandon our campus in the tremors of war. After fumbling several times for a worthy response I responded simply: "A soldier does not easily desert his post. I could not leave mine." Our rebel hosts seemed to accept that.

It was Commander Thon Agot who placed those questions to me on the second day of our captivity. Our encounter occurred after an exhausting night of trekking through forests and gardens by moonlight, we four interspersed among seventeen determined, armed soldiers. The commander bore an air of pride, sharp intelligence, and tender humanity. Interrogating us one by one, he probed my motivations for remaining in Sudan and asked after people that we both knew. We sat in a rectangular mud and thatch building that had perhaps been a large family house before the troops moved in. Strange, the gentleness mingled with severity I felt in the commander. His face was firm jawed, clear-eyed, and prematurely creased for his thirty-five years. We spoke of his uncle, Kedhekia Berech de Mabior, a well-known churchman, archdeacon of Bor, who had fled Juba town for the apparent security of rural Moruland. He had established his home and cultivated a massive garden less than a mile from my house on the college campus. "It means nothing to me whether my uncle lives or dies! I don't care if my own father and brothers are killed!" vowed Commander Thon. "No single life matters in this war: not one single person is of importance. Nothing is of value but our *liberation.* That is the only real objective!" A shudder went through me realizing that our four individual lives were naturally included. His words came like a rote creed, harsh and compulsive, something derived from socialist Ethiopia, not from

---

37. Traditionally the Jieng often liken humankind to ants. Both are black, small, and vulnerable when contrasted with the greatness of the supreme Divinity.

the soul of southern Sudan. Yet just beneath the dogma lay strata of sorrow, an intimacy with death, and, further down, maybe a thin vein of compassion.

Thon's words came back to me in the days that followed. We met other officers in rebel camps along the way. Some spoke confrontively, with sentences strongly spiced with Marxist phrases lifted from the SPLM Manifesto. Others had a quiet, almost formal, dignity as they contained the anguish of war. Still others, in camouflage fatigues, asserted their authority and spoke with speech slurred by *waragee,* strong local alcohol. Each dealt with his pain in his own way. However, none so perfectly blended the hard edges of rebel ideals with the pathos of a vulnerable human being than Commander Thon Agot. Several days later in our journey we heard it rumored that two rebel soldiers had raped a local girl. Both soldiers had been shot on orders from Commander Thon, ever unyielding in his mandate for liberation.

Undeniably, Thon's searing philosophy derived from the same turbulent world as the Jieng hymn I had suddenly found myself singing alongside our armed guards on our first day of captivity. The four verses of "Death Has Come" contain concepts deeply cherished by Jieng populations beleaguered by massive and apparently meaningless loss of life. I had first sung this vernacular hymn with Jieng students at Bishop Gwynne College. Alueel Garang, then a young, illiterate village woman behind Sudan's battle lines in north Bor, composed it in 1985.[38] When I first translated it and grasped the profound questions and assertions contained in its four verses I found myself weeping. Some months later the small Jieng minorities in towns like Juba and Maridi were beleaguered and terrified following a series of bomb attacks by the SPLA which had killed a number of local people. Jieng civilians had been accused of supporting the attacks and now were themselves under threat. When I paid pastoral visits to these frightened people it was this song in which they found solace. Now it was the same words that, to my astonishment, suddenly rose from the lips of guerrilla captors as they marched us eastward along Sudan's stony paths:

1. Death that has come to reveal the faith;
   it has begun with us and it will end with us.
   O you who fear death, do not fear death!
   It only means that you will disappear from the earth.

---

38. Mary Alueel Garang composed this song in 1985 shortly after her conversion to Christianity. Her rich language and idioms rooted in the dialect of the Jieng Tuic, Mary comes from a family of renowned vernacular composers. Though unschooled at the time she composed this song (Mary was born about 1966) Marc considered her the finest natural theologian in the Diocese of Bor. This was the first song of many remarkable compositions which have gained widespread popularity in Jieng communities rural and urban, in north and south Sudan. Marc Nikkel translated the hymn with the assistance of BGC students.

Who is there who can save his life and deny death?
We who live on the earth, we are mere sojourners in the world;
As the Lord has said: Let us serve the truth!
Upon the earth there is no man we can call our "father."
We abide together equally in unity as brothers.
God did not create us to be the slaves of mere mortals like ourselves.
This cannot happen upon the earth!

Chorus:
We are only the windblown dust rising from the black soil;
We have no one among us to save our souls.
We are blind and deaf within our hearts: We have rejected the words,
  the words spoken by our Savior are wonderful words!
The *jok* of deception has held us back from the light.[39]

2. Let us comfort our hearts in the hope of God,
   who once breathed life into the human body.
His ears are open to our prayer; the Creator of man is alert to see!
He reigns from his high throne; he sees the souls of those who die!
Turn your ears to us! Who else can we call for help?
You are the only one! Let us be branches from the vine of your son!
Jesus will come with the final word of judgment,
   carrying the book of judgment upon the earth,
   the book of peace and the life of faith!

Never did I expect that words I had once sung in Christian worship with our Jieng students might express the truth of the souls of SPLA guerrillas. However, here were values distinct from those of the commander. Where the highest objective to which Commander Thon aspired, to be attained through military force and for which anything — any human life — could be sacrificed, was the abstract concept of "liberation," Mary's hymn expresses the mystery of human suffering and finitude, affirms the struggle for good innate to all human existence and the ultimate ascendancy of a compassionate Creator, even over death. Time and

---

39. In the Jieng language (*Thuongjieng*) the term *jok* (singular) is the broadest generic designation for any unseen spiritual force or power. It may even refer to *Nhialic*, the "One Above," the Supreme Divinity, as well as the lowly earth powers with whom diviners have to deal. In the Jieng New Testament the term has been used to translate "evil spirit" or "demon" and so has taken on a distinctively negative usage among Christians. This composition speaks of the *jak* (plural) which Jieng traditionally venerate and propitiate through blood sacrifice. Having traditionally been perceived as the protectors and sustainers of Jieng society, they are, with the growing influence of the church, now perceived as malicious and death-dealing, deceiving the very people whose clans have in the past venerated them most faithfully (see Nikkel, "The Cross of Bor Dinka Christians"; "The Cross as a Symbol of Regeneration in Jieng Bor Society"; and LeMarquand, "Appropriation of the Cross among the Jieng People of Southern Sudan").

again the words of this hymn would rise among our guards, seeking the reasons for human oppression, the terrible logic of enslavement, be it spiritual or tangible, asking the great questions of our fragile existence.

Our first night, ripped from sleep and homes and a beloved community, we were thrust into a clammy nighttime wilderness. I had heard the clamor and seen the silhouettes of armed men pass my bedroom window in the moonlight. Bewildered, half asleep, I shouted, "Who is that?" They demanded I open up. I responded obediently and a band of ragtag soldiers came flooding into my dark house. At the same time my housemate, Akurdit, hid silently behind his locked door, thinking this was likely an SPLA military recruitment exercise in which he could be caught. Across the green rebels pounded on another door, demanding it be opened. "I will not!" responded Richard Morgan[40] ... and, quite remarkably ... they left him. On the far side of the same house Stephen was marched out of his room. Alert, sinewy Katie too had heard the clatter from afar, threw on her clothes, and was hiding under her bed while Heather remained in the next room still sleeping deeply. Heather had long years of experience nursing in Belfast's Royal. Growing up in Northern Ireland she had the capacity to sleep soundly even amid bomb blasts and street riots. It was only when her door was kicked in and she was dragged out of bed did she rouse to the urgency of the situation. Soldiers felt around Katie's darkened room and passed it by, so she could have remained behind, but when she heard Heather was being coaxed out into the night, she came out in solidarity.

It had rained the day before. On muddied paths we slipped in ill-chosen shoes. I wore only my *jalabiyya*, a loose Arab robe I used as a nightshirt, and a pair of *motokellie* (sandals made from rubber tires; the local Arabic name means, "when you die, they walk on after you"). This was to be my only garb for the next seven weeks. Heather, having thrown on what was near at hand, wore her satin dressing gown and paten leather shoes while Katie, best prepared of all, had donned jeans and hiking boots. Katie's marvelously appointed emergency daypack was taken from her during those first hours, but with my pleading, later returned largely intact. The *Good News Bible* she had snatched as she was bustled from her house remained a valued companion to all of us. On that first night we were given bundles of our own looted clothes to carry as well as mortar shells or metal boxes filled with rounds of ammunition. We became porters to our brusque, edgy captors.

After walking some ten miles, lost for a time amid densely cultivated Moru gardens, we took rest in a half-finished school building in the village of Bari.

---

40. Following this incident Richard helped in the evacuation of the college to Juba. For several years he taught at St. Paul's United Theological College, Limuru, Kenya, and is now a parish priest in England.

There we sat on a pile of bamboo poles while some guerrillas stood rigidly on guard and still others snoozed before the dawn. A boy sat next to me cradling his AK47. In Jieng I asked him for water. He brought a tin canful, and slowly we began to converse in Jieng. As it occurred, the boy was the son of a churchman, later bishop, the Rev. Gabriel Roric.[41] In 1982 I had stayed in his family home at Yirol, maintained by Gabriel's gracious wife, Ayong. "Don't fear," said young Marial, "you will be taken safely eastward, to Ethiopia. They will bring an airplane so you can be flown to the home of your father.... When you are free, please, telephone my father in Khartoum. Tell him that mother, Ayong, is well. The four children with her in the village are healthy. I have joined the SPLA to liberate our country. I am fine. Do not forget to contact him when you are free. Please don't forget!" Marial's father had been studying in Beirut and had had no contact with his family for years. "God is present.[42] He will protect you," he assured us. Marial was twelve years old.

Our first days were especially strained, our SPLA guards fearful lest government troops attempt a rescue operation, which, were it to occur, could see us all dead. Walking tensely through the chilled night for two days, we arrived at Wandi, a Moru village now transformed into a major SPLA staging post. Having not slept for two days, our bodies craved a quiet place to rest, but we were told to sit on mats at a busy nexus of activity, inquisitive young soldiers constantly passing to examine us and engage in what seemed utterly irrelevant conversation. Finally I asked if we couldn't be taken to the periphery of the camp to rest under a large tree. Yes, guards could be set to watch us. There we lay, drowsy and exhausted, on the edge of sleep, when, far across the clearing, we spotted an ancient woman in a brightly flowered dress, shuffling slowly toward us, crouched down on hands and knees. Reaching our resting place, trembling, the wrinkled old lady knelt before us. Slowly fumbling, she untied a tightly knotted crumpled handkerchief. Within she revealed five hard-boiled eggs and three pieces of cassava root, the finest offering her homestead could make. As it turned out, this was Dorcas, an elder in the local church, who had come to show her solidarity with four foreigners, her comrades in faith. The weathered old saint, radiant, fearful, dignified, took our hands and prayed in Moru, trying to console us. As she rose to leave she was apprehended by a couple of SPLA soldiers who crudely shuffled the fine old saint away. Dorcas was interrogated at length and harshly rebuked. Repeatedly in the weeks that followed civilians were warned against coming near us. Soldiers did not want to have our whereabouts circulated, or the route of our journey passed to government soldiers. No trust existed, not even for a weathered village

---

41. The Rt. Rev. Gabriel Roric Jur was consecrated in 1988 and became bishop of the Diocese of Rumbek in 1990. He is presently under discipline.

42. *Nhialic ato!* "God is present," a common Jieng affirmation.

woman. Greedily, thankfully, hungrily we parceled out our hard-boiled eggs and cassava root.

As the days wore on our diet was simple, bland, and adequate. The rebels provided for us as best as Sudan's sparse produce in a dry year allowed. On the first day we were told, "We don't know how to cook for *khawajet*.[43] These chickens are for you. You cook them yourselves." So it was that Heather and I plucked and gutted the skinny fowl. Stephen and Katie watched the pot and our captors provided firewood. Later, in the cattle country of the Mandari and the Jieng, a young bull would be commandeered from a cattle camp every two or three days of our trek. The bullock would be butchered in the morning. Customarily a calabash of meat roasted on the coals was brought for us to nibble, followed by liver and kidneys. After these came large quantities of boiled meat. No salt, no spices, rarely was there any form of vegetable or even sorghum available, but plain, boiled meat we had in plenty. Together with the fifteen to twenty guards who surrounded us, their capacity for boiled meat far exceeding our own, we would devour the entire beast by midday. When the gristle was too tough or entrails less than palatable, they were snatched by the emaciated young boys who watched on. On our departure, not a chip of bone or piece of hide, not a giblet or hunk of intestine remained in the radical economy of the hungry and destitute.

I recall that my emotions ran deep and angry during the first weeks of our "evacuation." Occasionally it was the being goaded and prodded like stupid calves. Our bodies, and especially our blistered feet, were not prepared to cover what would be 150 miles during the first thirteen days of our captivity. "You are now guerrillas! Be rugged! Endure!" we were chided. Our toughened guards could cover thirty or forty miles a day, and could exist for two and three days without food or water. We could not.

Perhaps the greatest humiliation, apart from taking an armed guard into the bush to observe you at your toilet habits, was seeing our clothes parceled and divided among the soldiers. The night we were taken our dwellings were looted: clothes, radios, recorders, bedding, whatever could be carried, all went. I had been fully acquiescent, yielding what was asked for. My shirts, most made by my mother in durable polyester, were bickered over, grabbed at, coveted by lanky Nilotic soldiers in an ill-clad army. One rude and abrasive lieutenant named Reuben refused me the pair of size fourteen running shoes he had snatched from outside my door. He strutted about in sneakers five sizes too large for him, proudly holding my cherished short wave radio to his ear. With a sneer he told me I could walk barefoot: he did not care what happened to my feet.

---

43. Plural of *khawajah*, the most common Sudanese Arabic term for "Europeans" or "white foreigners."

At the college Heather had employed her suitcase as a closet in which she stored a surplus of clothes. Now we saw it tied to the back of a bicycle weaving around us day by day, its contents to be sold or divvied out. One amiable, if tattered, rebel, Makur, ended up wearing Heather's brilliant magenta blouse, a man's green pajama bottoms along with his own dilapidated army boots. Her tape measure became a belt on another fellow's baggy trousers. We begged for a few more practical pieces of our clothing, some of which were returned, a few shirts, a dress. On our second day I also found myself requesting the peculiar items of feminine hygiene a bewildered soldier had stashed away from Katie's pack, thinking they might be oversized cigarettes. With my cautious explanation they were returned.

Returned to me without request was a tattered patchwork quilt, the handwork of my mother's mother some seventy or eighty years earlier. Wherever I have traveled overseas I have carried with me some object, some bit of family memorabilia, a tangible reminder of my past, my people, my roots. When I first went to Sudan I took this blanket, boldly squared off in strips of blue, each box containing a colorful multi-patch cartwheel. During my first couple of years in Sudan it hung on the wall of my sitting room, a peculiar use for a practical item most Africans thought. On the night we were abducted it covered my mattress and was swept away with all the bedding toward a new life warming guerrillas on the front lines. While our soldiers must have seen little use for this torn and faded old relic, its return brought me an enormous rush of joy. Here was some familial solidarity as I faced the unknown. In the days that followed it became a tent as we rested on the banks of the Nile, a thick turban-cum-sunshade on the trail, and a pillow by night. As the days wore on this heap of cloth became my constant companion, a shred of family history I consciously savored, a connection with those from whom I was now cut off. Very literally it became my security blanket.

Normally July marks the height of rainy season when there is an almost daily downpour, and mosquitoes rule the night. We had several virtually sleepless nights, relentlessly swatting by the hour. It was somewhere in Mandariland that our hosts presented us with two unbleached muslin mosquito nets: short, narrow, one-person models. There was but one for Heather and Katie to share and one for Steven and myself. Though far from adequate given my size, and useless in detouring the blood hungry insects when the cloth rested on exposed skin, these were far better than nothing, another sign of the concern of our captors.

Undeniably, our greatest pain was in what had been left behind, the abrupt severing, the loves and shared life suddenly terminated, the chaos that we knew followed in the wake of our abduction. This violation ate at me and kept me from easy conversation, from the friendships that might have grown with soldiers in those rugged days. The sense of violation never fully left. Or perhaps it was simply the ever-present AK47s that dampened our spirits?

Behind us, at Bishop Gwynne College, we've been told, all of our expatriate colleagues evacuated within a dozen hours after we were taken. In confusion a few of our things were thrown together and hoisted on overcrowded lorries. Akurdit was in our house that night. He had awakened, gone out, and, thinking the soldiers were coming to take him, ran in and bolted his door. After our release he wrote me: "I could not express the panic I felt that night I went to your room, calling for you, my heart pounding . . . I later ran to Kedhekia's compound to find Nyaluak (his wife) and the other girls weeping, crying out of control. They broke my heart. I am unable to describe the terrible emotions of those days until I meet you personally." Within three days all Sudanese students and staff of the college had been evacuated, the families leaving behind possessions that took years to collect and gardens that had been expected to bear foods to survive the coming year. I am told that seven hundred local people scrambled with possessions to board the last lorry heading out of this rapidly erupting war zone. As our quartet sank into sleep under glistening skies on the nights that followed among our ever-present guards, our legs and feet, our entire bodies aching, we could only try to imagine events in Mundri, and pray.

For me our eastward path was not unfamiliar. The first eighty miles, at least, I had traveled before, with Mandari and Jieng Aliab friends before the war.[44] Several of our nights were spent near the mixed cattle camps of the Mandari and the Jieng Aliab. In one of these I met Bongatoich, a Mandari friend, his once massive wrestler's frame now withering with age. He told me of friends I had not seen in years. I met his own two-year-old son, the joy of Lau, his diminutive wife, who had lost five of the seven children she had borne. As I drank a gourd full of sour milk he told me of Ija, my closest friend from those years. He had married two wives. Each had born him a son. In the last year, the Mandari girl, the beautiful wife, had died. Both of their sons, each less than two years old, had also died. "This is our life," said Bongatoich as I recalled how small my own personal losses had been.

We left cattle camps behind as we moved out to the vast flood plains that, over many miles, evaporate or drain gradually toward the Nile. We were among the few who could be thankful the rains were sparse that year. There was but

---

44. The Jieng can be divided into at least twenty-four subgroups. The Jieng Bor inhabit regions east of the Nile; the Jieng Aliab are another subgroup on the west side. It was among the Aliab that Marc first had intimate contact with traditional Jieng cattle-centered life and was adopted into an Aliab family. Their territory is separated from that of the Moru by the Mandari, also a significant cattle people.

one night we lay under a drizzle filtered by mosquito nets at the heart of a cattle camp, soaked in rain and muddied in dirt and cow dung.

Our guards knew the distances we must cover between each humble "staging post" on our trek, vast regions void of any cattle camps or homesteads, sometimes consisting only of flood plains punctuated by slight rises of dry land. Gazing into muddy water as we trudged on, I found, fouled the weary soul, but there were also those stretches of perfectly clear, slowly moving, transparent waters. My eye took refuge in the varieties of greens and delicate shapes of leaves, the underwater garlands, the occasional blossoms of standing plants, the lilies that lolled along our watery path. Nonetheless, our feet became sore, cut, and infected as our guards pushed us on with their peculiar combination of condescension and compassion.

Often we stayed overnight in the compound of a chief or headman into which we had stumbled unannounced, usually after dark. By morning he would collect food from among his people as a sort of tax contributed to SPLA authorities, his armed guests. Ground nuts or grain, an occasional chicken, rarely a goat, or fresh maize from the gardens might be brought. Local people usually complied with little argument through thinly veiled resentment. For the four of us there was a real discomfort in eating our fill on whatever simple rations were brought while emaciated children and gaunt mothers looked on nearby.

One night, after a day trekking through waterless thorn forests and grass-lands we came, desperately thirsty, into a barren, disheveled compound. In the moonlight we saw shriveled, half-grown corn stalks. On the small, low hut was a tightly fastened reed door. The guerrillas shouted in the dry night demanding some response. None came. They shook the door. Some rustling within betrayed the sleepers who, in fear, held their silence, hoping the storm of voices would pass. An order was blurted, the door kicked in, and with shouts and slaps the naked inhabitants were dragged and chased from their hut. A withered old man came stumbling out, a child, a man, all emaciated. One younger man was beaten and then chased with a fistful of burning grass, singeing his buttocks and genitals. Women were sent far into the night to obtain water to satisfy our parched company. We drank, tied up our mosquito nets, and settled into a numb, uneasy sleep.

Heather's feet suffered terribly with stiff, once shiny, patent leather shoes never intended for a hundred-mile stroll through the bush of southern Sudan. After seventy miles the shoes fell apart and her feet emerged, a mass of infected, torn, blood blisters. She lost most of her toenails. Painstakingly, she rinsed brown and bloodstained socks at the end of each stretch and tried to pull them back on, a futile attempt at cleanliness and preservation. Guards glowered over her ablutions, impatiently cursing, prodding her on, in languages she could not understand.

It must have been over a week into our trek that we had especially grueling expanses of knee-deep, near stagnant waters. Several times in the blistering heat I pleaded that we stop to rest in the shade of an island of trees. It seemed that we had been assured we were "near," "very near" for the past fifteen miles. The lightly complexioned, freckled skin of Stephen's face had peeled for the third time despite his relentless efforts to shield it from the sun. My heart pounded heavily in the day's heat. We trudged on. Dryer lands emerged. Cattle tracks showed we had crossed the flood plains and were, hopefully, coming within reach of cattle camps. Heather drew up the rear followed, at a good distance, by two guards who customarily filled time by squatting down and twirling the sticks they carried to spark a fire and light up their pipes stuffed with potent Jieng tobacco. Stephen and Katie were half a mile ahead lacing their way through fields of warm mud churned by cattle hooves. Into a dreadful area of knee-deep mud we waded, Heather moving painfully, trying to support herself with her stick. Once through the sludge she sat in the burning sun as I attempted to rinse her shoes and socks. She dabbed her sores and I went ahead to take shelter in a tangle of thorn bushes. In the distance I heard Maker shouting angrily at Stephen and Katie. When, at last, Heather and I limped along, he was back cursing us. He broke off a thin branch and began whipping us like wayward calves. Maker had often been hard on Heather, but I had come to like the toughened, sinewy fellow with the cattle camp wisdom of an old man at eighteen years. Just now, in my exhaustion, I was furious. I told him to hold his mouth, discard his stick, and respect his elders.

It was only around another thick stand of trees, however, that a large clearing opened up, alive with the dust and activity of cattle camp; our next destination came into sight. Bleary eyed, we saw our captors clustering tightly in the sparse shade of a few trees. We were led to mats laid out for us in the only shade remaining. There we collapsed. Now it was Maker who hovered over us. He unbuttoned Stephen's shirt and fanned his overheated frame. He called for pots of water and gently helped remove Heather's shoes. Out of necessity he had driven us hard, we felt beyond our strength, to get us to the shade and water he knew would be our salvation. The young guerrilla now cared for us like a tender mother.

We were nearing the Nile with its grass-lined tributaries. Heather's feet were in such pain that she could hardly hobble along. At one point the heavyset young nurse, so capable in her element, simply sat herself on the ground and began to cry. She declared that her hip was in such terrible pain that it must be broken. Of the four of us Heather, with years spent in the urban hospitals of Northern Ireland, was the least prepared physically for this arduous journey. Finally our determined companions resorted to a technique used across southern Sudan to transport the sick (or corpses). A sturdy pole was cut from the forest, and from it was tied a large blanket, a sort of massive enclosed hammock, in which Heather was told to sit suspended. Sinewy young men from a Mandari cattle camp were coerced into shouldering the weighty bundle. After stumbling for a couple of hundred yards stronger men were brought on. Amid a crowd of laughing rebels and passersby from the cattle camp, they too capitulated. Heather well outweighed the emaciated bodies of sick Nilotes transported by this means. Humiliated, Heather determined to plod on unassisted . . . until we arrived at a small overgrown fishing village on the banks of one of the Nile's many tributaries. There we waited two days for the arrival of dugout canoes.

Just as the sun was gliding out of sight on that first evening on the water's edge there arose a dark veil shrouding our entire world. Amid the all-encompassing whirr of Equatorian insect chatter I felt vaguely uneasy as I realized we were within a seamless veil of mosquitoes rising from the dense grasslands in precise timing with the receding light. By evening in these parts every human arm becomes the suckling place for thirty or forty famished insects. Though only six o'clock in the evening, thousands of tiny needles drove us to our coveted, if inadequate, muslin mosquito nets.

Mosquitoes notwithstanding, once the canoes arrived we were wondrously rewarded for our three-day wait in purgatory. In slender dugout canoes we glided out through narrow waterways amid the plush bird life and exotic undergrowth that line the Nile's tributaries in these parts. Night was spent on a well-cultivated island of the Jieng Thany, the fishing clans of the Jieng who, having no cattle, survive on the fruits of the land and fish. I recall sitting solitary in a dugout canoe on our second day, a boatman at his leaf-shaped oar before me; these were my most pleasurable moments of our weeks in the company of the SPLA. Here I was away, for some moments at least, from guns and guards. With the oarsmen I spoke easily and felt a new kind of freedom, the first I had experienced in these "liberated areas."

Once back on land we were marched into the parched rebel camp of Baidit, its zinc-roofed, cinder block buildings originally built by the Dutch to house a medical training center. On the edge of the squared compound we were presented with our own small concrete box, one of the few that remained secure enough that we could be locked away by night. Again, as guerrillas passed by our plot, single or in clusters, we were often made to feel as if we were on exhibit, objects to be prodded and inspected. More desirable were the careful ministrations of a rebel medic as each of us had our wounds carefully cleaned and bandaged. Capsules of tetracycline were broken, their contents sprinkled on open sores to help them heal. Back in our concrete cubical by night we tried to sleep, twisted and cramped two each in our midget mosquito nets. On hot nights the sweat rolled off our bodies as Stephen and I each sought desperately neither to touch nor awaken the other. As our hips became increasingly sore, sparsely padded on a concrete floor, so increased the torture of moving and keeping utterly still.

Most disturbing — to the point of driving me to distraction — was the "music" of Baidit. Fifty yards from our cubicle was a grass hut that housed a loudspeaker that belted out cassette recordings hour upon pulsating hour. Thanks to a large solar panel and lavish sunlight the volume remained high throughout the day. Audio offerings comprised an incongruous combination of rhythmic rebel marching songs in vernacular languages, a sermon by an American evangelist (intended for our spiritual edification?), and a medley of cheery Christmas songs, all repeated relentlessly, morning to night. I found no place to hide from the all-encompassing sound. The camp's entertainment center constituted a proud novelty to most guerrillas but was a painful thorn in my throbbing cranium that only craved silent solitude. My daily lamentations finally saw the broadcasts cut to the bone, leaving only the SPLA radio broadcasts from Ethiopia between 1:00 and 4:00 each afternoon. For me the cutback was an enormous relief.

As days of waiting lengthened I found myself waking each morning to ask, "How long, O Lord?" We filled our hours with a sort of order as each bit of personal space, each simple possession, took on increasing significance in our impoverished world. Simultaneously personal idiosyncrasies seemed to grow more pronounced, those of our companions, more irksome. Cleaning chores emerged. We took turns leading daily meditations for our quartet, Katie's Bible growing more tattered by the day. Stephen delicately excised the entire book of Philippians as well as each blank page in his attempt to copy and memorize the entire epistle... until his only pen ran dry. Later he surgically removed the entire book of first Peter and sat alone, committing it to heart. Heather and I read nearly the entire Old Testament with oral readings of the books of Lamentations, Job, and Ecclesiastes, which somehow soothed our souls. We begged for books from Mabior, our most regular guard at Baidit, who, with his raspy-voiced, assertive manner, became a friend. It was he who would supply us with bathing water, nail clippers, a hair pick, as requested. Books, however, were at a premium. "We smoke the books!" declared one guerrilla, meaning that they tear out pages in which to role their powerful, locally grown tobacco (the thin paper on which Bibles are printed being much preferred). Strangely, a fat volume of Jane Austen's *Pride and Prejudice* had somehow survived, each of us reading as much of romantic eighteenth-century England as we could endure, strangely juxtaposed amid a Sudanese rebel camp of the 1980s.

On the compound was a handful of boys, some as young as four or five. Older ones spent long hours over boiling pots cooking what scraps of food, often strips of hide or entrails, were left to them. The sturdy, unclad boys had made the transition from the serious responsibilities of cattle camp to the routine of SPLA camp life. Studied, if playful, goose steps replaced the night dances of cattle camp. At five o'clock each evening a battered trumpet played reveille as the troops assembled. Every soldier stood stiffly in his place and gave a salute. Simultaneously, every naked little boy also stood erect, utterly serious, saluting, utterly committed to the work of liberation.

I have said that there were four abductees. This is accurate if one is concerned only with aliens, the non-Sudanese, who were taken that night in Mundri. During 1986 and 1987 there were thousands of Sudanese also on the move, old people, emaciated women and children, the last survivors fleeing the slash and burn raids of the Morhaliin and the Rizigaat then sweeping down into western Bahr el Ghazal. Still others moved under mandate of the SPLA. Occasionally, moving with or around us on the same eastward bound trails were dozens of boys destined for the training camps of the "Red Army" (*Jiech Amar*) in Ethiopia.[45] As many as forty thousand boys between the ages of six and fifteen moved eastward, ostensibly to obtain the formal education unavailable in their homeland. Of these as many as a third were to die on the arduous trail.[46] Among the chaotic and ever-changing entourage of soldiers, captives, and civilians in transit that always surrounded us, were two individuals who had been taken from their homes on the same night we were. I became distinctly aware of them only when we were imprisoned in the same small concrete cubical at Baidit.

Lieutenant Colonel Martin Kajevora was a Moru of the Sudanese government army who was on home leave during the time of our abduction. Martin was articulate in English, jovial, intelligent, and worldly wise. His family home had been adjacent to my house in Mundri. According to Martin, he had taken extended leave in the south with the intention of deserting the army to join the SPLA. He had not, however, made his move and the guerrillas determined to hold him as a military prisoner until his loyalty could be determined. A well-provisioned

---

45. "Those who survived experienced appalling hunger, thirst, danger and sickness, arriving exhausted in Ethiopia. SPLA commanders, inspired by the Marxist thinking prevalent in Ethiopia, saw the opportunity to forge a new, tightly disciplined force out of the thousands of displaced and homeless young boys. Many of those who arrived in Ethiopia had been recruited and organized by the SPLA into bands for the grueling walk to Ethiopia. Cut off from family and community, isolated and vulnerable, the vision was to create out of them a *jesh ahmar* ['Red Army' in Arabic, which became *jiech*, or *jiec amar* in Jieng]. The young Red Army soldiers would become the military and political 'shock troops' of the Movement, totally committed to the cause of liberation and loyal to the leadership" (Werner et al., *Day of Devastation*, 528–29). With the overthrow of the Marxist regime in Ethiopia in 1991 the SPLA largely abandoned its Marxist veneer. Ironically, these same boys also came under the influence of the Episcopal Church of the Sudan while in the Ethiopian camps. Many became devoted Christians. When the refugees were forced out of Ethiopia, many returned to their home areas and began to preach the gospel of Christ and to form churches. At the same time, those boys who remained in the SPLA were a major evangelistic influence on the rebel army, which has now been largely Christianized. Contrast the image of the SPLA found in this letter with Marc's letters after his return to Sudan in the 1990s.

46. For more on these "unaccompanied minors" see the letter of April 1994 (p. 108).

and experienced military man, Martin had assembled his bush travel bag before his forced departure. Better prepared than any of us *khawajet*, he had a short wave radio, a couple of changes of clothes, a toothbrush, and mosquito net. The four of us "expats" were begrudgingly resupplied with essentials from the ample provisions soldiers had cleared out of our houses, ostensibly for themselves.

With us also was Sebit (meaning "Saturday" in Arabic, recalling the day of his birth), a malnourished, knock-kneed boy of perhaps fourteen years, the pathetic product of a union between a Moru woman and an Arab merchant. As an insecure half-caste Sebit was not trusted by some SPLA soldiers and quickly labeled a spy. In Mundri they had debated if they should simply shoot the lad but then decided better use could be made of him as slave labor. In exchange for his life Sebit was forced to carry massive loads, ever stumbling before us down the narrow paths we trod.

Our weeks in the bush proved to be an uncompromising — often humiliating and sobering — sort of tutor for my soul, one that has in some cases rippled on for months or years since. Particularly poignant was a memory of my behavior toward young Sebit that came starkly to consciousness as I sipped a beer in a Virginia café some six months after our release.

At Baidit, Martin and Sebit shared the same small concrete cell in which Heather, Katie, Stephen, and I were locked away each night. It is startling how, even in such stripped surroundings, we — all equal in captivity — could so quickly begin to class ourselves and our meager possessions, superior and inferior. Martin, with his radio and change of clothes, was clearly in the lead. The four of us expats had each assembled a small bundle of objects that were "our own," mostly bits of clothing we would have discarded in any other circumstance. Of us Katie was at the fore, still possessing remnants of her well-provisioned daypack which she, with unstinting generosity, shared with any of us as need arose. At the other end of our pecking order was impoverished, smelly, parasitic Sebit.

The one really significant contribution the SPLA made to our possessions had been mosquito nets, something without which we could hardly have survived. Sebit, of course, had no mosquito net. Each night he crawled into a concrete trough, a sort of sink, which extended the length of the room at waist height. There, above our heads, as we lay on the floor, we could hear Sebit swatting mosquitoes through the night. Given their ravenous determination it is unlikely he ever slept. It should not have surprised me then, that one hot, sunny morning I returned to our cubical to find Sebit sleeping in Stephen's and my spot on the floor. Gazing down at him with a degree of disgust I suddenly realized that there, folded beneath Sebit's scrawny body, was *my* blanket, *my blue patchwork blanket!* Here was my heritage, my connection with the broader world, my sense of past and present, symbol of my home and ancestry, all contaminated by this little creature!

In an instant I was filled with rage. Certainly, Sebit had not taken this liberty on his own. Someone must have told him to take my blanket and catch a midday nap. Only Stephen Anderson, eternally good-hearted, well-meaning Stephen, would have been so naïve! I spun around and stepped outside to Stephen. I was right. It had been he who invited Sebit to take rest…at my expense! Abruptly I chased Sebit from my blanket and reclaimed my heritage for myself alone.

Only six months later, in a very different atmosphere, did this small incident rise to consciousness…and when it did, I wept, and wept bitterly. How could I have been so arrogant, so utterly inconsiderate toward this young life? Me, the compassionate missionary, the open-minded teacher? The incident suggests something of the possessiveness, the arrogance, that I saw as so fundamental to my character, made all the more bold for our poverty and the meagerness of our possessions. Since that memory dawned and I have reflected on Sebit's tragic life he has become for me a kind of Christ figure for his pathos, his poverty and silent suffering. Some years later I learned that he was still alive, having gone through the military training camps and still among the troops in Ethiopia.

Such incidents aside, life at Baidit tended to be tedious. The monotony was broken one day with the shattering sounds of a sonic boom as two Sudan government MiG jets darted across the skies. Almost simultaneously a flurry of machine-gun fire erupted from gun sites mounted all around us, an utterly impotent response to the high tech wonders overhead. Missiles were fired as we felt the dull thud of bombs half a dozen times or more, under our feet (or through our bellies if we'd been quick and clever enough to dive for cover). More rockets, more mind-rattling machine-gun fire…continuing long after the jets had disappeared. Such manic activity seemed both a frantic response to the unanswerable threat overhead as well as a catharsis for soldiers too long away from the battlefront. In small clusters across the compound guerrillas laughed nervously as they scanned the serene and empty skies. Such intermittent air raids, we were told, had done no great damage, no lives lost. Aim is poor. Mabior and others laughed at our timidity. We were rightly shaken.

After perhaps ten days in this otherwise bland environment — even the maggot-laden dried fish had no salt — we were separated from one another for what was called an "interrogation." A thin, well groomed, if nervous, civilian-clad young soldier asked the second most frequently asked question of our sojourn: "When you are free, what will you tell the world about being taken by the SPLA? Why do *you* think you were taken?" It was clear our captors were concerned about their image beyond Sudanese borders. I tried to feed back what we'd been told from the first night. We had been "evacuated" for our own safety from an area that was rapidly becoming the battlefront. For their own safety the SPLA wanted all civilians, especially foreigners, out of the way. "Yes, but what do *you* say? Why were you taken?"Well, no, we were not "prisoners of war" because we were simply civilians taken from our homes. We were not "hostages" because that implied a ransom of some sort: I knew of none. If, however, it was an *evacuation,* I said, I did not like having my possessions looted. I had been angered by the arrogant and twisted Lieutenant Reuben who had commandeered my shoes, my radio, and who knows what else. My interrogator instructed me in guerrilla tactics and their repercussions, concluding that looting is never condoned by SPLA policy. At interrogation's end I was asked to read the form our young interrogator had written full. "Sign your name on the line below," I was told. At the bottom of the page it read: "Name of Hostage ________." Perhaps SPLM chairman Colonel Dr. John Garang clarified this some days later in a radio report of a speech. He said that we were *not* the "hostages of the SPLA," for we were only innocent civilians. Rather, we were "hostages of the situation in Sudan."

Every day had its periods of conjecture when the four of us wondered how much longer we would be held and just what we might do to "encourage" our release. It was something of a relief when, at the end of two weeks in Baidit, the towering (six feet eight inches) commander of the base, Kwol Manyang, surrounded as ever by six armed body guards, came to meet us. He told us that a truck was now available to transport us eastward toward Ethiopia. In part this was a response to Heather's determined declaration that, with shoes in shreds and feet still tender, she would *not* walk another step. No, Heather had not been transformed into a rugged guerrilla. Though delays seemed to multiply, it was only two days later that we were loaded atop a Russian-made lorry heaped high with hundreds of parachutes, packed tightly with some thirty-five armed guerrillas and civilians. With every stop on our journey there erupted the customary vying for space, the small wars and fiery words, common atop all overcrowded Sudanese market trucks. We were told the lorry was provided solely for us four, for our safe transport, but that did not assure us of any more comfort or space.

Like the Nile crossing, there were marvelous and memorable moments as we crossed the expansive plains of the Murle.[47] Incomparable were the elegant herds of *tiang,* resplendent in black, white, sienna, and gold; there were the enormous herds of white-tailed *cob,*[48] smaller and more delicate antelope, that surged around our truck in their tens of thousands, like rushing rivers in the night. It appeared our movements coincided with their annual mass migrations. The jar to reality

47. The two groups of Murle people are spread over a wide area of southeastern Sudan. The "lowland Murle" are pastoralists and the "highland Murle" are farmers. The two groups speak a common language and maintain close ties in spite of cultural differences.

48. *Tiang* and *cob* are species of antelope found in northeastern Africa.

came when soldiers began firing into the herds of *tiang*. With the poor accuracy of AK47s few were killed, but many were maimed, left to die in the savannahs. Then the lorry would verge off the dirt track toward the herds and volleys of gunfire dropped a dozen large antelope seemingly without discrimination (male and female *tiang* are not readily distinguished). Ultimately eight *tiang* carcasses and two wild geese were hauled up, blood oozing, onto the lorry, food for the rebel outpost ahead. We struggled to perch ourselves atop them, avoiding the spiraling horns of the *tiang* pointing in all directions. A rugged reserve for wildlife, this stretch of southern Sudan seemed untamed Eden, its major threat being humankind and our indiscriminate guns.

With the lorry under us heading eastward, our hopes again surged. Release might be near. It seemed we were being hurried along, having but one night on the road. Would the sounds of the airplane or helicopter we had often been promised suddenly come into earshot? We arrived on the edge of the village of Pibor, captured just three months earlier, under a waning moon at about one o'clock in the morning. We picked our way through a tangle of spiraled horns, over the cooling carcasses and dismounted. After much discussion among our captors we were led on a circuitous footpath down to the river. In boats we were ferried across and brought to the old compound of the "American Mission" (the American Presbyterians), home of successions of missionaries in more peaceful times, many of them known to me.[49] Here we spent our first night in a dusty, pre-fab oval tin hut. The morning revealed that a well-appointed pit latrine, lavish by guerrilla standards, had been dug for our use. Apparently we were not leaving immediately.

In this new abode we slept in what seemed luxurious beds, locally hewn wooden frames webbed with strips of cowhide and padded with layers of sienna and white *tiang* skins. This was in stark contrast to the cement floor of Baidit. We met our first rations of tea and sugar, captured government army supplies we were told, provided with a dented black pot. Rebel wives cooked the most savory food we had eaten thus far and a small pot of milk was brought for our consumption each morning. A dense, far-spreading tamarind tree offered cool shelter through long days and the brown river below provided a daily bath. It was strange, sometimes whimsical, how fragments of European-American life, the refuse of decades of missionary inhabitants, surfaced on the old compound; bits of a past readapted, discarded, or burned as firewood in a sleepy rebel camp. A sizeable machine gun was mounted just beyond the shrubs. As might be expected of our Nilotic rebel

---

49. The American Mission among the Murle people began at Pibor in 1952 (see Partee, *Adventure in Africa*). For a discussion of recent the Christian experience of the Murle see the article "Bringing Christ to the Murle" by Jonathan Arenson. Arenson estimates that as many as 50 percent of the Murle became Christians during the civil war.

hosts, every patch of garden being cultivated so carefully around the compound was given to mind-numbing tobacco. Armed guards rotated shifts outside our hut night and day.

It was in our fifth week of captivity that I began to have stomach pains. Throughout our journey we had thanked God for the miracle of good health. On the trail we had often had to skim water off mud puddles or stagnant ponds. Never was water purified. Both Katie and Heather had had less than four months to adapt to the varieties of parasites so plentiful in Sudan, but I was the first to succumb. With the appearance of blood, mucus, and diarrhea it was clear some bug had taken hold in me. After a few sleepless nights, much complaining, and several visits from an SPLA "doctor" in whom I had little trust, some blue and pink capsules they called "measles" appeared in small quantity. Amazingly, thankfully, the pains and diarrhea subsided.

Many soldiers rotated guard duty or walked through "our" compound. Mathiang was a gentle, good-natured guerrilla in his tattered khaki military jacket and torn shorts. "Don't fear," he assured me in Thuongjieng (Jieng language) from the first day, "God will take care of you. He is here and he will see you safely to your homeland." His were familiar Christian phrases. As we became more friendly I asked him why he wore a charm dangling from his neck, a bulging pouch of "medicines" supplied by a *kojur* (a traditional diviner-healer). "I kill Arabs," was his response, meaning government soldiers, be they Arab or black. "I cannot take the cross of Christ into the killing fields." "Do you pray?" I asked. "Oh yes, I know God is always with me. I pray constantly: I could not live through this war without the power of Christ, but I cannot take his cross into the battle. When the fighting is ended," he explained, "when there is peace, then I will wear the Lord's Cross again." Always Mathiang treated us with gentleness and respect.

Strong and broad framed, Mangarowit was a soldier only two years out of cattle camp. He was about thirty years old and, like many others, had left a wife behind in the village. Newly married, he had no children. Others had left several wives and offspring they hadn't seen in three or four years at this stage in the war. Some would never see their families again. On Mangarowit's neck, suspended from a leather cord, hung a shiny black plastic object, like the finger grip from a syringe, I thought. This was his cherished black cross. He polished it regularly. Early in our stay Mangarowit asked if we four could accompany him to the inter-tribal church service on Sunday morning. Even with additional guards, however, this was not allowed, our captors anxious lest knowledge of our whereabouts be circulated beyond this rebel enclave. Often I saw him reading, slowly mouthing each word, from his tattered, loose-paged Jieng New Testament, his only book. He, like many, struggled to teach himself to read. In the evenings I heard him sing church songs composed in wartime. "Death has come to reveal our faith," was often on his lips.

There was a simple and endearing goodness about Mangarowit, a man who had left familiar life for the strictures of the SPLA, who knew he could easily end his life in the "armed struggle for liberation" like tens of thousands of his comrades, equally uneducated, having only a couple of months in military training camps. With little knowledge of a world beyond cattle camp or of national politics, his goals were immediate: to keep the land of his people, the God-given land of their ancestors (along with the vast oil wealth beneath it), for their children to have freedom of religion void of Islamic *shari'a* law, to have equal economic development with the north (whatever that might mean), and . . . to be respected as equals with all Sudanese: not to be called "slave" (*abed* in Arabic). SPLA Radio states their goal as the "liberation of the oppressed Sudanese masses from the elite bourgeois ruling clique in Khartoum."

Often we sat with our guards to listen to BBC World Service as well as SPLA and Juba Radio on their irrepressible little short wave radio. We heard in those days what were said to be documented descriptions of between one thousand and three thousand southern civilians — men, women, and children — who had been massacred amid racial tension exacerbated by the war in the town of Ed Da'ein in Darfur on the weekend of March 27. We heard of the slaughter in Wau of three hundred (some said six hundred) men on one day in August. There were installments read about present-day slavery in Sudan. Young people, it said, are taken for slaves by nomadic bands as their parents are killed, their cattle raided, and entire villages wiped away.[50]

There were some days I found myself revolted, disquieted to the point that I could not go near the radio. The carnage was too close, too all-encompassing to absorb. Evening news reports blended with the firsthand narratives of men coming in from the battle-front, merging daily with the sight of dozens of young (some *very* young), naïve, emaciated new recruits passing through our camp as they trudged toward rebel training camps. All this combined with the intimate, daily reflections of our all too human captors.

Compassion for the men who held us — for all the desperate people who surrounded us and passed us by — the enormous suffering of this war, blended with our longing for our own little "liberation." Though brief (we hoped) and limited, our vulnerability merged with the vulnerability around us. The myriad participants in this war had faces. The scale of our discomforts seemed inconsequential

---

50. Tens of thousands of southern Sudanese, mostly women and children, were enslaved during the civil war — most of these have not yet been returned to their homes. At least two former slaves, Francis Bok and Menda Nazer, have written the stories of their captivity: Bok's *Escape from Slavery* and Nazer's *Slave*.

in the midst of a bleeding land convulsing with famine, mass slaughter, forced abductions, and destitute refugees. "No one matters in this war; not one individual
life is of importance." The cold, emotionally sterile words of Commander Thon
Magot came to mind as youngsters marched by us wearing only rags, the future
"Red Army" going to war.

While in detention how should we or could we pray? How might we find God's
presence in our own sorrow, our relentless desire for release, our parasites inner
and outer, against the vulgar grind of war? We would gather our little group for
prayers that often seemed insignificant, misdirected. From our one tattered Bible
we read of the wilderness wanderings of the Jews, of Jesus' temptations among the
"wild beasts." As stricken widows passed us by eastward Heather, a midwife, would
read about the miraculous birth of Samson and remind us of the joy of barren
women when at last they conceive, as well as of the intense sorrow of every
woman whose children die. I think each of us, at various times, felt guilt about
our own selfishness, our possessiveness of our meager rations and our carefully
apportioned space in the tin hut. We bemoaned the pettiness of our personal
conflicts. We pitied our parents and loved ones who, we suspected, suffered more
than we — totally severed from us and knowing nothing of our well-being. How
could we pray? How is God present amid this web of petty conflicts, still more
amid irrational, undeserved suffering all around us; our Sudanese kinfolk's so
much more than ours?

In our attempts to hold it together we made communion. There was no bread
or wine. What we did have was *kissera,* ground sorghum made into paper-thin
brown crepes, made by the hands of rebel wives. And we had our small daily
ration of fresh milk. In a land of hunger and destitution this somehow seemed an
appropriate image of the suckling of God. These became for us the Body and Blood
of Christ, body and blood in the ruthless carnage of war. In those moments, as
we sat around our altar, a battered ammunition box with Russian lettering across
its sides, we tried to open our hearts to the suffering around us. The old woman,
Dorcas, had brought us eggs and cassava root. Like her wrinkled handkerchief,
we tried to unfold our soiled hearts. There was little to give from our anxiety and
lethargy, but many broken fragments to receive, to hold in the presence of God.
We imagined people across the world gathering close with us...from home in
Northern Ireland and across America, our beloved colleagues and students who
had probably fled the college within hours of our abduction; we imagined warriors
in an array of hues in government and SPLA forces, and young soldiers in the
making, our occasional companions, all somehow bound together in an utterly
impossible hope for reconciliation and healing.

August 25, the forty-ninth day of our captivity, began with the monotony
of every other day at Pibor: the erratic discomfort of parasites in my belly, the

endless pinpricks of the ticks that inhabited every seam of my *jalabiyya*, a breakfast of gruel, our uneasy cohabitation with our guards. Several times during preceding weeks small aircraft had passed overhead. If they tarried for more than a few minutes, a flurry of machine-gun fire rose from the gun mounts hidden in the bush around us. As at Baidit, these volleys did nothing to threaten the aircraft overhead, but evoked wild spurts of adrenaline among the otherwise lethargic soldiers on the ground. On this particular day the purr of a small Cessna arose from the south, the little aircraft beginning to circle, like a lonely, red-bellied mosquito overhead. In seconds the loud clamor of machine gun fire was unleashed, at first in the distance at the main rebel base, then from gun mounts in the bush that surrounded us. Impervious to the clatter we endured on the ground, the persistent little insect kept circling, occasionally flying out of sight, then returning: ten minutes, fifteen, twenty. The ground fire blasted on noisily wasting vast quantities of ammunition. Some two miles away, at the heart of the military base, the commander gave orders that a heat-seeking missile be fired, a weapon precise and powerful enough to down the intruder. For some reason the firing mechanism failed and the missile fizzled in its mechanism. Still the little aircraft circled.

At last the base commander, realizing something very strange in the aircraft's peculiar persistence, gave orders to build a fire on the airstrip indicating an invitation to land. Making a wide loop, the Cessna came in for a quiet landing. As it touched ground a large number of armed soldiers flocked around the aircraft. On board were two men, one a pilot from Mission Aviation Fellowship (MAF) which owned the airplane; the other, Mr. Daniel Butrus of the Christian relief agency known as ACROSS, under which Stephen, Heather, and Katie had entered Sudan.[51] The reception was initially tense. Gradually the newcomers explained that negotiations for the release of the one British and three American "hostages" had been underway for weeks between the U.S. and British governments and the offices of the SPLA in Addis Ababa and Nairobi. Only the previous day had the SPLA granted clearance for a plane to enter Pibor to evacuate the four. As it turned out, approval had indeed been granted in Nairobi and in Addis Ababa ... but the radio message had never reached the SPLA base at Pibor. Realizing the international debacle that would have erupted had he succeeded in shooting down the Cessna, the commander was visibly shaken. Immediately soldiers were sent to tell us, over a mile away, to prepare for departure. Again, crossing the Pibor River by canoe, now in bright morning light, our motley quartet walked toward deliverance on a little Cessna airplane.

This was an abrupt end. The evacuation we had waited so long for seemed inconsequential in contrast to all we had encountered, all the facets of Sudan at

---

51. ACROSS: Association of Christian Resource Organizations Serving Sudan.

war that had become part of who each felt himself or herself to be. I remember well the peculiar blend of wistfulness and exhilaration that filled me as I gazed down over the flat, uninterrupted vastness that is south Sudan. On the one hand I was deeply grateful to be getting out, to be able to reassure my family and friends of my well-being, to have the parasites that inhabited every seam of my *jalabiyya* as well as my bowels eradicated, and to have a fresh change of clothes. On the other hand, our weeks in the hands of the SPLA had served to bond my soul, like nothing previously, with the suffering of the people of Sudan. My sense of identification, indeed of participation, with this traumatized land and its remarkable peoples had not diminished but become far more intimate.

And...*why* had we stayed in Mundri? Ultimately each of us had our own distinctive motivations for holding on. Yes, the elders of the village and church had been indecisive. All of us preferred to deny reality. None of us wanted to capitulate. Yes, it seemed preferable to deny our fears, to forego the reality mounting all around us and persevere with what was familiar. Yes, we feared that our dispersion could bring some students into far greater danger than what we knew as a tightly knit college community.

Beyond these concerns I speak only for myself. After our abduction I would not reenter Sudan for six years. Nonetheless, in retrospect these events were not so much a termination as a culmination of all that preceded it, an anticipation of all yet to come.

I had first gone to Sudan in 1981 in the belief that in returning to Africa there was still a great deal to challenge and transform me.[52] This may sound self-centered but I had come to believe that it is always in the dialogue, the shared, mutually transforming experience, that the most significant work of learning is done — never more so for me than in Africa. Though I might be awkwardly labeled a "missionary" as if I were *taking* something to Sudan or *doing something to* or *for* its people, I knew that in reality my primary purpose was going to be in encountering facets of the spiritual, the Divine, hitherto very rare in my experience. Soon after my arrival in Sudan this was amply confirmed. While I knew I had things to offer as a teacher, an artist, a pastor, the real benefit would be in the *shared* venture, the chemistry that would transform both student and teacher together. While there is no question that some refraction of the Christ is to be met in every human community, every society, every culture, it seemed as if these "small incarnations" were an almost daily occurrence during my years

---

52. Marc had been in Zaïre (now the Democratic Republic of the Congo) in 1970 working with his sister and brother-in-law, Mavis and Sam Bergen, who were missionaries there. He had also spent time in Nigeria in 1975. Each of these two stays had been for a period of about nine months. Marc described these times as "deeply formative periods of my life."

in Sudan. There was no encounter, no event, which did not possess its spiritual dimension, revealing something of the presence and nature of God.

For all its bland uncertainty, all the raw emotions and abrasive encounters, our experience as "hostages" brought these experiences to their culmination. The soles of our feet had felt the great beauty as well as the desolation of this land at war. We had eaten the food of starving people. We heard the gunfire and felt the thud of bombing raids. With virtually every common, sensual encounter the Creator seemed tangibly present. Heather had experienced, as she said, the life of a refugee who leaves all, trudging into the unknown. There were moments — talking quietly with a sullen soldier, too familiar with death for his years; observing a destitute young widow struggling to suckle her emaciated infant — that the Christ in his vulnerability and pathos drew exquisitely near. It was these tender encounters, laced with the Divine, more than anything else, that had drawn me to Sudan . . . and held me . . . and have drawn me back time and again. Those long and volatile days "in the bush" with the SPLA, continually mingling with the dispossessed and suffering, were touched with the immediacy, the efficacy, and the passion of Christ, like none other in my life.

Surveying the billowing chaos that is Sudan my mind goes back to the song of Mary Alueel. Rising from the mouths of SPLA soldiers as we marched on, the final two verses describe, through visionary Sudanese eyes, both the battle and its resolution:

3. Evil and good are competing. The earth will stand still
    and the blood of mankind will cry out: "O Lord, Lord!"
   People are crying out all over the earth: "God, do not make us orphans
    of the earth!
   Look back upon us, O Creator of humankind!
   Evil is in conflict with us tying heavy burdens upon our necks which no
    person can bear."

4. Let us encourage our hearts in the hope of God who once breathed into
    the human body.
   His ears are open to our prayers; the Creator of humankind is watching;
   He reigns from his place, seeing the souls of those who die.
    Turn your ears to us: upon whom else can we call?
   Is it not you alone, O God? Let us be branches of your son.
   Jesus will come with the final word of judgment, bringing glory to the earth,
    peace and the truth of faith.

This is an apocalyptic vision from the heart of a child of Sudan in wartime. All the inhabitants of the earth are engaged in terrible conflict, combat both physical, in the body, and spiritual. Then in one great, culminating moment they all, with one united voice, cry out, pleading that they not be made "orphans of the earth," not be abandoned, made destitute, landless, as it seems so obviously they are.

In the final verse there is an abrupt step back, taking in the larger, encompassing reality: Above and over all is the Creator God brooding, listening, intently gazing on all that occurs. Under his eye *none* is bereft. *None* is orphaned. The compassionate, creating Father is attentive to each loss, each soul that dies, be it that of a young solder, infant babe, or destitute widow, whether by bullet or through starvation: each is known and beloved. With confidence we affirm that Christ will intervene, will arbitrate and establish that glorious peace which is longing to be born.

Throughout our wilderness wanderings with the SPLA, both of these dimensions seemed to encompass us, the battle that has left two million corpses in its wake . . . and awareness of a compassionate God who knows all and is concerned with each life's demise. It is this mystery that held me, this enigma that transfixed me. God is intimately present even amid what appears to be his utter abandonment. Transfixed, I could not leave. This is why I stayed.

Marc Nikkel

Part Three

Pilgrims and Refugees

Letters of Longing for Africa, 1988–93

The years following Marc's release from SPLA captivity were horrific for southern Sudan. By 1987 the last NGOs and Christian organizations seeking to bring relief and development to southern Sudan, including ACROSS, had been expelled, with the result that "there were virtually no witnesses to the colossal human tragedy unfolding in the country."[1] Government-funded militia groups were given free reign not only to attack military targets of the SPLA, but also to raid Southern Kordofan, the western Upper Nile, and Bahr al Ghazal. "The result during 1987 and 1988 was a bloodbath across wide areas of Bahr el Ghazal. Countless villages were destroyed, cattle killed or looted, young children and women taken off as slaves. . . . Many thousands were killed, others died of starvation, many thousands more fled."[2] By the end of 1988 as many as a quarter of a million people had been killed in these areas of Sudan. Most of this carnage was invisible to the outside world.

In June 1989 Sadiq al-Madhi's government was overthrown in a military coup. Omer al-Bashir assumed the leadership of the country, but it soon became clear that the power behind this new government was the National Islamic Front led by Hassan al-Turabi. The regime of al-Bashir and al-Turabi must be described in the harshest terms. Declaring the war against the south to be a jihad[3] the National Islamic Front formulated a process of Islamization of the south through what can only be called genocide. In 1997 political theorist Paul Marshall wrote,

> The word genocide is a harsh one, thrown around too frequently and too cheaply. In the case of Sudan, however, it is simply a factual description. The United Nations describes genocide as "attempting to destroy a group by killing its members, causing bodily harm, subjecting it to conditions which cause its physical destruction, preventing births, and forcibly transferring children." This is a systematic

---

1. Werner et al., *Day of Devastation*, 525.
2. Werner et al., *Day of Devastation*, 525.
3. *Jihad* is the Arabic word for "struggle" and has a variety of meanings, including the interior spiritual struggle against one's own sinfulness in the quest to be submissive to the will of Allah. In forms of radicalized Islam, however *jihad* can also mean literal warfare against those who oppose or who are viewed as opposed to Islamization.

description of the current situation in southern and eastern Sudan. . . . The government restricts the activities of outside aid groups so that it can control the supply of food to groups of refugees. . . . Non-Muslims are given the choice of converting to Islam or being denied food, clothing and shelter. . . . Others, especially women and children, are enslaved, either for labor or sex, or both.[4]

During the late 1980s and through the 1990s the Sudanese government waged a war not only against the SPLA but also against its own civilian population. Even when atrocities became known, the world was largely silent. "Under an arrangement the United Nations made in 1989, Sudan was given power to veto when and where aid could be delivered by Operation Lifeline Sudan, the consortium of relief groups working under the Untied Nations flag."[5] The Sudanese government regularly used this veto to keep relief workers (who could have functioned as witnesses) out of areas where the government was launching offensive actions, thereby keeping food and medicine away from the people who most needed assistance.

Although the south was filled with the violence of war and the Episcopal Church was still living with the effects of schism, the churches, amazingly, began to experience unprecedented growth. "Before the war the [Anglican] Diocese of Rumbek among the Dinka consisted of nine congregations. . . . The number may now [1996] reach 400."[6] Figures like these can be produced for most people groups and most areas across the south.

But during the period of 1988–93 Marc was unable to return to the Sudan. Having been "with" the rebels, his visa was denied. He spent much of 1988 in Kenya, teaching at St. Paul's United Theological College some twenty miles outside of Nairobi. He continued to cultivate relationships with Sudanese students and refugees living in the area, and even managed to visit Kenyan cattle camps of the Turkana and Samburu people during holiday breaks from teaching. Marc then migrated to the U.K. to study for a doctorate, a project which surveyed the history of Roman Catholic and Anglican mission work with the Jieng, with a special focus on the indigenous theology being produced by the Jieng through their newly composed hymns. And Marc remained a pastor, in Britain and in Italy, reaching out to Sudanese, gathering refugee communities to pray, to search the scriptures, to mourn, and to celebrate.

Limuru, Kenya
August 25, 1988

One year ago today: the deafening roar of the small yellow Cessna shifts to a steady purr as it lifts six shaky and relieved passengers up, over the flat grasslands

4. Marshall, Their Blood Cries Out, 20–21.
5. Mary Ann Glendon, "Sudan's Unpunished Atrocities."
6. Wheeler, "Church Growth in Southern Sudan 1983–1996."

of southern Sudan. The terrain below, in this year of sparse, retarded rains, is broken by the occasional dull, brown stream and a sprinkle of tenacious trees. With effort a mud and thatch hut can be seen, linked with others by narrow paths, radiating like spiders' webs. This is our departure from Sudan — the four "hostages" or "evacuees" or whatever they call us — on August 25, 1987.

Like a determined mosquito over a formidable ear, the pilot had kept his small plane circling the rebel-held village. For half an hour he awaited some sign of permission to land, spotting bursts of gunfire from only one of the four or five machine gun mounts that spewed impotent rebel warnings. The clattering guns caused far more excitement among teeming guerrillas down below than in the cab of the deafened pilot high overhead. When the plane at last landed a couple of trembling rebels confessed that it was by God's grace and great good luck that the plane had not been downed by the heat-seeking missile trained on it. The base commander called a halt just as it was being fired: the missile fizzled in the mechanism. Had the persistent plane been swatted from the sky there would have been far-reaching repercussions. In this, the seventh week of our detention, rebel communications had not successfully relayed the message that a small, civilian plane would be allowed to land and rescue the four "hostages" between 8:30 and 10:00 a.m. on this day.

A swarm of soldiers provided the four of us with a chaotic escort from the place we had been secreted a mile away. We folded our disheveled, untrimmed selves into the airplane and rose from the strip of low grass bordered by crowds of tattered rebels. Some waved farewell, ever present Kalashnakovs flung over their shoulders. Was it from the relief of tension after weeks of waiting or the thought of a "final" departure from Sudan and from beloved people that I found tears coming to my eyes as I surveyed the stark land below? It was a relief, certainly, to be away from AK47s and the ever-changing shifts of guards around our hut.

Suddenly we were puttering toward "freedom," toward phone calls and publicity, toward family and loved ones. I recalled in that cushioned seat how I had perceived those long days we had been prodded on. As we trekked knee deep in the flood plans of the Nile I had, perhaps too romantically, thought of the floods of Noah's day, of Moses' crossing of the sea, and of the baptism in the Jordan. It had become for me a kind of baptism, a passing through the waters, the seas of Sudan's troubles. In a small way I was participating in this dying... holding, in God, to the hope of rising again. Those days were a sort of submersion in this gasping struggle to survive. For me there was a tangible sense of Christ, amid, within a ravaged people, whatever their tribe or race, civilian, rebel, or national army. In that small airplane surrounded with smooth, molded plastic, vinyl seats, and glass windows — already a world apart from huts and sleeping mats of *tiang* hides — I felt as if the loving identification with Sudan had intensified in these weeks. It had not diminished. Was it, I asked myself, cheek against the cool glass of the airplane's window, a baptism that marked an end of my life in Sudan, an end to relationship with many people of the church, and with the indomitable Jieng? If it was a baptism, was it an end or a beginning? If a dying... then a rising to what?

It is ten months since I have written one of these long letters. Eighteen days before our release, my mother, Rosie Nikkel, was found to have cancer, which had spread throughout her abdomen. She had prayed during those days of high local California publicity around our "captivity" that she would live to see me again. On our release I returned quickly to California. We had ten formative weeks together. She died on December 7. My first Christmas "home" in some eight years followed fast on the funeral and all the tender emotions in which a family is bonded together in pain and love. Amid my completion of a thesis, my preparations for another departure, packing up all remaining possessions in "Marc's room" of the past twenty years, and much public speaking, there were those good and solid times with my father, Reuben, with sister and brother-in-law, Marvis and Sam. They now live together, the three of them, in my parents' home of fifty-four years.

Since mid-March I have been back on African soil assisting the overtaxed teaching staff at St. Paul's United Theological College, Kenya, twenty miles north of Nairobi. While courses I have taught have comprised a variety I would not have chosen, we have made it through the third term. Hearts and minds have been shaped a bit. Friendships have emerged, new and continuing, in this beautiful and exceedingly complex land of Kenya. Occasionally I ask myself how it is that I have taken up quite such a challenge — another web of cultures and relationships — for a mere six months in a year already so fragmented. For many reasons, however, this interlude has been precisely right, even providential.

I still ask myself: was the walk through those waters a baptism marking an end... or a beginning? How does the past relate to the future? Five months in Kenya have provided remarkable contacts not only with the diverse peoples of this country but also with Sudanese students, "asylum seekers," refugees and professional people. It is my reflections on two of these new friendships, beyond Sudan's borders, that I write.

Thomas lives the precarious life of a foreign student-cum-refugee in Nairobi. Despite his tidy grooming and prosperous ponch at thirty-eight years, his life is as precarious as that of most Sudanese who are separated from family and homeland in wartime. Thomas anticipates the likelihood of a sort of "baptism" other than mine. As we walk along the red gravel path near the college, he recalls a traditional Jieng proverb: " 'I am your grave,' says hyena to dog." One imagines that omniscient hyena grin consuming the scavenger's face. The corners of his glossy, laughing lips turn quizzically as he breaks into his hyena's howl. Thomas is silent for a few moments, leaving me to discern the truth in hyena's words. "If the dog should die in the house, the people throw out the carcass ... and hyena will be there to devour it. If, on the other hand, the dog wanders too far into the forest, there too, patient, persistent hyena will pack him into his belly. No matter where dog goes, where he hides, he must know his end: 'I am your grave.'"

An easy grin breaks on Thomas's own smooth, broad face. He speaks with careless bravado about the life of a guerrilla, about the great warring traditions of his people. He will not speak about the destitution of his wife and two kids silently hanging on in the Khartoum rains, about a ravaged homeland, or slavery or starvation. Like rebels around a nighttime fire he says: *"Ma batal!"* "Take it easy; we don't talk about bad things; that just makes you unhappy; you feel weak." Only recently has he learned that, two years into his course, the Sudanese government has cut off all funds for completion of his studies. The old proverb of hyena and dog is conjured in memory by young men, those from cattle camp or town and students like Thomas, away from their homeland, as they consider the narrow options of the future. The war, the liberation movement, the likelihood of death, awaits them, most of them. Once he completes his course in business administration Thomas anticipates this baptism in war: "I am your grave." The hyena is waiting.

During these months in Kenya there is still another sort of Sudanese initiation I've encountered, that of the "asylum seeker." For many it is a baptism of severing, a cutting away from all that is familiar ... and the feeling of one's own final rejection. *Refugee.* I have found that the designation carries enormous stigma: the dispossessed, the freeloaders, the homeless, the despised, the maltreated, the jobless, those perceived as without the rights of citizens. These are they who wait in the long lines of the destitute from many lands. Day after day, month after month, they wait for some paper document that so inadequately tells others who they are, or the crumb of allowance, twenty-four dollars a month (in five months to be totally cut off). I survey the few, mostly young, Sudanese I have come to know, who have taken this course. The pressures upon them, inner and outer, seem never to subside.

Kuchtiel (the name means "one who does not know jealousy") is a fellow of twenty-three years. Perhaps six feet six inches tall, he often folds his thin, basketball-playing frame into a contemplative pylon, a posture which carries that blank, faraway look of the dispossessed. There is a lethargy, a quiet desperation, his brow creased, as he considers the carnage in his homeland. He does not know if his mother — most beloved of all people — is dead or alive, nor his brothers or sisters, or even if they linger in the mud and pollution of Khartoum during the recent floods. He frequently suffers from severe headaches. The other day Kuchtiel said, "I cannot think clearly; sometimes I feel like I am going mad."

He held a prestigious position and good salary, by the standards of Khartoum, the only southerner in a massive office block, the employee of Arab government officials. After two years he, with his quiet, conscientious manner, could bear the discrimination no longer. Three times he was accused of being a spy and interrogated, held for days and weeks. Twice he was severely tortured by government security, a criminal because of his color and his tribe. In the end he disappeared without notice. His first choice, like all of his agemates, was to join the movement, to find his way out of Khartoum to the "bush," to enter the belly of the hyena. Five times he attempted. Each time his way was cut, and he was discovered by the army. Each time he was able to bluff his way out of a silent execution.

Kuchtiel's father, an Anya-nya guerrilla, was killed in the first civil war, in the late 1960s. By age eleven Kuchtiel had set out precariously and utterly alone to obtain an education. With some periods of near starvation he made it through secondary school and a further certificate. For fourteen years he has not seen his family. Try as he would, the war severed every homeward journey. Now, in June 1987, his uncles, those surviving, displaced in Khartoum from their scorched and decimated land, consulted together. Kuchtiel, age twenty-six, was called to a special meeting to receive their wisdom. A few of them are educated, one with two doctorates. Their sons and nephews, nearly every young man of the clan — some four hundred all counted — had already joined the movement. Most are dead. The hyena is finished with them. The elders gathered their authority in their long, tattered *jalabiyyas*. They brought together what little money they could spare for purchase of Kuchtiel's air ticket. With one voice they declared that their son Kuchtiel was not to join the war. He, for one, would preserve their line. He must go out to obtain an education. He must advance himself so that his people have a foundation in the future. His life is to be preserved.

For much of the past year Kuchtiel sat behind the prison-like fences and guarded gates of a "refugee receiving center." With him were a couple of thousand other asylum seekers of many nationalities, among them perhaps a dozen Sudanese. They are allowed to leave during specified hours, but only in extreme emergencies are they allowed a weekend pass. "Being a refugee has taught me to do things I never would have thought of," says Kuchtiel. Among the new skills are those of lying, making up stories for the sake of a pass. Three or four weekends he, with two Sudanese camp mates, have come to visit their "uncle" at my house.

Kuchtiel's agemates back home — those who survive — now live the stoic and deprived lives of guerrilla fighters. The couple of letters that come from them denounce Kuchtiel: he is no longer their friend. He is cut off without honor or respect, called a betrayer and a coward with no place among them. He has fled, a soft asylum seeker. Bearing the rejection of his all-important agemates, the wretched news of his charred and depopulated land, as well as the negligible identity of a jobless refugee, Kuchtiel now lives in a tiny one-person room in Nairobi. This he shares with three other refugees. He has written over eighty letters seeking entry into degree programs, whether in Africa or overseas . . . and searching for funding. Always the first obstacle is funding. To date not one positive response has arrived. This is Kuchtiel's silent, long-suffering baptism as an alien in a strange land.

These are small images of individual suffering I see rippling out at the periphery, myself now a year outside Sudan's borders. At the heart of the country the trauma seems only to increase. Three days ago a Kenyan newspaper began an article with the words, "It is as if there is a curse upon Sudan." The writer went on to describe civil war and continuing famine. There are those who die of malnutrition and related diseases by hundreds and thousands during the present weeks. Bodies are strewn along the railroad tracks and footpaths that lace northward. The last rem- nants of human life crawl along seeking food and security they will not find. The article described the dark blankets of locusts that spread out for dozens of miles to devour every blade of cultivated life . . . and finally there are the floods which now melt the mud homes of hundreds of thousands leaving their inhabitants — especially the displaced southerners — stranded on garbage heaps in northern cities. These plagues, said the article, are "of biblical proportions."

What sort of baptism is this for the peoples of Sudan as the Nile floods its banks? There is no simple, symbolic sprinkling here. Some estimates suggest that over five hundred have died in Khartoum during the past two weeks (contrary to official statements of ninety). One agency states that forty thousand children are at immediate risk with the spread of diarrhea and cholera in polluted waters.

Whether in Old Testament biblical or in African traditional thought it indeed seems to many that God has forsaken his people in Sudan. He bestows curses rather than blessing. Withered elders of the Jieng and Shilluk[7] peoples declare that they wish they had not lived to see the present devastation. The question turns over time and again in the minds of many, "Why has God forsaken us?" A pastor in Khartoum, a former student, writes that for many Muslims, Christians, and traditionalists alike these tragedies are perceived as God's punishment. As in years past many continue to search their souls, confess, and repent. The tragedy continues. It seems a baptism unto death, the decimation of entire peoples.

There are those few, however, who witness to signs, even if small, of a rising from the waters, a glimpse of redemption. I close with one more image from the

---

7. The Nilotic kingdom of the Shilluk is on the west bank of the Nile. The Shilluk are among the most organized of Nilotic cultures. They have a divine king who symbolizes the whole realm and whose rituals and physical well-being are believed to affect the kingdom for good or ill.

periphery of Sudan. During our captivity last year we saw a few of the emaciated mothers, among thousands, trekking alongside twelve-year-old rebels-to-be eastward, toward Ethiopian refugee camps, where well over three hundred thousand southern Sudanese now live, some in appalling conditions. Many of their mud and thatch dwellings have also been washed away in recent rains. In one of the four camps, Pinyudu (meaning "the land of the ostrich"), huddle over thirty thousand inhabitants, 60 percent of whom are children under fifteen years of age. Many sit numbed both by malnutrition and by the atrocities they have witnessed. In these camps — now somewhat more stable than a mere two months ago — churches are being built of mud and thatch and ever larger congregations of displaced, disenfranchised people gather together.

Recently I received a letter from one of my closest friends, a former student. We have had no contact since his graduation four years ago. His is, for me, an eloquent statement of hope contrary to the prevailing sense of annihilation. Zechariah writes the following from one of the worst of the refugee camps:

> Thank the Lord our Christ that he has joined us through the message I received from you though we spent a long time without meeting each other. It is only your name which I heard over Radio during your sojourn in 1987.
>
> For our Father to bless and empower me in my ministry I want your uncountable prayers to him for me and my family. Pray for me as one of the church elders. He is using me to do his work throughout these years since I have been given the name "Abuna" as you know [meaning Pastor; I heard this of him when held by the rebels].
>
> The theology and practical teaching of God are being revealed to the people in these times. They are being seen during this difficult time of sorrow and pain. This leads to a change of life and to faith among our people. The more there are sorrows and pains, the more the faith of each person grows firm. Now many people are asking God to bring peace to the Country through the way he has chosen, in order to stop the death which is prevailing.
>
> Many people have changed their traditional beliefs in created things as their gods to faith in the Creator. They are now believing on the true God the Creator, through our Lord Jesus Christ. It is now being witnessed in Rumbek, Bor, and other areas of the Sudan. The church of Christ is growing very rapidly. This is confirmed by the Jieng song you know well, "*Thon ce ben e nyoth de gam...* " (death has come to reveal the faith...). It is really true. The death which is now prevailing has shown a strong faith among our people. If you once visit Sudanese Refugee Camps you would

believe it. There are many churches functioning in the areas as well as in the Refugee Camps. God is doing his work because he is perfect.

[He then makes some harsh complaints against UNHCR's service among them].... Food items and medicine are given to us like one bone thrown to many dogs and the people laugh at them....

So, being a Christian this is my appeal to all of you Christians who are filled with the Spirit, in the name of our Lord Jesus Christ. Don't forget that we are not totally orphans because the Holy Spirit is with us, and we hope that the Christ will be with us again. We should remember the song which says, "We are one in the Spirit, we are one in the Lord." If we are one according to that song then let the aids be given to our people abundantly.

Christina Halima is asking some gifts from you if they can reach us here in the refugee camps. The children born during your absence are: Sunday Marial (a baby boy) and a newly born baby girl, Alek Marial. Halima is requesting some clothes for men, women, and children because we are naked together with our neighbors. There is also need for bedsheets and blankets.

We are still remembering you always in our prayers. *Athiei de Nhialich abe ya to ke yen aluot ku jol a kockuon kedhia. Yenekan.* [The blessing of God be with you always and with all your people. Amen]

Here is one image of hope that the waters will recede and that from them something new might be born, indeed, is being born.

On that day one year ago, in the small Cessna, I asked myself if my own "baptism," splashing through the flood plains of the Nile as "hostage," was one that marked an end or a beginning. It seemed for a time I could identify intimately with those around me struggling for survival. That image of my baptism now seems insignificant in contrast to the continuing trauma in Sudan. Regardless, whether far out on the periphery with students, refugees, and the displaced, or nearer to the center, the impact of Sudan and of the sense of Christ's faithful presence there marks my soul. I believe he is present even, perhaps especially, among those who sense they are a forsaken people. Only he has the power to redeem a curse, power to transform drowning floodwaters into a redemptive baptism. In ways I could not imagine events of the past year prove to be only a beginning.

In early September I will return from Kenya to the United States to spend the month with my father, family, and friends. Colleagues in the Overseas Mission office of the Episcopal Church have graciously agreed to maintain me on salary as I begin a doctoral program at the University of Edinburgh. The course will commence on October 10. My Diocese of Southwestern Virginia, under Bishop

Heath Light, has been exceedingly generous in seeking funds to assist in the coming academic year.

My deep thanks to each of you who has held me, my family, and the peoples of Sudan in prayer especially during the past fourteen months. May the blessings of Christ's cool, redeeming waters of life be poured out upon us all.

Love,

Marc Nikkel

June 3, 1989

Dear Friends,

After eight months in Edinburgh, Scotland, it is again time to try to stitch together beloved people and places through a duplicated letter. I greet you in the love of Christ, as always grateful for your thought and prayer for me and for our Family in Sudan. It has, thankfully, been a mild winter in Edinburgh. I am not certain how I would face up to a severe one. Spring has introduced me to varieties of blossoming trees and flowers I didn't know existed. At 4:30 a.m. old stone buildings are aglow with the morning sunshine as new leaves wave and billow under winds sweeping off the Firth of Forth. In a small apartment, one corner of a century-old house, behind tall glass windows I spend days pecking away at my computer, wrestling with the history of missions in southern Sudan. It's always a little disorienting given a heart and mind so linked to friends in Africa and a body relishing the sensation of an Edinburgh spring.

Just now I'm writing from my family's home in California farm country. For five months my father, sister, and brother-in-law had planned to visit me in Britain. Along with sightseeing this was to offer an opportunity to meet Sudanese and Sudan-related friends of whom they had only heard. During their preparations it was found that my dad, Reuben, had a blockage in his heart and would need bypass surgery; the trip was canceled. They offered to cover the cost if I would come this way. So it is that I am with my family for eighteen days expecting to return to Britain on June 11. Dad is recovering in good form; it has been great being together. He is more expressive, more full of humor and spontaneity than I have known him before.

At the Centre for the Study of Christianity in the Non-Western World at the University of Edinburgh I have more joy in academic work than ever before. There is the feeling I am doing precisely what I am called to. A couple of solid papers have been produced on the early days of Anglican mission in Sudan, which was, for its first ten years, primarily among the Jieng. There is an exhilaration in working through the original correspondence of people I have heard about for years, preserved primarily in the archives of the Church Missionary Society in

Birmingham. My research has several times taken me on forays into England both for work in the archives and to meet the surviving Sudan missionaries of earlier years, some now in their eighties. Several young families with whom I have worked in Sudan provide open hearts and door during my travels — in their fellowship I find myself very much at home in Britain.

A major portion of my dissertation will involve analysis of Jieng indigenous Christian songs. Some 350 have been collected to date from as early as around 1910. At present friends are recording contemporary pieces in the refugee camps of Ethiopia, in the shantytowns of Khartoum, and in southern Sudan. With some two million people now displaced, complex traditional structures wear thin. But even here the church of Christ is growing, taking new forms, providing a modicum of stability. The songs provide insight into an evolving Christian identity and theology and the survival of the Sudanese church through these turbulent years. While my work focuses on Christianity emerging from the efforts of the Anglican Church Missionary Society I hope to compliment this with study in the archives of the Verona Fathers in Rome, the major Roman Catholic resource on Sudan. Toward this I am trying to acquire a bit of Italian.

My hope, finances allowing, is to continue through the three-year doctoral program without a break. Because there are few Sudanese nationals resident in Edinburgh, but a large population in London, I have enquired about a non-stipendiary position with the Diocese of London which might provide accommodation. It seems a position has opened up in a multi-ethnic church in north London where I will serve as a supporting minister two days a week. That covers accommodation in a location which is, providentially, near the homes of several Sudanese friends. From there I will commute to Edinburgh for consultations with my advisor every two months or so.[8]

In Scotland a fine harmony has come about between the academic press and Christian ministry. I have been assisting at the "Piscy" (colloquial for Episcopal) Church of St. Peter's, finding a warm welcome as I fumble through the subtleties of the Scottish liturgy and preach a time or two each month. St. Peter's is an old church coming to new life. In the Dioceses of Bradford, Salisbury, and Edinburgh I have had more opportunities to speak on Sudan than I can handle, continuing that "stitching together" of friends near and far.

In correspondence as well, I find a fulfilling sort of give and take. Dozens of letters come from Sudan, north and south, each month, offering moving accounts of a people's struggle for survival. I close with an excerpt from one letter written

---

8. Marc's supervisor for his doctoral dissertation was Prof. Andrew Walls, who founded the Centre for the Study of Christianity in the Non-Western World. Walls is perhaps the most important scholar of missionary history, and his two volumes of essays are considered seminal in the field (see *The Missionary Movement in Christian History*, and *The Cross-Cultural Process in Christian History*).

by a former colleague at Bishop Gwynne College. Gordon, with his lovely wife and six bright kids, is among the two hundred thousand souls who try to hold themselves together in Juba, a town for months under siege.[9] Hemmed in behind two concentric circles of land mines, residents cannot venture out even to collect firewood for cooking. Food is supplied solely by relief planes that spiral precariously overhead on entry to besieged territory.[10] Gordon's daughter, five-year-old Rejoice, sees the anxiety as neighbors frantically dig foxholes for safety around their homes. One day in March a brief barrage of missiles killed twenty-two civilians. She sees her mother faint when the shelling starts again. Her father describes Rejoice's vision for peace making:

> Do you remember Rejoice, my second youngest daughter with her question about the Easter drama BGC students presented in 1987 on the brutal killing of Jesus? Her question was [at age three], "Why did God allow Jesus, his own Son, to be brutally killed by those people? And why did people leave Jesus to die without taking him to hospital?" Rejoice, distressed with the shelling of Juba, one day tried to propose a plan to stop the SPLA and the government soldiers from killing people and each other. Her plan was:

> Let us buy enough ground nuts [peanuts] and Mommie can make *kaimot* [stone ground peanut butter]. Then we will fill the empty milk tins with the *kaimot* and take them out to where the SPLA are calling us to go, and we will give it to them to eat so that they may not shell Juba again. Then we must do the same for the government soldiers and tell them to stop shooting at the SPLA but allow them to come out of the bush to come home and sleep in their houses.

A little girl longs to bring peace and reconciliation among combatants in a war-torn land. Rejoice offers even *kaimot*, her favorite food, that enemies might sit and eat together. I pray there are others of us who offer the best we have in the search for peace and equality. I am profoundly grateful to hear that with increased awareness there are efforts underway — if all too belated — in London, Washington, and other capitals, that may contribute to an agreement to end the war. I hope that my work over these years may add to a foundation for mutual respect between those who are far and those who are near. Thank you for your love and support.

Love,

Marc Nikkel

---

9. Gordon Abina later became the principal of the college (1992–94).

10. The government-held town of Juba was under siege by the SPLA for several years during the civil war. Relief planes delivering food would spiral down in order to avoid anti-aircraft fire from rebel positions.

Edinburgh, Scotland
November 8, 1989

As the blue airport bus glided away from Rome's Termini Station last Friday it was easy to imagine I was on one of those guided tours, except for the slight queasiness of yet another departure. I went to Rome to study the 140 years of the Comboni Missionaries in Sudan,[11] not anticipating how past and present would flicker before me at every step. Passing the grand facade of St. Mary Major, the bus lumbers down Via Cavour. We pass the rubbish-littered stairs that lead up to the church where Michelangelo's marble Moses sits in all his contained fury. There also a gold-and-glass casket display of the chains that are said to have bound St. Peter.

Behind and between the spots on tourist maps are places where modern-day itinerants try to hold flesh and spirit together. At the edge of the park, not far beyond Moses' church, is "Caritas." Here the pockets of Pope John Paul II offer a noontime meal to refugees from Africa and Eastern Europe. Each day at noontime they swarm in their language and ethnic groups or stand in queues to receive a free lunch of pasta. This became one of my points of pilgrimage in Rome.

The bus moves haltingly through traffic two blocks from the Roman Forum. There, just inside the alleyway, Father Bresciani offers a sort of frayed lifeline to Ethiopians, Somalis, and Sudanese. With some thirty-five years in and out of Africa, he is known by all the Africans. In his chaotic chapel-cum-office they battle for his attention in search of housing, health care, funds for short-term survival, or a night off the streets. New arrivals have it rough. They often spend wary nights in some corner of Termini Station or huddle in a stone portal of the Coliseum.

As we roll into the wide avenue a vista of rubble — the Forum's stones and pillars, skeletons of pagan temples — comes into view. My mind traces its way through the ruins down to the stone chamber where Peter and Paul were, by tradition, imprisoned along with the numerous deacons and bishops who followed after them. We swing around the ever-startling Coliseum, where souls of martyrs and tourists mingle through the centuries, down the parkway and between the edifices of old smudgy mustard, orange, and peach-colored residential Rome. For me these dwellings still have more the feel of North Africa than of Europe.

It was on my first morning in Rome that I stumbled into Charles at the door of St. Paul's Within the Walls, the Episcopal church in town, my home for three months. By Sunday Charles had assembled most of the available Sudanese for a welcoming feast out in the suburbs. What a moving time it was as these fellows,

---

11. Founded by Verona missionary Daniel Comboni, who first went to Sudan in the 1880. See Nikkel, *Dinka Christianity*, 74–75, 85–89, and the articles by Francesco Pierli ("Daniel Comboni"), Giuseppe Caramazza ("Comboni Brothers"), and Maria Teresa Ratti ("Comboni Sisters").

surviving so precariously, pulled together the best cooking they could muster for this transient American. Into the evening they told me their stories and I told mine. We prayed.

It was on mere whim that, on my second weekend in Italy, I joined Angelo (a refugee for six daunting years) for a two-hour train journey to the rural village of Villa Laterno, near Napoli. There we met the other half of the Sudanese refugee population camped at the edge of peach fields among rows of ravaged tomatoes, trying to eke out some cash for the winter. Conditions were rugged in the summer heat, reminding me of desolate refugee camps in the Horn of Africa or maybe of a rebel camp. Men on the move, they knew they would endure it for only two or three months. Most slept on makeshift mattresses under the stars; no electricity, no shelter except a small, unfinished, cinder block cube. They carried their water from the village (when the spigot had not been locked by residents), cooked over a wood fire, and worked long hours picking tomatoes at half the wages an Italian would receive.

I was deeply impressed. Here these guys built their own United Nations from five countries and two dozen ethnic groups, the majority Sudanese. How remarkable, I thought, that they can support each other, work and cook together, and live with a modicum of harmony in this rugged environ. Despite the neglect and prejudice of rural Italians, these are survivors in a strange land, pilgrims en route. Most have dreams of education in the West; all endured the long, painful wait in Italy (often having spent years traveling through Iraq, Syria, Turkey, Yugoslavia). On Sunday we talked from scripture about trying to live as sojourners with Spirit-filled integrity, as people of God.

It was not until Friday, back in Rome, that I chanced to hear of the killing. Tuesday night four Italians, sixteen to twenty-four years old, had tried to rob an African work camp near Napoli. One twenty-nine-year-old South African, Jerry Essan Masillo, had been shot dead, others wounded. It was Villa Laterno. Apart from those being held as witnesses, the shaken refugees came streaming back to Rome. Suddenly Italian papers were full of debates over African refugees. Some residents of Villa Laterno described them as animals, living like savages, wild beasts. Government officials proposed tighter entry restrictions and immigration policies to keep them out. Some groups, mostly Christian, called for facilities to care for them. Through the gauntlet of interviews and cameras we attended three memorial services for Jerry on my third Sunday in Rome. At St. Paul's we prepared a *karama*, a time for the African community to remember, to pray, to weep, to eat together in their own more familiar way.

Statues of Peter, massive keys in hand, and Paul, sword at his side, are everywhere in Rome, exalted on pedestals or beside altars. Sometimes I reflect on my new refugee friends, young men I came to love and respect — Macar, Angelo,

Jacob, Makur, Caesar (who had held dying Jerry in his arms) — as sort of itinerant evangelists. Each of these is a man of Christian faith, though none preaches gospel sermons on Roman street corners. Their message simply confronts us with who we are. Perhaps because they are dark and destitute, vulnerable and transient their presence unsettles us. We are so much like them; we try to put our evil on them. They speak of countries divided, of brothers and sisters — we ourselves — at war, of prejudice without impulse to understand. Like Peter and Paul they call us to repent, and we hate them for it.

From tomato picking the refugees were tumbled into "temporary" lodgings in northern Rome with the aid of UNHCR (temporary, because in just five weeks efforts were twice made to evict these fellows who have no legal employment and little money). Six to a tiny room in a massive apartment complex they spiced the blend of Filipinos, Russians, Ukrainians, Poles, Somalis, Ethiopians, on and on. What an education in refugee aspirations this was: the "American dream" shines on! Most hope fervently for immigration or studies in the United States or Canada. The plump, great-hearted Ukrainian Pentecostals, already with eight to fourteen kids to a family, adopted the Sudanese, sharing their pre-cooked refugee vittles each day. This also became for me a place of pilgrimage, of hope, and of prayer. I would sit at table with Russians and Sudanese and ponder my own immigrant ancestors from the Ukraine.

Wonderful it is when deep-flowing joy and laughter can spring up from life in the margins. We planned a farewell dinner with all the Sudanese in Rome and others who had been in Villa Laterno, some fifty altogether. Since Jerry's *karama* we had not assembled in that pink velvet parish room at St. Paul's. A visiting Sudanese friend, Gai, cooked a marvelous feast that near brought tears to the eyes of some. Old Bresciani gave news of peace talks; I spoke with more passion than I expected; several of the guys prayed for survival, for a future, for peace. I remarked to Father Ted that the hardwood floors just might not endure Jieng dancing in full flight. He invited us into the church proper where our crew let loose. Before ornate nineteenth-century mosaics, drums roaring, the Jieng stripped into shorts and gave a potent rendition bursting with cattle camp passion. Then came Bari, English, Moru, and Kikuyu[12] songs and Danish dancing. Into the night we laughed and sang and nearly cried for joy.

These people and events enlivened my work, those long hours plodding through books in my faltering Italian, photocopying reams of paper or provoking fifty-year-old memories from whiskered Catholic Fathers. There were the writings, in Italian, by the first southern Sudanese Catholic priest, ordained in 1887. Young Daniel Deng Farim Suror, a Jieng, was bought out of slavery by Daniel Comboni

---

12. The Kikuyu, or Agikuyu, are one of the major ethnic groups of Kenya.

and taken to study at Propaganda Fide.[13] Each time I walked by the old Vatican Seminary I wondered how Daniel felt on Roman streets over a century ago. Reading his plaintive words — the cry of a liberated slave to European Christians — I began to realize how much things have changed . . . and how little.

Love,

Marc Nikkel

London, England
St. Francis Day, October 4, 1991

After eighteen months I bid greetings to family and friends across the globe. Ties continue to deepen with the Sudanese community in London among whom I serve informally as pastor or, rather, as "Abuna." We meet in my flat for what has become the Ecumenical Sudanese Christian Fellowship. While refugees are better cared for physically here than in many lands, the spiritual and emotional toll is enormous. Couples stumble and divide, bereft of the structures that would hold them secure at home. Kids grow up with an indistinct identity as "British Blacks." Through them I learn the gnawing pain of separation, rootlessness, and loss. I offer prayers at our all-too-frequent *karamas,* memorial gatherings for relatives who have died at home, through illness or in battle.

Occasionally we gather for more joyful occasions. Some weeks back St. Olave's was rocked by a Sudanese wedding at which I officiated, assisted by two Sudanese clergy. The bride flew in from Khartoum and the groom from Austria. There are also celebrations of baptisms and birthdays and, most movingly, the reunion of families long separated by war. Recently a courageous and resourceful mother, with her four children, celebrated their reunion with her husband, a commander fresh from five years on the battlefield. Even Nilotic men had difficulty restraining their tears as the children presented Dad with flowers and songs and speeches they had composed themselves. In mid-September I was privileged to set foot, if only for eleven days, back on African soil as I attended meetings of the New Sudan Council of Churches (NSCC) in Nairobi. There were joyful reunions with former students, now visionary Christian leaders of the "Liberated Areas." Being cut off from the rest of Sudan and needing links with the outside world, churches of seven denominations in the SPLA-controlled areas are organizing themselves. Together with their expatriate colleagues, Sudanese leaders form a vigorous and

---

13. Daniel Deng Farim was liberated from slavery by Bishop Daniel Comboni c. 1873. He received catechesis, was baptized in 1874, trained for the priesthood in Rome, and was ordained in 1886, the first Roman Catholic priest from southern Sudan. He served in Cairo and in Beirut but, sadly, never returned to his native Sudan. He died at the age of forty in 1899 (see Nikkel, *Dinka Christianity,* 91–94).

creative lot, thoroughly ecumenical, committed to peaceful reconciliation and the rebuilding of a ravaged land in the Spirit of Christ.

Images of the desolation of war, famine, and natural disaster are sobering. Two pastors, former students, now work in the vast territories of the Upper Nile, which have been thoroughly inundated by floods. Life is conducted on ant mounds or by building barriers against the mud. In many regions, war and disease have eradicated once flourishing herds of cattle; pestilence and floods stultify the crops. Into this swamp have come four hundred thousand refugees fleeing the camps of Ethiopia. Food is almost nonexistent except for a trickle of relief aid. The Sudan government has, on occasion, taken to aerial bombing of these concentrations of the dispossessed, and the threat of chemical weapons remains high.

And yet, from this quagmire of misery, come glimpses of the miraculous resilience of the Sudanese spirit. Over vast territories people are constructing hundreds of churches as Christian faith replaces ancient systems of belief. Schools flourish where naked children seek to learn, having nothing but the ground to write upon. The Diocese of Bor, with perhaps 10 churches in the early 1980s, today has over 120, as well as innumerable preaching centers. Accounts of mass conversions, miracles, visions, and the renewal of life are thoroughly reminiscent of the formative years of the church in the book of Acts. Amid all the challenges of mere physical survival, Sudanese leaders have set theological education as the first priority of the NSCC, an effort in which I hope, one day, to offer my support.

As might have become obvious, it is no easy task keeping my dissertation at the center of daily life. I am grateful, however, that so many relationships and duties dovetail with and inspire my writing. The days in Kenya provided opportunity for taping many hours of valuable interviews. Along with the bonds that have developed with an elder generation of British missionaries, I have been grateful to become part of the sizeable academic community committed to Sudan. Likely it will be another eight to ten months before my dissertation is finally completed.

As much as you remember me, pray also for our kinfolk in Sudan, desperately in need of your fellowship and support.

Cheerio,

Marc

October 5, 1993

"A pilgrim from a distant land travels to his home...."

Dear Friends,

After a long silence — in terms of duplicated letters — time has come to put finger to keyboard and restore our ties once again. The mundane life of a doctoral student in London, spending most days before a computer screen, is over. My thesis was submitted in August and another phase of life is near completion. As I return to Africa, the first joint appointment between the Episcopal Church, U.S.A. (ECUSA) and the British, Church Mission Society (CMS), I again invite your prayer and solidarity.[14]

No question, I will *miss* London. An apartment in an old Victorian vicarage became, with some renovations, a fine abode in which to work and welcome friends, not a few of whom stopped in transit between the United States and Africa. In north London I served as assistant minister in the multi-ethnic parish of St. Olave's. Strangely, it was only a few months ago that I examined the oak chair in which I have sat each Sunday. There I saw the date "1636" carved squarely in its time-darkened back. In London terms my sojourn has been brief indeed, but for me, an extremely formative four years.

The Sudanese Christian Fellowship (SCF) began in 1991, a small cluster of refugees meeting in my flat. It now continues to develop under its own leadership, drawing as many as two hundred for worship and communal meals in a central London church. In August 1992, we were invited to present a service of solidarity with Sudan at Westminster Abbey. It was for each of us a wonderfully affirming opportunity, but no small challenge to compress Sudanese spontaneity within the strictures of British punctuality! Keep the SCF in your prayers as they seek to console one another in the hope of Christ amid continuing news of conflict and death back home.

Next week I return to Britain for my oral exams (October 20) and several weeks of speaking in "Link Parishes" from London to Edinburgh. Also awaiting me are several farewell parties and services of commissioning. In Britain I have been engrafted not only into the refugee community but also into a marvelous intergenerational family of men and women who have served in Sudan across the decades. Many have welcomed me into their homes and occasionally their churches, as I have traveled and conducted research. Now they join with the Sudanese community in Britain, and you in the United States, in sending me out.

At present I am writing from the abode of my sister and brother-in-law, our "family home" in a small California farm town. How good it has been to renew ties, especially with my dad and Maria, his remarkable wife of four years. Both are

---

14. Because Marc was the first appointed missionary to the Sudan from the Episcopal Church of the United States of America, he began to wonder, during his time in Britain, whether it would be more appropriate for him to return to the Sudan as a missionary of the Church Mission Society. The CMS had had a long and fruitful ministry in the Sudan and several dioceses in England, especially Bradford and Salisbury, had historic links with the church in the Sudan. During this period Marc sometimes felt that his ministry was better understood in Britain than in the United States, but eventually it was decided that a joint appointment between ECUSA and CMS would be the most helpful way for him to maintain the many international relationships he had developed.

a winsome eighty-one. Maria, like our Mennonite forebears of the last century, was born in the Ukraine. During the Second World War she saw the menfolk of her family taken to Siberia never to return. Amid the tumult of war she, with three young children, endured an arduous journey westward and, after several years, was granted asylum in California. Here she worked as a baker and cook, and raised a fine family. Only in her seventies, however, did she decide to remarry, much to the enrichment of my father and our family.

It is in part because of encounters with resilient people like Maria that I have sought to reclaim aspects of my Anabaptist heritage during this visit home. Over some four hundred years our Mennonite forebears sought freedom to live and worship as they chose, migrating first from Holland to Prussia (sixteenth century), then to Russia (seventeenth century), and finally to North America. As I have been conversing with our elders and reading a bit of history, I find that themes of spiritual pilgrimage, peacemaking, and reconciliation relate as much to the displaced of the late twentieth century as they did to our forebears. Such gleanings will, I believe, inform my life with Sudanese Christians on their arduous journey, one not dissimilar to that of the saints of past generations.

As I anticipate a return to Sudan sometime in early December, it is difficult to offer a precise job description. For my colleagues and I, our primary hope is that I will serve at a small pastoral training college called Dhiaukuei (meaning "the cry of the eagle") which has sprung up in rural Jieng territory. There some 160 mature students, many of them women (most of the men are in combat or dead), are preparing to serve as church workers and pastors. If this location should prove inaccessible, I may reside among refugees in camps near the Ugandan border. Broadly, I expect that my contribution will be in three areas:

Solidarity

Recently Jimmy Carter observed that of the thirty-four civil wars currently being waged around the globe, the conflict in Sudan has endured the longest, been most destructive (leaving an estimated two million dead), and is least known to the outside world. During the devastation of the past decade many southern Sudanese Christians have felt extremely isolated, neglected by the very churches that once brought the gospel to their lands. They plead for solidarity and invite individuals who will share their difficulties and provide a link with Christians beyond their borders. Many of my former colleagues and students recall the life we shared together during the 1980s. They anticipate and welcome my return.

Documentation

It is unlikely that there is another branch of Christ's Body worldwide which is growing more rapidly, or whose people prove more resilient in the face of great suffering and oppression, than in Sudan. With virtually no external assistance they are developing ways to propagate their faith and to survive. They are evolving fresh forms of ministry, developing a distinctive theology, and creating a vast corpus of vernacular music. Much of this goes on unrecorded and unrecognized. Among the many ethnic groups whose churches are growing at an unprecedented rate[15] are the Jieng, whose century-long dialogue with Christianity was the subject of my doctoral thesis. If I am based in Jieng areas I will continue documenting their pilgrimage, believing that the church worldwide has much to learn from their tenacious commitment to Christ.[16]

Theological resources

Many of us who have worked in Sudan are reluctant to impose the structures of the West upon Sudanese Christians. Since 1964 when all European missionaries were expelled from the country, indigenous believers have proven their single-minded commitment and creativity. The vernacular songs I have translated reveal their vigorous theological debate, concerning issues such as the meaning of ancestral land in the economy of God, the return and coming judgment of Christ, and the presence of God amid armed conflict. While I will take a range of theological and other reference materials, I anticipate that the most significant developments will arise from dialogue and shared reflection among a people for whom the drama and poignancy of the biblical narrative is daily experience.

Packing for this journey seems, on the one hand, quite simple. Since I will be airlifted to my location I will travel as lightly as possible: some vitamins and medicines, lightweight clothes, boots, possibly a bicycle … and not a lot else. The one major investment I am making is in a new compact computer, software, and a solar panel to support it. This, together with new eyeglasses and clothes has come to over US$4,000, no small investment for an unemployed student (during the past three years I have been sustained primarily through the generosity of friends in Britain). Until now I have rarely, if ever, made financial requests through duplicated letters. However, my savings are meager, and the financial resources of my mission(s) are more limited than a decade ago. I would welcome any assistance toward outfitting for my new posting.

---

15. On church growth in various ethnic contexts in the Sudan, including the Jieng, the Murle, the Nuer, and the Uduk, see the articles in Andrew Wheeler's *Land of Promise*.

16. Marc produced several published articles addressing issues of the theological reflection of the Jieng people in response to the massive changes which had taken place in their culture because of the war. See especially "Contemporary Religious Change among the Dinka" (1992); "The Cross of Bor Dinka Christians: A Working Christology in the Face of Displacement and Death" (1995); "Songs of Hope and Lamentation from Sudan's 'Unaccompanied Minors' " (1997); " 'Children of Our Fathers' Divinities' or 'Children of Red Foreigners'? Themes in Missionary History and the Rise of an Indigenous Church among the Jieng Bor of Southern Sudan" (1998); "The Cross as a Symbol of Regeneration in Jieng Bor Society" (1998).

Again, I am profoundly grateful for your solidarity with me and our kinfolk in Sudan. Reading family histories I was moved to find that my great grandfather, Cornelius Nikkel, having traveled halfway around the world (remarkably, his Ukrainian home was at precisely the same longitude as my destination in Sudan), asked that a particular German hymn be sung at his funeral. The lines at the head of this letter reflect his sense of pilgrimage, ever holding in sight his permanent home in heaven.

Faithfully,

Marc Nikkel

Part Four

"God Has Not Deserted You"

Letters in the Midst of Devastation, 1994–98

Throughout the twenty-year conflict I have heard a common theme from Sudanese: "Why does the world not act?" "If the world is concerned about Israel, Palestine, Kuwait, Iraq, Kosovo, and Serbia, why do they not care about us?" As I was leaving Kakuma refugee camp after a visit there in 1996, I was stopped by a woman who spoke to me in a language I did not understand. My companion interpreted: "When you go back home, do not forget us . . . pray for us . . . do not forget us." The Christians in the Sudan have felt largely abandoned by the world and by the church.

Therefore it was of immense importance for the Episcopal Church of the Sudan during this period that the archbishop of Canterbury, George Carey, made two visits to the Sudan. The first visit, which Marc describes in his letter of January 1994, was to the south, in December 1993 and January 1994. According to Andrew Wheeler, the government attempted to control the archbishop's visit and use it to win international support for the regime.

> The Archbishop resisted this arrangement, and when the Government appeared unwilling to give way, he cancelled his visit to the government areas. His decision to proceed with a visit to the South caused an uproar. To Southerners, many of whom, of course, were Christians, the visit of George Carey to Nimule, to Akot, Dhiaukuei, and Yambio, whilst refusing to be manipulated by the Khartoum government, was a huge affirmation.[1]

There was fallout, of course. The authorities expelled the British ambassador and broke off diplomatic relations with Great Britain. But for the people of southern Sudan the mere presence of the archbishop, even more than any words that were spoken, was a sign of solidarity and encouragement. "We are not alone . . . we are not forgotten."

Archbishop Carey made a second trip to Sudan in October 1995, this time visiting government-controlled Khartoum and Juba. Far from being controlled by the Sudanese

---

1. Werner et al., *Day of Devastation*, 626.

103

regime, however, he took his visit as an opportunity to be critical of the government's dismal human rights record. And during his day in Juba, in a sermon to a crowd of eighty-six thousand, he described the Sudanese church as "the Crucified Church" and said that his lasting impression was "of the triumph of Christ crucified and raised from the dead."[2]

The archbishop's visits were important "events" for Sudan, symbolizing that the outside world was aware and concerned. During this time Marc, like very few others, was a more constant sign of the presence of Christ and his worldwide Body among the displaced people of the Sudan both inside and outside of the Sudanese borders. Marc's work of theological education in refugee camps and in war zones was carried out without the accoutrements that usually accompany such a task — blackboards, books, lecterns, lecture halls, desks. The textbooks were the Bible and the songs that the Sudanese themselves had composed to express their lament and their praise to God. The blackboard was often a cowskin stretched between trees and the chalk was cassava root. The students, lacking much formal educational training, but eager to learn, sometimes walked for days to get to a seminar where food was often in short supply. The emergence of a new generation of pastoral leaders, many of them women, had come suddenly as, especially among the Jieng, almost the entire people had abandoned their old divinities and taken up the cross. Marc, like them, finds himself, in his vivid description, "nestless," without a permanent home, always on pilgrimage, but in the end, not abandoned.

Nimule, Southern Sudan
January 17, 1994

New Year's Greetings

It is somewhat tentatively that I begin my first "link letter"[3] unassisted by my computer and back in the dark ages of the manual typewriter. Given the volatility of this dry season friends advise me neither to carry valued possessions, nor, for the present, to establish my "permanent" home within Sudanese borders. It is, then, as a sojourner among displaced sojourners that I have made my first foray across the frontier into a beloved land.

My welcome has been profoundly moving, meeting former students and colleagues I have not seen since our abduction in 1987, events they recount in great detail. (Indeed, I have several times been greeted by well-groomed young men who were once our armed guards.) Among Nimule's largely Jieng displaced

2. Werner et al., *Day of Devastation*, 601.
3. The term "link letter" is used by the CMS to describe the missionaries' correspondence home to friends, family, and supporters.

community it often seems as if biblical characters have come to life. For my doctoral thesis I translated and analyzed the songs of gifted women and men I am now meeting for the first time. As I learn of the experiences that inspired their compositions my admiration only deepens. Reentering this world — much transformed from the one I left six years ago — it frequently feels as if I am entering the epic events of the Old Testament: war, exile, and the promise of Yahweh's divine intervention are in the air, the subject of spontaneous, communal prayer and song from morn to night.

I arrived in Nairobi on December 15. On the 22nd took a train journey to Kampala, Uganda, and by the 24th was driving northward in the company of Roger Schrocks of the New Sudan Council of Churches (NSCC). We arrived at Nimule, just inside the Sudanese frontier, by 6:00 p.m. on Christmas Eve, and after a flurry of welcomes, went to the nearby Catholic mission for a multilingual Mass under the stars (given the curfew we could not attend the midnight Anglican service).

With the coming of the archbishop of Canterbury set for December 30 the compound of the Episcopal Church was a hive of activity: posh new *tukhls* of mud and thatch were being completed and decorated, grass was being cut; and the adequacy of chickens, goats, and sheep ready for slaughter continually reassessed. The compound, as with the three neighboring displacement camps (the "Triple A" region: Amay, Atepi and Ashwa) have a quality of permanence that makes it difficult to recall that these are the habitations of people who have been displaced three and four times. (Most of the native peoples such as the Acholi[4] fled to northern Uganda prior to 1989; most of the present, largely Jieng Bor population took refuge in Ethiopia during the 1980s, fled back to Sudan in 1991, and, by stages, have established themselves near Nimule since mid-1992.) Surveying the ample array of exotic foods on offer for His Grace and companions (fresh tomato salad, turkey, bottled soda, stuffed egg plant, numerous varieties of cakes and biscuits), it was hard to comprehend that these were provided by people so recently near starvation . . . and who are still thoroughly reliant on relief supplies. Church folk had scraped the bottom of their resources to import foodstuffs from Uganda: even in destitution Sudanese receive their guests with honor and panache. When the great day arrived only the dust devils were determined witnesses to the holocaust of recent years. Sweeping in with vigor, they threw up their dry clouds of grit together with the ashes rising from the seasonal burning of surrounding grasslands, a terse welcome to His Grace.

---

4. The majority of Acholi people are from northern Uganda, an area which has itself been a place of much insecurity in recent years.

With hardly a pause, the entourage of churchmen and journalists passed from airplane to Land Cruisers, bumping down the road toward Ashwa, the first of two displacement camps they would visit in the neighborhood of Nimule. Here, as elsewhere, the road was lined with white clad Mothers' Union workers and armies of singing, dancing youth. Forests of long, thin crosses bobbed in rhythm above the singers, the hair of many adorned with delicate crosses, also made of reeds. So different from a decade ago, the cross has become a pervasive symbol of salvation in all its varied dimensions.

It is difficult to assess the significance of the archiepiscopal visit. George Carey's addresses were clear and concise, reaffirming the solidarity of the church worldwide with a people whose trauma has been so little known outside. Bishop Nathaniel Garang of the Diocese of Bor was euphoric, often translating for his guest and adding his own supporting commentary. As happens, ponderous formality occasionally overshadowed public statements making the relaxed encounters at meals and in the evening under moonlight all the more important. The archbishop's questions were penetrating, frequently returning to issues of theological education, remarkably, the first priority which Sudanese church leaders have set toward the healing of their wounded peoples.

Theological discourse is everywhere underway but, framed in vernacular language, is little accessible to outsiders. For this reason I asked youth leaders to provide the lyrics of songs they planned to present during the tour. These we translated into English and presented to the archbishop. For Bishop Nathaniel as with many of his flock, there is one lengthy composition (six verses and chorus) which captures the spirit of this time. After each of the archbishop's addresses Bishop Nathaniel prompted the assembly to raise their voices and sing:

> Let us give thanks: Let us give thanks to the Lord in the day of devastation:
> Let us give thanks in the day of contentment.
> Jesus has bound the world round with the pure light of the Word of his
> Father.
> When we unite our hearts and beseech the Lord, and have hope
> then the bad spirit [*jok*] has no power.
> God [*Nhialic*] has not forgotten us.
> Evil is departing and holiness is advancing;
> this is the transformation which throws the earth into convulsions.

This first verse conveys some of the complexity of Jieng Christian thought. The past decade of war has brought death, loss of cattle and a beloved homeland, and massive displacement to Sudanese peoples. Indigenous social and religious institutions have been uprooted. This traumatic period, "the shaking of the earth," is understood, first, as the long predicted judgment of God against Sudan (Isaiah

18 is a passage widely known and frequently invoked[5]), and, secondly, as the means through which God is bringing about the spiritual transformation of his people. Old allegiances to spiritual powers (the *jak*), once perceived as essential to survival, are now repudiated and are being supplanted by the "Word of the Father." Since "holiness" is advancing and evil is receding there is reason for thanksgiving even in devastation. This does not, however, suggest that Christians do not plead with *Nhialic* to have mercy and "look upon us." Daily they plead for peace and a just end to war. As with the ancient Hebrews, severe judgment, compassion, and restoration are integral to the nature of the God "who has not forgotten us." It is at this level of discourse that I hope the archbishop will have had opportunity to engage the Sudanese church. Clearly, his visit was perceived as a sign of divine compassion and reason for massive celebration: at last the pilgrimage of this remnant people is known around the globe. Solidarity has been confirmed; advocacy and tangible intervention are expected.

For the present I remain a sojourner among sojourners, still undecided where to establish "home base." I hope to spend February at Dhiaukuei Bible College amid the Jieng on the west bank of the Nile. Bishop Nathaniel has advised me to travel with him, explore the Jieng church across Upper Nile, Bahr el Ghazal, and (as at Nimule) in displacement… "and then you will think what you will do." Most daunting has been the bishop's habit of introducing me to congregations as "the Second Macuor," the second Archibald Shaw,[6] pioneer missionary among the Jieng (d. 1956; since 1959 the CMS has had no missionary committed to Jieng territory). I am not Archibald Shaw nor are the Jieng who they were eighty years ago. Nonetheless, it will be a poignant experience discovering what chemistry develops between us in the coming months through the providence of the one who has "bound the world round with the pure light of the Word of his Father."

Likewise, may your New Year be bound round with his light,

Marc Nikkel

---

5. Marc notes here that Isaiah 18 is "invoked" as an oracle of judgment against Sudan. Indeed the Good News Bible heading for that chapter is "God will punish Sudan" and the New International Version entitles the chapter "A Prophecy against Cush." Several biblical scholars, however, argue that the word of judgment in this chapter is not against Cush/Sudan, but rather against Jerusalem and that Cush functions in this passage as the agent of judgment. For details see LeMarquand, "Bibles, Crosses, Songs, Guns, and Oil."

6. Archibald Shaw was a missionary of the Gordon Memorial Sudan Mission of the CMS from 1905, when he and a group of British missionaries sailed down the Nile from Khartoum, until his retirement in Nairobi in 1940. His Jieng ox-name, *Macuor* (or "*Machuor*"), is the name given to a bull the color of a gray vulture. Shaw treated the Jieng people and their culture with seriousness and respect and was known among the Jieng as "the only white man with the heart of the Jieng." His grave on the outskirts of Nairobi is still "a place of pilgrimage and prayer" for displaced Jieng living in Kenya (see Nikkel, "Archibald Shaw 'Machuor,'" 103; cf. Nikkel, *Dinka Christianity*, 103–29).

Nairobi
April 15, 1994

> Lead us to your good land, O Lord.
> — from a hymn of the "unaccompanied minors"

Greetings all,

Contrary to hopes expressed in my last letter, I have not been in Sudan since January, but just returned from six weeks at the heart of Kakuma Refugee Camp, among yet another community of Sudan in Diaspora. Established between two wide riverbeds in the desert lands of the Turkana[7] in northwestern Kenya, the site is but seventy-five miles from the Sudan border. Our international time zones declare that there is one hour's difference between Sudan and Kenya. Resetting one's watch is simple enough, but this variant offers many Sudanese a way of asserting their ties with home, defying their refugee status, and, almost daily, provoking the consternation of non-Sudanese. "We keep our watches and our hearts in Sudan," I was told early on my arrival, and so they do. I was deeply impressed by the ways through which a people reconstruct and order their lives in a foreign land...even when they have been displaced three and four times. The term "refugee camp" once suggested a disquieting netherworld betwixt and between the places where "real life" occurs. No more: I found a people who retain with defiance much of what they hold dear.

Kakuma is home to some forty thousand refugees, all but six thousand of whom are Sudanese (others include Ethiopians, Ugandans, and Zaïrois). I flew in on February 24 in the company of Archdeacon Peter Bol, the most prominent of Episcopal churchmen during the Sudanese sojourn in Ethiopia (1987–91) and so the focus of a resounding reception. On our first Sunday morning I was sobered to find some six thousand people assembling for the 6:00 a.m. (here, as below, Sudan time) service in the largest of three open-air churches. These massive forest chapels are set among the thorn trees and spindly, fine-leafed acacias of the region; their meager shade encourages worship in the cool of early morning. (I later realized that youth are up as early as 4:30 a.m. laying out handkerchiefs to reserve their places.) The pews are long, smoothed loaves of dried mud, occasionally marked with crosses molded in relief. It was in these churches I preached each Sunday, and on weekdays I sat among the three hundred to five hundred "minors" who gather for prayer at 5:00 a.m. As we sang we would watch the eastern sky ripen to orange and mauve over riverbed cliffs, forests, and hard-edged Turkana mountains. Sudanese friends predicted that I would not long endure the

---

7. The Turkana are a nomadic pastoral people who live around the area of Lake Turkana in northern Kenya just south of the Sudanese border.

withering heat of Kakuma nor the wind, laden with fine dust, that blows for several hours each morning. Nevertheless, the land — and the spirit of the place — has its compensations.

The Spirit

Song and prayer pervade the ECS compound in which I was hosted amid a maze of mud and thatch houses and coarse, brush fences. In January Stephen Dit Makok, compiler of the new Jieng Bor songbook, had begun a class with fifty young evangelists and Christian leaders, teaching, among other things, the 662 compositions of the new volume. Each night from 7:00 to 9:30, they surrounded the house in which I stayed ("The Right Rev. Bishop's House" scrawled above the door), saturating its mud walls with their contagious rhythms, occasionally breaking into dance. Later, in the quiet night darkness came the plaintive sound of a solitary lyre, marvelously constructed from catgut, goatskin, and a soldier's military helmet. On several nights I was awakened at 2:00 or 3:00 a.m. by the songs of folk gathering to minister to some ailing soul. And again, the pre-dawn darkness carried the low rumble of young male voices. Dispossessed of the rhythms of their homeland, a people mark out time in patterns which, I believe, are essential to their survival. Their song, ever straining toward homeland and heaven, affirms the divine presence, assuages pain, and gives meaning to their communal journey.

This is not to disregard the complex social and political currents which surge through Kakuma, nor the ethnic, cultural and, generational tensions inherent in so diverse a community. The great sacrifices required for military victory and political ascendancy are constantly in the air: hearts and minds are frequently tuned toward the war zone. Religion is, then, but one aspect of refugee life, but an exceedingly important one. I came to believe that there are but two institutions which hold the passions of Sudanese in exile: One is the varied political-military structures of the SPLA/SPLM. The other is the unifying ethos of the churches. Only these two have sprung directly from the Sudanese soul and are sustained by them alone. Only these will be carried back to Sudan when exiles return. Alongside them all else is secondary.

The NGOs (Non-Governmental Organizations) and related agencies (among them, UNHCR, Lutheran World Federation, and Swedish Save the Children) must be commended for the diverse services they provide at Kakuma, encompassing food, water, housing, health, education, feeding centers for children, and therapy for amputees. Essential as these services are, however, they are temporary. Developed and sustained by "aliens," they do not, by and large, arise from the impulse of Sudanese. Even the schools, so greatly valued and so important for the formation young minds, are less potent than the two forces which presently drive the psyche in exile. Given the sustenance which most Sudanese derive from

the church, I was saddened to hear some NGO staff denigrate the religious expressions of refugees as transient and superficial, a product of boredom. In some
quarters there was enthusiastic talk of the "psycho-social activities" provided
for troubled "minors," but little willingness to recognize that the most dynamic
systems for social, psychological — and spiritual — well-being are those which
refugees themselves create and sustain. It is in the churches that souls well up in
prayer, retelling and relieving the trauma of the past. Here hostilities of clan and
tribe diminish as a surrogate family affirms its common vision. Here exiles cast
themselves upon a God who transforms suffering through love.

This yearning of spirit is especially poignant among Kakuma's eleven thousand "unaccompanied minors,"[8] a phrase which becomes increasingly euphemistic
as these remarkable boys enter manhood. It was their arrival in Kenya during July
1992, then numbering some nineteen thousand, that first formed the nucleus
around which Kakuma developed. The saga of most began amid the escalating
military conflict of 1987 when they were between four and fifteen years of age.
Some lads fled the carnage, having witnessed the massacre of kinfolk. Others
were sent away by parents desperate to preserve a future generation. Most lads
dreamed of education in Ethiopia, while many determined to defend their homeland as liberation soldiers. Their eastward passage, covering hundreds of desolate
miles, saw the death of thousands, still more starving during early months in
ill-equipped reception camps. Boys recall how the young cried when they first
confronted death...until it became so commonplace they disposed of friends'
corpses without emotion. With the support of the UN the camps gradually stabilized, food arrived, and rudimentary schools emerged. Still, after four years in
Ethiopia the lads endured yet another harrowing trek in 1991, back to Sudan,
and ultimately to Kenya. Moving in their thousands, lacking food, they again fed
on leaves. They were often under gunfire and aerial bombardment. Some were
swept away in swollen rivers. Again, many died.

---

8. The amazing story of these "unaccompanied minors," often called "the lost boys," is now
becoming better known in the "outside world." There may originally have been as many as forty
thousand of these young people who left their homes in southern Sudan for various reasons during
the upheavals of the late 1980s. Some had left hoping to be trained as soldiers. Others had fled their
villages when raiders invaded — slaughtering their fathers and taking their sisters and mothers as
slaves. Since young boys were often sent to take care of livestock, many were in the fields when the
villages were destroyed. In the trek through the Sudanese bush to Ethiopia, many died of starvation
and not a few were eaten by lions and hyenas. Apparently many of the boys found their way to Ethiopia
by following the trail of bones. After years in the camps, the boys were driven out of Ethiopia when the
Marxist government of Mengistu was overthrown. At gunpoint they were forced to swim across the
crocodile-infested Gilo River back into Sudan where, once again, they were forced to walk through
Sudan for hundreds of miles while trying to avoid wild animals, rebels, and government soldiers. Since
many of the so-called "lost boys" have been received into Western countries as refugees, their story
has now been told many times. See, for example, the firsthand account of Abraham Nhial in Nhial
and DiAnn Mills, *Lost Boy No More*.

Today it is difficult to reconcile these tall, slender, relatively healthy young people with the emaciated, bloated, and dying children photographed in 1988. These survivors are clean, often scrupulously well groomed (even if they must wash and dry their single change of clothes by night). I was continually impressed that, for all they have lost, suffered, and gone without, most carry themselves with dignity and self-assurance. During six weeks, often in their company, I found them gentle of heart, compassionate, and generally obedient to their elders. If their pride was offended, however, or injustice perceived, they could flare with indignation. Highly intelligent, most are desperate for education. Through adversity they have become highly self-reliant; virtually never did any make tangible requests of me. Camp regiment requires them to build their own mud houses, carry water, and (though resentfully) cook their own meals. Older boys frequently oversee the young, providing support, correction, and guidance. What struck me most, however, was their seriousness in worship and urgency in prayer.

When, at dusk, I would sit on the edge of the riverbed, boys would gather around. Occasionally I would ask what has made them who they are. Most had experienced the rigors of cattle camp in their early years. The SPLA organized them in groups and appointed caretakers; most have been under military discipline. But their responses pointed elsewhere. One said, "We've left our parents and our land and have gone to the bush. Our lives are in the hands of God. He has given us the Bible to guide us." Soon after their arrival at Pinyudu, "the camp of children" in Ethiopia, two Sudanese pastors went to live among them. During 1988 the lads, most having come directly from rural Nilotic life, sought baptism, three and four thousand entering the church in a single service. Today, many draw upon the gospel and the biblical narratives to articulate their identity, to explain their pilgrimage, and to express their hope for the future.

On several occasions I was asked to answer questions arising from the Bible. I expected a meeting of perhaps twenty. Over four hundred gathered, their penetrating questions a challenge to any scholar. And in smaller groups I would ask, "What biblical passages do you like most?" The Psalms and the book of Lamentations, responded a seventeen-year-old. Here is nourishment for beleaguered souls wise beyond their years. One paraphrased Psalm 27 and expressed the thoughts of many: "Because my mother and father have left me, the Lord will care for me when I am in trouble" (Psalm 27:10). Another recollected the words: "My sin has become heavy upon me, and all my neighbors see me like a wild animal, yet I will rely on the Lord." A lad of fifteen wondered if God might not raise up a prophet like Isaiah from among themselves, one who will speak words of warning and comfort to his people. Many boys, having survived their tortuous pilgrimage, perceive themselves as a chosen people, a new generation at the dawn of an age when the Spirit of Christ is powerful in Sudan. In the climate of war, with all the tensions which surge through Kakuma, the Bible provides an alternative vision, a glimpse of a larger reality.

Perhaps my portrayal of this "yearning of spirit" is too biased. Each young man is a complex individual filled with the tensions of late adolescence. Camp managers must confront the dark side of unsettled youth. Numerous and complex questions surround their future. Still, it is this spiritual dimension, its pervasiveness, depth, and authenticity, which took me by surprise. Often I would ask, "When peace comes, what work do you want to do?" A remarkable number of these young warriors declared their hope to be pastors and evangelists.

Early on arriving at Kakuma I accepted Stephen Dit Makok's invitation to teach a daily class in the history of Christian mission in Sudan. (What delight to find one's doctoral thesis eagerly devoured, my one copy passed around, read even through the night.[9]) As Easter approached I asked our students if they'd like to merge a study of theology with worship and prepare a series of services for Holy Week, something none had previously experienced. Within days I was stunned to find some five thousand people carrying branches, singing at the top of their lungs, and marching three abreast in preparation for Palm Sunday. On Maundy Thursday we washed feet, and I celebrated communion in a crowded forest chapel. On Good Friday a Passion Play took on Sudanese flesh, our six-foot-eight-inch Jesus wearing his T-shirt on the cross, and Roman soldiers goose stepping in SPLA uniforms, after which thousands sat in meditative silence for nearly two hours. The week culminated in a nine-hour Vigil, beginning at 11:00 p.m. By 4:00 a.m., on the morning of the resurrection, we processed our paschal candle, followed by baptism, and communion for over seven thousand. Bishop Nathaniel had arrived on Friday, adding to the exhilaration, and stayed on conducting confirmations. Our candlelit service was spectacular: the glow of thousands of candles turned the trees of Turkanaland white, this after eight hours of reading the great acts of God's liberation in the Old Testament.

My present work is one of expressing solidarity and exploring options for the future. At Kakuma there are but two ordained ECS pastors and nine young evangelists. They minister to a church of well over twelve thousand souls. Rich in experience, none has more than two or three months of wartime Bible training. They plead for further education to help bring this great yearning of the spirit toward maturity.

I write, ever in the resurrection hope,

Marc Nikkel

---

9. The interest of the Jieng in Marc's scholarly work is paralleled by Marc's own love of the subject. In a personal letter of December 8, 1992, Marc commented, "My life contains not a whole lot else apart from tapping out my dissertation.... It has become the work of my soul."

Nairobi
June 9, 1994

> *God has not thrown you away . . . God has not deserted you.*
>   — a recurrent theme in the sermons of
>   Bishop Nathaniel Garang in the Diocese of Bor

Dear Friends,

My heartfelt thanks to those of you who have written in recent months. Know that your jottings comfort my soul, providing some continuity during a period with no fixed abode and little in the way of a predictable schedule. My movements have generally been at the behest of Bishop Nathaniel Garang, with whom I continue to meet the pastors and churchfolk of two vast Sudanese dioceses. With such scattered populations, undergoing profound culture change, ever beleaguered by war, we ask ourselves what form and content theological training might take, with what personnel, and in what locations. Our encounters have taken us to displacement and refugee camps and, most recently, to the bishop's own Diocese of Bor.

On April 28 Bishop Nathaniel, young Jon Magac (pronounced *Magash*), who recorded our visit on video, and I climbed into the Spartan cargo hold of a Hercules relief flight. Stacked high with LWF sorghum, the plane was destined for Panyagor (four miles from the better known town of Kongor), some 250 miles inside Sudan's southern border on the east side of the Nile. With most of its population dispersed during successive waves of military conflict, it had been three years since the bishop last visited his diocese. Everywhere our welcome was rapturous, with all the singing, marching, and cross- and flag-decked processions these remnant communities could muster.

Even as our entourage processed from the airstrip to church compound, however, the sobering reality struck home. Walking beside me a young fellow glanced toward the white outcroppings in the grass and said in Jieng, "bones of men." Only a year ago the entire area of Panyagor had been the site of a massive battle between factions of the SPLA, leaving untold numbers of combatants and civilians dead. When I asked why the corpses had not been buried, the answer was consistent, "there were too many." (It is also true that Nilotes tend not to bury those fallen in battle.) Several times I picked up and meditated on the bleached skulls of adults and children, now indistinguishable by tribe or factional loyalty. Later I saw a cluster of Panyagor's four hundred orphaned children (there are an estimated twenty-five hundred in the district) fashioning small cattle byres of mud, filling them with clay cattle, this only a few yards from heaps of human bones. In their determination to survive, young and old seem numbed to the abiding presence of death. Here, as everywhere we went, houses of mud and thatch were quite new, people having felt secure enough to return and rebuild only during the previous eight months. In the center of Panyagor's killing fields stands a large new cruciform church finely roofed in grass, still gold in color.

I had not previously been with Bishop Nathaniel as he moved freely among his people, at ease in his own language, preaching, counseling, ordaining (three deacons; eight pastors), and confirming (about two thousand). A superb pastor in this context, he has the capacity to buoy up the spirits of his people with his own authentic vision of a nurturing, protecting . . . and victorious God. Echoing lines from familiar songs, he would declare to those who see themselves as the last remnant of holocaust, "God has not discarded you, he has not forgotten you, you have not been forsaken. God is doing a new and marvelous work beyond our understanding: He is transforming the peoples of Sudan." In churches crammed to overflowing old and young hung on his words, seeking some tangible expression of divine power. They also wanted assurance that they are part of a widespread family of faith who stand with them, a fact my presence helped affirm. At the fulcrum of a momentous social and religious movement, Nathaniel's energy seemed inexhaustible.

Throughout our journey I was surprised by the pervasiveness of Christian symbols and expressions of faith, arising in even the most remote areas. As our vehicle later jostled through open savannah land, naked lads would sprint to the roadside shouting, "Bichip! Bichip!," fully aware of the identity of this purple-clad elder. Sinewy, ebony children at the riverside look precisely like their ancestors have for centuries . . . except that, hanging on a string around the neck of each, is a cross, hand fashioned of white plastic. (Etched with hot metal on fragments of imported plastic pipe, they appear in a plethora of designs.) While on a day's trek to villages in the *toc* (flood plains, dry season pasturelands), I was moved to meet older women who, with serene dignity, greeted me with the words, *A thiei wun de Benydit,* "Blessings on you, servant of the Lord." (Even in the *toc* there are now 129 churches.) Among the wide range of people who came for confirmation were village elders, old men wrapped in blankets kneeling alongside green-clad SPLA combatants, their arms left among the walking sticks outside the door. Undeniably, there's a new spirit moving in the land of the Jieng Bor.[10] On arrival at Panyagor we were in the care of Archdeacon Daniel Dau, who, with his companions is proud never to have fled his country, opting rather to retreat

---

10. A fact sheet prepared by Marc in 1996 reported that "in 1993 Bishop Nathaniel Garang confirmed 10,000 at Kakuma Refugee Camp; in the Diocese of Bor 5,300 were confirmed, Dec. 1995. In the Diocese of Shuei Bet [or Cueibet] Bishop Reuben Machir confirmed 16,000, Oct. & Nov. 1995. . . . In the Diocese of Bor 8 churches in 1983 have increased to 280." Similar statistics could be provided for most Jieng areas. According to Wheeler, "The result has been the almost total conversion of a people to Christian identity and allegiance in a 10 year period" (Wheeler, "Church Growth in Southern Sudan 1983–1996," 23).

into the inaccessible *toc* during each successive wave of conflict (a tactic used by their ancestors for centuries).

Amid the endless visitors, handshakes, and embraces of those first days, one sobering little figure stands out, that of Jakob Jaw (pronounced *Joo*), an old man at seven years of age. In his tattered *jalabiyya* Jakob stood before a room full of adults articulating well-honed opinions, able, on request, to recite extensive passages from the Koran. He had been one of the many Jieng boys rounded up in the garrison town of Bor for Muslim indoctrination. As a lad of five he had openly challenged — on the grounds of Islamic doctrine — the system whereby food was allocated to children who embraced Islam and denied those who did not. For his insolence he was tied in a burlap sack and flung into the Nile. (One consistently hears that this method has been used to dispose of "large numbers" of malnourished children in recent years.) The irrepressible Jakob Jaw survived. When his companions were herded onto a military plane headed for Khartoum Jakob escaped. Today he is a solitary figure ("like a ghost" said one observer), highly intelligent, with no peer to comprehend the forces moving within his singular soul. Reports proliferate that in every government-held garrison town — Juba, Malakal, Wau, Torit — southern boys are routinely gathered and shipped northward to be groomed as the vanguard of Muslim fundamentalism in the future southern Sudan. Strangely reminiscent of the Nile slave trade of the last century, military barges on the Nile reportedly stop to abduct children on their northward passage.

Our hope was to visit not only regions near Panyagor but to travel further south, toward Bor. With the only available transport that of the SPLA, we found ourselves, half a dozen churchfolk among an equal number of soldiers, atop a military vehicle. The five-hour journey to Yomciir (pronounced *Yom-cheer*) traversed open plains which, in four months time, will be thoroughly flooded. Time and again my companions pointed toward expanses of high ground, often marked by mounds, once the site of vast seasonal cattle camps. Here the soul of Jieng life once pulsed, with the fine-tuned ecological precision evolved over millennia. That entire manner of life was brought to a cataclysmic halt in 1991 with the massive armed raids of the neighboring Nuer.[11] Unprecedented in known history, the region was utterly stripped of cattle, the central symbol of spiritual, social, and economic well-being, for some three hundred thousand people.[12] Everywhere the

---

11. Numbering approximately a million people, the Nuer are the second largest ethnic group in southern Sudan, after the Jieng. As with the Jieng, their culture revolves around cattle. The Nuer do not have a centralized political structure but live in relatively autonomous villages. E. E. Evans-Pritchard's books *The Nuer* and *Nuer Religion*, although now fairly old, are still the most important ethnological works.

12. It is difficult to overemphasize the importance of cows for traditional Nuer and Jieng societies. Speaking of the Jieng, Nikkel writes, "their herds [embody]...the most profound social, religious,

bones of beasts, exhausted by the northward trek, littered the roads we traveled. It seemed quite inconceivable that traversing sixty miles at the heart of the land of the Jieng, *we did not see a single cow, sheep, or goat* (though a few head had been gathered near Kongor). It cannot be denied that, in their intense passion for the gospel, the Jieng Bor seek some compensation for the traumatic losses of recent times.[13]

With the onset of rains the famished people of Yomciir were cultivating intensively, as were communities across the *toc*, desperately hoping for a plentiful harvest. Because they are bereft of cattle, agriculture takes on new urgency among the Jieng Bor. Here too church people assembled for services in considerable numbers. However, my sights were set on a visit to Pakayo (pronounced *Pakeeo*), some twenty miles further south, and the place of worship which has become known as Zion (transliterated in Jieng as *Dhion*).

For many, Zion is the site where, across all of Jieng territory, the authority of ancestral powers (the *jak*, singular *jok*) have been most dramatically supplanted. The first impulse toward the creation of Zion arose in 1987 with the night visions[14] of a newly baptized layman, Paul Kon Ajith.[15] Believing himself divinely inspired, he proclaimed that all people must turn to God, renounce their *jak*, and cast them into the fire. If they obey, Sudan will receive God's immeasurable blessing. If they do not, his punishment will intensify. Undertaking two prophetic journeys,

---

and economic assumptions of Jieng communities. In bride price these were knit together and political alliances formed. In cattle a man had a grasp upon perpetuity, for to have descendants who could bear one's name, wives and cattle were the prerequisite. . . . In blood sacrifice, the central rite of Jieng religion, an ox assumed the place of a human life, reconciliation between communities was enacted, and unseen powers were propitiated. In an inhospitable land where human beings could not exist without cattle and cattle could not exist without human care the Jieng had evolved an extraordinary, symbiotic relationship with their herds, rich with symbolic meanings which penetrated every sphere of life" (" 'Children of our Father's Divinities' or 'Children of Red Foreigners'?" 68). The political background to the split between Nuer and Jieng factions of the SPLA and the resultant "Bor Massacre" are described in some detail in the Human Rights Watch/Africa report: Jemera Rone, et al., *Civilian Devastation*, 91–112.

13. The Nuer and the Jieng, although very similar peoples, have often been in conflict, usually over cattle. The civil war with the north has complicated what has always been a tense relationship. In the 1980s "numerous East Bank Dinka were seeking asylum to Ethiopian refugee camps. By May 1991 the Mengistu regime in Addis Ababa had fallen and refugees surged back to their homelands en masse. Within six months . . . fighting erupted between SPLA factions on the East Bank. In October 1991, trial raids executed around Bor left an estimated 3,000 civilians dead and prompted yet another exodus, this time toward the southern borders of Sudan. . . . Virtually all cattle were raided or wantonly slaughtered and women and girls abducted. . . . Some estimates suggest that over 5,000 were killed" (Nikkel, *Dinka Christianity*, 245). Many observers at the time believed that the Nuer who launched these raids were armed by the Sudanese government.

14. A common feature of African Christianity, as with traditional African culture, has been a worldview which emphasizes the reality of the invisible world. Many Africans identify strongly with biblical stories concerning dreams, visions, miraculous healing, and the reality of spiritual beings.

15. For a fuller description of the ministry of Paul Kon Ajith see Nikkel, " 'Children of our Father's Divinities' or 'Children of Red Foreigners'?" 71–74, and Werner et al., *Day of Devastation*, 545–47.

Paul traveled widely, reaching Nuer and Mandari[16] territories. Moved by Isaiah 18:7, "gifts will be brought to Mount Zion, the place of the Name of the Lord Almighty," he instructed his followers to build a massive, cross-shaped church, itself called "Zion," construction of which began in November 1992.[17]

Paul's message drew a zealous response across Jieng Thoic and Jieng Gak areas, so much so that the Sudan military, garrisoned at Bor sixteen miles away, determined to suppress this popular Christian movement. On December 26, 1992, soldiers came for Paul. He was killed, and, in an apparent effort to extinguish his influence, his body was cut into pieces. Within months three other Christian leaders were singled out and killed. But passion for the destruction of *jak* gained momentum, and the sacred pegs, forked poles, fetish bundles, and spears, symbols of some of the most venerable and reputedly powerful divinities of the region were amassed at Zion. On February 6, 1993, some thirty-three thousand people reportedly assembled for a massive bonfire, followed by Christian worship under the leadership of Archdeacon John Kelei.

Because our visit to Zion raised concerns of security, our entourage walked the twenty miles from Yomciir by night. At dawn I was astonished by the sight of Zion, more substantial than I had envisioned, with its numerous outbuildings and fenced compounds, all of mud and thatch. Certainly the church is the largest and most impressive building of local construction I have seen in Sudan, the labor of thousands of committed souls. Beautifully thatched, it rises to perhaps thirty feet at its center. Amid a forest of supporting poles, like a primitive cathedral, the congregation (numbering some four thousand on our visit) fills the arms of the cross, all facing toward a central octagonal dais. Outside, the site of the holocaust remains untouched, its rubble of rusted spears, bones, and beads a stark reminder of the subjugation of *jak*. Next to Zion is the grave of Paul Kon.

The theology and practice which evolved at Zion have not been without controversy, though its proponents are now thoroughly within the fold of the ECS. During recent Sudanese history the movement probably constitutes the most radical departure from European forms toward a distinctively indigenous expression of Christianity.[18] Across the Jieng church today, but especially here, the

---

16. The Mandari are a group of Bari-speaking people.

17. A sketch of this massive traditional structure is found in Kayanga and Wheeler, *But God Is Not Defeated!* 150. In 2003, in a conversation with Archdeacon John Kelei at St. Andrew's College in Kabare, Kenya, I was told that although the building was bombed by government troops several times in the 1990s, the people of the area always have managed to rebuild the church and that it is still in use.

18. Most African Christians south of the Sahara are vividly aware that the message of the gospel of Jesus Christ that they received was brought to them by people of a radically different culture, people who did not always respect or admire things African, people who often confused Christianity with *Western* forms of Christianity. The attempt to "indigenize" has long been an important agenda item for African theologians (see, for example, the wonderful book by the Ghanaian Kwame Bediako,

supplanting of the *jak* is the central and most radical event in establishing a new spiritual order. Believers speak of the "cleansing" of the land and proudly list the prominent shrines which have been demolished (though we listed some seventeen which continue to function). Some SPLA officials spoke as enthusiastically about the defeat of the *jak* as they did of their military victories. Even among individuals with a more secular outlook these phenomena are often considered an essential foundation for the social development of their people.

I have tried in this letter to illustrate something of the complex dynamics and motivations underlying the widespread growth of the church during this period. Some observers have said that the church in Sudan is today the most rapidly growing Christian community in the world. Likely this is true, but it is also a vulnerable community, with many unsettling questions surrounding its future. Often I sat with several of the twenty-four, mostly young, pastors I met during this tour. I asked them to list the most challenging questions raised by their people. Among those concerning church order, spiritual powers, and the divisions of the church, the most frequently asked was: "Why does God continue to punish us?" How would you respond?

Faithfully,

Marc Nikkel

Nairobi, Kenya
September 1, 1994

"Are you a white foreigner ... or are you a person?"

One evening in late June I was walking along a dry riverbed bordering Kakuma Refugee Camp in the company of a cluster of young Jieng children, talking playfully as we went. Suddenly a small girl looked up at me and asked seriously, "Are you a *khawajah* [a white foreigner] or are you a *person*?" Suspicion had dawned that I might be a human being. Until that moment the peculiar appearance, erratic behavior, and incomprehensible speech of white foreigners had not seemed compatible with the category of "person" as she understood it. Now I was beside her; I held her hand, and importantly, I spoke in the tongue of human beings she knew. We laughed at the time, but her question still tumbles in my mind. As aliens entering a society for the first time each of us is appended to the complex backlog of people and events which have gone before. I recoil when, in a rural Jieng area, a venerable patriarch greets me respectfully as *Turuuk*, a remnant from the Turkish-Egyptian era of the last century. While I acknowledge that I, like

---

Christianity in Africa). The case of the indigenization of Jieng Christianity is clearly an example of a grassroots transformation.

the Turks, am a light-skinned foreigner, I impulsively disclaim associations with the exploitative empires they lorded over. The perceptions people carry within themselves may be far from what I would like to believe they are.

For the past six weeks I have been in Panyagor, Upper Nile Province. Here, as in neighboring Kongor, succeeding waves of aliens — be they colonial rulers, relief and development cowboys, missionaries, or high-flying entrepreneurs — have each left their mark, tangibly, and in the psyche of the people. Viewing Panyagor from afar one sees a sprawl of mud *tukhls* and foliage, dominated by the domed skeleton of an abandoned warehouse, like a huge silver spider harboring its prey. In the early 1980s Panyagor was base for the billion-dollar Jongelei Canal Project (JCP), extinguished, as so much else, by war. The decaying paraphernalia of the JCP dominate the place, its most lavish monument being several miles away: the gargantuan "bucket wheel" stands rusting in the gaping scar it slashed across the earth.

Among Panyagor's relics nothing retains the meanings or uses intended by the alien civilizations that brought them. Today human life flourishes out of doors, under trees, in community, not fortressed in concrete dwellings. Hundreds of people occupy the space once dominated by a handful of whites. The spacious oval living room of a JCP employee is darkened by smoke, its windows hung with burlap sacks. Empty in the daytime, it shelters dozens of souls during the rains and at night. Prefabricated metal sheets become foxhole covers heaped with dirt. Zinc water pipes are curved to shape the church's cruciform grass roof. Enormous pieces of earth-moving equipment, motionless now for a decade, have had their six-foot tires hacked to the metal core, to be transformed into rubber sandals. More recent is the influx of white synthetic grain sacks, unwoven strand-by-strand, to make fly swatters and dancing skirts for young warriors. As the refuse of passers-through is continually recast, one is tempted to imagine that what is "concrete" and "permanent" has all been brought from outside, by aliens. That is an illusion.

Now, in wartime, no one imports cement or zinc. It is the fleeting visitations of those huge iron birds disgorging sacks of relief grain that epitomize the aliens beyond. Immaculate Red Cross planes sweep in, deposit or collect their health workers, and evaporate in minutes. Rural Jieng, having relied on relief flights for survival, can distinguish the sounds of airplanes from afar: Buffalo, Antonov, Hercules, passenger jet, Red Cross. When someone leaves by air they say, "he has gone up," as if he had ascended into some mysterious supply depot in the heavens. Many assume that every light-skinned foreigner has his own airplane and boundless hoard of supplies. These birds of steel communicate vast wealth and power . . . and infinite transience.

Nonetheless, memory of some distinctive *khawajet* lingers for years. The LWF's irascible John Parker (known everywhere as *Jon-paakuh*) is spoken of with wary admiration. For a year John succeeded in airlifting sorghum to the district's starving populations, often during brief intervals in fighting. A dozen babies are named after him. But, for the present, attitudes have soured. UN officials and their donors have been enraged by what they perceive as the duplicity and brigandage of the SPLA. In June the liberation movement contravened international agreements and commandeered an enormous UN barge destined for the starving towns of Bor and Juba. In response all relief deliveries were severed across vast swaths of southern Sudan. In Panyagor, Parker closed operations in a fury, leaving local people bewildered and apprehensive. Unaware of international wrangling, they see themselves as victims of prejudice, perhaps because they are black, or Jieng, or because theirs is the home turf of SPLA commander John Garang. Sadly, a pilot's miscalculations saw the last departing Hercules drop sacks of sorghum through the roof of the ECS church, leaving ten gaping holes. On the ground this was an irrefutable sign of the fickleness and arrogance of the region's ephemeral benefactors. Are you a *khawajah* or are you a human being? There is no simple response. How can we "Europeans" compare ourselves with the people on the ground, the unquenchable survivors? Through decades of devastation they are where they are, war and no war, aid and no aid, cattle and no cattle, starvation and bullets.

It is in this context that Archdeacon Daniel invited me to "do theology" with the thirty-seven pastors in the ECS Diocese of Bor (as distinct from those serving among refugee and displaced communities). Their call went out on foot and by SRRA radio. Over ten days, at the peak of rainy season, they came trekking and canoeing from as far away as eighty miles. Through downpours they crossed flood plains and swollen rivers and miles of remorseless knee-deep mud. *Abuna* Matthew hobbled forty miles on a leg bloated with Guinea worm infections.[19] They came barefooted and in rubber sandals, wooden crosses in hand, worldly possessions in a backpack (again, refashioned from grain sacks; "He carries his home on his head," is a common expression). As each individual or group of clergy arrived they would proceed silently into the church, lay down their loads, and pray. Only then, on reemerging, did the scene explode with laughter, flailing limbs, and song.

Their average age is thirty-nine. The youngest is twenty-two, and the eldest sixty-four (our elder, sinewy, wry, spry and whimsical David was addressed as *ran thii*, "young person"). Bishop Nathaniel ordained most during the past four years

---

19. Occurring mainly in Africa, Guinea worm disease is contracted by ingesting water fleas, usually found in stagnant water. The worm matures inside the human body and can cause intense pain and severe scarring, and may cripple the patient.

to meet the immense demands of a burgeoning church. Their education aborted by decades of war, over half have no formal schooling, but learned to read in the voluntary, self-help "clubs" of the churches. Eighteen have some primary schooling; only one had completed secondary education. Yet each pastors one or a cluster of churches, which have an average Sunday attendance of 538 souls. Three of their churches have congregations of over a thousand.

Few pastors have known a "missionary," the last CMS emissary to the Jieng having departed in 1959 (though some have of course met visiting churchfolk). Here suspicion takes another cast from that suggested above. One pastor asked bluntly: "What have we done to make the white people hate us?" and another, "Who can cultivate a garden and never come to tend it?" Expanding on this image was a pastor's parable: "A man planted a fine tree but went away, neglecting to clear the weeds around it. The grass grew, and it was burned during the dry season, but the tree was not destroyed. In time it even bore fruit, good fruit. If another man comes and wants to cut down the tree, what will the original owner of the tree do?" This was Rev. Jakob's question to me, to CMS, to the church worldwide, perhaps to God. Maybe few of us had realized a tree had been planted in Dinkaland, or even in Sudan . . . or we had assumed the root had died out long ago. Three decades after the "missionary era" a small bud has sprung to life, and we are held responsible. Today the seedling once nurtured by our forebears is the flourishing tree that some would like to sever at the root.

Expectations surrounding my arrival were substantial. I am to impart the knowledge and the benefits of "those who have learned." Some, I am sure, wondered where my airplane was. On our first encounter a rural dean asked for five wrist watches (so his pastors would know when to begin their services). Others longed for shoes, a pair of trousers, a shirt, a bed sheet, theirs being in shreds or nonexistent. It is not easy to disappoint so frequently. Many asked for eye glasses. (In morning prayers leaders passed a pair of spectacles back and forth so each could limp through the reading of the service; poor Archdeacon Simon cherishes an ancient pair of women's horned-rims, a lens half vacant, frames broken, limp as a squid, but his only access to the scriptures.) I am, it is hoped, a link to "enlightenment," to the storage depots "above" . . . and most of all to the compassion of those who preserve and cultivate trees.

We held classes in the church (which doubled as dormitory), sun and rain streaming through the roof until teams of pastors completed reparations. With the cancellation of LWF flights none of the supplies Daniel had purchased in Kenya — blankets and used clothes to barter for food, soap, basins, notebooks and pens, ledger books, oil, salt, and sugar — had reached us. The archdeacon begged and borrowed. Chairs were few and most pupils sat on mats, discarded oil tins, a gas tank. Painted plywood pallets from relief shipments served as black-boards. Three times it appeared lessons would terminate due to lack of food. Then, unexpectedly, a small band of folk from some distant church would be heard singing in the distance, advancing with sorghum and dried fish, some maze or pumpkin or groundnuts. In the absence of salt, gravy was seasoned with packets of oral rehydration salts extracted from medical stores.

It was at first suggested that I would be one of four teachers for a three-week course. In the end I was one of two for a five-week course (the other providing rudimentary English). I would come prepared with well-tried material, Sudanese — especially Jieng — church history. But horizons soon expanded. We made a time line that stretched four thousand years from Abraham to CMS pioneer Archibald Shaw to help these pastors apprehend this branch of their spiritual lineage. We labored with the thousand years of Nubian church history, comparing its strengths and weakness with the church today . . . and then they wanted the history of the Hebrews, the Exodus, and the Babylonian exile, and God's words of comfort to a decimated people. They wanted the prophets, notably Isaiah and Daniel. We surveyed the Old Testament and did a study of Levitical blood sacrifice, contrasting it with Jieng sacrificial rites. Eighty-eight years after CMS arrived among the largest tribe in Sudan the Old Testament has never been published in Jieng.[20] Today its imagery pulses in their blood, and they are desperate for it.

These men, too, are re-creators. Morning prayer may be cassock, surplice, and the vernacular 1662 Book of Common Prayer, but ejaculatory prayers are heartfelt and topical. Each hour of the day is punctuated by song, and no pastime is more loved than the learning and teaching of new compositions. Every day began and ended with an outpouring of song, as did prayers and every classroom lesson. In the dark of night sleepers would rouse to sing, sometimes one of the women's *tukhls,* sometimes a men's . . . and again fall off to sleep. In the evening, under the moon, several pastors would take up drums. Young people gathered from neighboring compounds. Younger clergy stripped down and led in dance with all the spiritual and libidinal dynamism of centuries past. Rhythms, movements, and pulse are those of cattle camp, while the lyrics are richly Christian, touting the spiritual victories of the church over *jak* and the joy of Christ the King reigning in wartime. An hour or two of dance was followed by a homily around the fire and focused, passionate prayer, ever punctuated by the swatting of mosquitoes.

The question remains — am I a person, or am I a *khawajah?* If the bestowing of names is a sign of adoption then I must be part of the human family. To

---

20. This is still the case, although some portions of the Old Testament have now appeared for experimental use.

date I have four or five Jieng names. In Panyagor I am most widely known as Manguangdit, an appellation bequeathed by students in the 1980s (suggesting a bull with a particularly aggressive curve of horn). Among the pastors I am *Thondit Akon*, Great Bull Elephant. A diminutive but gifted young pastor, Peter Yuang, became *Thon Awaan*, Male Fox. Each morning we awoke with, "Have you risen, Male Fox?" and "Have you risen, Bull Elephant?" Indeed we had.

Love to you all,

Great Bull Elephant

Nairobi, Kenya
December 1, 1994[21]

> *The sins of the generations have awaited my coming,*
> *but your word has also come to me*
> *amid this death and poverty, amid hunger and nakedness.*
> — from the prayer of a Sudanese widow

To many of us from northern climes Christmas in Sudan — there the most widely celebrated of Christian feasts — seems an incongruous affair, occurring, as it does amid the withering heat and stillness of dry season. Only occasionally do parched winds rise to resurrect inert waves of dust and grit. This is a season bereft of green. Throughout December the plains and hillsides are increasingly blackened, not whitened, as they undergo their seasonal burnings, the cyclical incinerations of centuries. Yet amid this appalling barrenness, expectant bodies glow black with anticipation. Here, in this place, on that night, the irrepressible Sudanese soul runs in torrents, breathless through the darkness, singing, dancing, celebrating, with sweat and parched throats, the fact that God has become flesh, the fact that we wear new clothes just off the tailor's table, and there will be rounds of games in the local playing fields for days and eternal days. Such images derive from peacetime . . . but the spirit of celebration is hardly less resilient even in war, amid hunger, in the aridness of refugee and displacement camps.

During recent decades Christmas has also been the season for the enforcement of curfews, for the firing of tear gas among defiant, celebrating masses, a time thought particularly appropriate for bombing raids, armed attacks, and torture. It was on the night of December 26, 1984, that church folk assembled in Bishop Nathaniel's compound at Bor found themselves surrounded by government soldiers. Gunshots fired in the dark missed the bishop by inches but disgorged the brain of evangelist Jakob Akech.[22] Bullets shredded grass mats where children

---

21. Most of the footnotes in this letter were written by Marc Nikkel.
22. Jakob was the son of the respected pioneer evangelist of the 1940s Mordekai Amol.

Sudanese Nativity, Marc Nikkel.

slept, but miraculously, none were harmed. It was on the same day in 1992 that soldiers apprehended and killed the young prophet Paul Kon. Hundreds of such late December incidents could be recounted among the peoples and regions of Sudan, the sobering counterpart to nativity, the season of Holy Innocents.

As has happened for two millennia Mary yields up her cries of joy and pain and Jesus enters our worldly war zone in the pliant ooze of a mother's flesh and blood. Mary, clad only in her radiant blackness, lies breathless on the soil of Sudan, having seen her child, half her children, all her ripening fruit, wither and die before her eyes. She prays.

Founder of two missionary churches, Rebekah Lueth is a respected and much loved matriarch of the Bor Jieng. A guide and consolation to women and children, she is a formidable counterpart to Nilotic men. She is the consummate mother, embracing virtually everyone with word and gesture, greeting them as her *own* children, the issue of her womb. She is not old, perhaps in her fifties, but the flesh bound round her still stately frame has been scarred and weathered through calamity. When she speaks she is unyielding, fixing her listeners with eye and word, hammering her conceptions with incontrovertible clarity. Never is this more so than in prayer. Going before her God this elegant woman kneels, folding herself down, down into the earth, her face buried in the soil that receives her tears. Before her on the ground she stretches out her hands, parched palms open, supplicant, expectant. The following is my translation of her prayer at Lebone, a camp for the displaced in Equatoria Province, on the morning of September 23, 1994:

> Lord, hear our prayer.
> (*Those assembled respond,* And let our cry come unto you.)

> We give you thanks, our God. We give you thanks, Almighty God. We give you thanks, Father of our Lord Jesus Christ. We give you thanks, Lord of life. We give you thanks, God of the deaf, God of the blind, God of those who are stranded. You are the God of those who are utterly helpless. You don't retreat from evil people, O Lord. That is why I call upon you. I am not good, O Son of God. Almighty Lord, how can I place my petitions before you, for I am a mere widow? There is nothing good, O God: I am impoverished. I go to sleep with nothing in my stomach but water. I collapse in your presence.

> Merciful Savior, you came in the form of a human being: you came through Mary. Mary has cut the first flag for all women.[23] You have taken all the sins of women to the cross for you have passed through woman. I give you thanks, O my God, O my God: I too am a person of value coming from people of worth, for you passed through the body of a woman.[24] You have passed through the body of your daughter, a servant, and you left your message when you rose from the dead in Jerusalem. At that time you spoke to the daughters of Jerusalem, saying, "Do not weep because of me, but cry for the sins of your children as well as for your own sins." Those sins have by-passed the generations and awaited my coming.[25] Those sins have

---

23. This translation derives from a cassette recorded during an early Morning Prayer service led by Bishop Nathaniel in an open-air chapel in the forests of the Imatong Mountains. Here Rebekah declares that Mary has created the banner which all women now carry throughout the generations.

24. Though women may be abused and suffer indignity, their flesh, their very reproductive organs, their bowels, are hallowed ground because God has made his home within them: He "passed through" one of them.

25. Previous generations were numb to their ever-accumulating sins (seen especially in defiant veneration of ancestral divinities). Only now, in war, has the terrible impact of sin been realized. The widow weeps for her sins and those of all generations who have preceded her. Underlying this is the belief that God's judgment, constrained throughout the ages, has now descended upon the peoples of Sudan. Nonetheless, God is also the redeemer and liberator who employs such devastation to bring about the conversion of his people and the dawn of a new age. This theology of judgment and restoration of the Sudan is seen as based on Isaiah 18.

waited for me, but your word has also come to me amid this death and poverty, amid hunger and nakedness. I am able to rejoice because the Lord has blessed me. Your word has come to me during this time of death.[26]

If your word was not there I would have hung myself from a tree. There would be no old women who followed after the Lord. We are dried up. The life of young children is pleasant, and the life with one's husband is sweet, but these are finished, all of them.[27] If it were not for your word I could not cry out to you today, so you, God of the generations, have mercy, for you are one who shares fellowship with the blind. You share with the deaf. You share with those who are mentally unbalanced. I am the deranged one among your sisters. I am your handicapped one. Today I have climbed the sycamore tree like Zacchaeus[28] so that I could see afar. I thought of your servant, and now he has come to us, to gather us for a new meeting, and he has fed us, and I have become joyful. He came on the very day that I thought of him, so my faith in the Great Spirit who has ears to hear is reconfirmed.[29]

I am only mud, for I have come from the dust and I will return to the dust. You, O God of widows, you God of women who live among the thorns, God of the women who live in the rocks, I give you thanks and I call out to you on behalf of the children, these whom you have sent us in human form ... for that was the way you yourself came. I know, O my God, that the dawn is coming, the dawn is coming because you have given me hope and courage. I have accepted you, O God. If there is anything I have failed to accomplish, fill out my deficiencies that I may be strengthened. Give me the capacity to pray so that I can truly pray. Have mercy on me, O my Father.

If you were not present to whom would I compare myself? If I were not here and if you were not present upon the earth, O God of Israel, then

---

26. Much of the first section, above, suggests a form of confession, a pattern which, with much thematic diversity, is typical of Rebekah's prayers.

27. In another prayer Rebekah says, "My house is now down, sunk in the hole you have dug, the hole now filled with the bones of my children.... My children are finished in my hand, the children with whom I ran away. The birds have finished them [Isaiah 18:6].... They talk about me around the fire, saying, She is the woman whose children have all died.... The children to whom I have given birth are taken by the son of El Bashir [the president of Sudan]. He sat at the door of my house and scattered all my children, and people say, 'If they pass your way, be sure to kill them.'"

28. Luke 19:1–10

29. This prayer was offered three days after Bishop Nathaniel Garang and Marc arrived at Lebone at the beginning of a five week tour through some six camps, most of which have developed since February 1994.

"America" could not come to see me.[30] Who am I? I am a woman who dresses in rags, the woman who cannot speak a foreign tongue: I am blind, and I am unschooled. My survival has always relied on cattle, but now all our animals have been raided. My children have been bribed to come and torment me.[31] My God, my God, have mercy on me. It is you who will raise me out of this suffering. I endured ten days without eating and I lived on the water you brought, and then "America" came and saw me. O God don't let me be deceived. People ask how I will find knees to crawl to "America." Do I have a car to take my children and hide them? Do I have a car or an airplane to take me? You, the God of generations, you are my airplane, for the widows here in Lebone whose eyes are red with weeping, you are our airplane. You are the house in which I hide myself. Open the door, my Lord, so that I will be hidden in your bosom. Open the door so that the orphaned will be protected. Open the door, my Lord, so the widows may be covered by your embrace. I need your arms now.

I want to converse with you, O God of the generations. I give you thanks for you have brought Nathaniel[32] to be born among us, himself sinful as we are, and you have caused John Garang de Mabior to be born among us, himself sinful as we are. You have brought them to stay among their people and love their people so they are not worried about their own lives.[33] Therefore, O God, I have cleansed the earth with my prayers so your servant John can proceed through unharmed. I have cleansed the earth with my prayers, O my "bad God,"[34] so that your servant Nathaniel Garang Anyieth will

---

30. In Rebekah's thought "America" is more a concept and a force than a country or nationality. Here, as in other prayers, she uses the word to encompass all foreign NGOs and relief organizations she has encountered during years in displacement camps (no U.S. agency had yet worked at Lebone). Still more widespread is the notion that something called "America" provides liberation — primarily through military means — for oppressed peoples. "America" is still perceived as a force of "Christian" justice and good which is believed to have aided Somalia, and particularly Kuwait (there, it is noted, against a brutal *Muslim* oppressor). Southern Sudanese typically ask why they must wait so long for the liberation of "Christian America." In this context the word was here specifically associated with Marc's visit.

31. In another prayer she says, "My children are hired to kill one another. They rob each other. The cows on which I once lived have all been raided." Rebekah embraces all people of southern Sudan as her offspring (in other prayers she suggests that people of virtually every race and nation are her issue) while she laments the interethnic and factional hostilities that have brought death to tens of thousands. She here asserts that some of her progeny have offered themselves up to bribery and are being armed by the Khartoum government to kill their own precious siblings.

32. Bishop Nathaniel Garang.

33. As her prayer intensifies Rebekah's voice breaks with emotion, her words pound rhythmically between each breath. She begins to weep, as do women and men around her. Speaking of "cleansing the earth" she moves her arms in large circular motions over the dirt floor on which she kneels, sweeping, cleansing, and smoothing the surface of the earth with word and gesture.

34. This type of Jieng affirmation-through-negation is usually reserved for children. Such names express affection through opposites when conventional words seem banal and inadequate. English

advance on a smooth mattress, unobstructed, O God, so he can go to visit the people of Mangalatoria, he can visit those who are in Nimule,[35] visit the widows who are in Kakuma, so he can visit, O God of the generations, the people remaining in our homeland. Lead your servant, our God.[36]

I have grasped your hand, my God, my God. I have caught your hand, O God of the generations. I kiss your mouth. Discover me unawares in the place where I have been lost. Now I wear a dress I did not bring with me. Now I eat enough to sleep soundly, leaving food to remain, the clothes and food which "America" has brought. So, O God of Israel, listen to my cry: I will return to the soil with my stomach filled with green leaves.[37] Have mercy on me, my Great Lord. If you have discovered me and I have grasped your hand, then clutch my hand firmly.

And I greet you, O Great God of Israel, in the name of the Father and the Son and the Holy Spirit. Amen.

Rooted in a particular place and time, merging a vigorous and desperate faith with a specific political vision, this is *not* an easy prayer. Rebekah's words reveal a God of judgment and love, of annihilation and redemption, as she has come to know him on her arduous journey. As a maidservant offered her body to become the channel through which Salvation passed, the widow prostrates herself and cleanses the way for the Lord's liberator, a military commander. Again, by prayer and gesture, she smoothes the earth that God's appointed prelate may pass through unobstructed, proclaiming the Day of the Prince of Peace among the poor and brokenhearted. The virgin who sings to the Lord while giving suck to Immanuel is mirrored by a widow weeping over the accumulated sins of generations

---

equivalents might be the African American "he's so-o b-a-a-d!" meaning he is good and worthy of admiration, or "my little devil" for a beloved child. In Africa such usages often derive from the tendency to speak of children in negative terms lest some malign spirit, on hearing words of praise, might seek to harm the object of affection. In Sudan such names for God also reflect an ironic play on the Muslim exaltation of *Allah* and denigration of the divinities of African peoples, be they Christian or traditionalist.

35. Rebekah lists several camps that the bishop and Marc were to visit. From Lebone they flew forty-five minutes to Nimule, and then drove to neighboring Magale; southward into Uganda to the camps at Adjumani and, crossing the Nile Westward, to Koboko; then northward, again into Sudan and Mangalatoria (near Kajo Keji). Scattered across Equatoria and northern Uganda, all of these camps have substantial Jieng Bor populations.

36. Again, typical of Jieng Bor Christian thought is the linking of "the two great Garangs" (a common personal name deriving from a primal ancestor and divinity) whom God has raised up, John Garang of the SPLA and Bishop Nathaniel Garang of the Episcopal Church in Sudan, both sons of the Bor area. It is believed that God is using these two very different men to bring about the liberation of his people.

37. In apparent contrast to the preceding line, Rebekah now laments that she will die with nothing in her stomach but green leaves, a diet associated with utter impoverishment, according to the meat-loving Jieng.

and the corpses of those to whom she once gave issue. Can we, in confronting Rebekah's synthesis, still in gestation, not confirm that the Magnificat, the Song of Mary,[38] itself derives from the longings of a people who sought to reclaim a homeland, both eternal and terrestrial? Rebekah, mother of Israel, searches out a future for her children.

This comes with every good wish as you hallow and exalt the Prince of Peace, once born, once crushed in this, our worldly war zone . . . and ever risen,

Marc Nikkel

Nairobi, Kenya
May 1, 1995

— *Of rootlessness, frustration, and hard-heartedness*

I greet you with love in the weeks after Easter, ever in the resurrection hope. It is now sixteen months since I returned to East Africa. It seems time for a more *personal* appraisal of my life in Sudan, specifically with the Jieng, than I have offered thus far. Some of you have written thanking me for my *particular* reflections on the Sudanese church . . . but asking, "What about *you*? What are *your* highs and lows during this period?" A response does not come easily, especially when I place my petty ordeals alongside those of my Sudanese kinfolk. Nevertheless, I will try to describe three areas among many, with which I grapple . . . spheres where I feel my soul is gradually undergoing its own reformation. I will write, first, of my ongoing sense of *rootlessness*, second, of my not infrequent feelings of *frustration* with tasks before me, and, finally, of my wrestlings with my own *real — or perceived — hard-heartedness* in the face of seemingly boundless needs. You might receive this as something of a confession. If so, that is much to be preferred over an index of personal gripes.

Rootlessness

"Where do you live?" a Sudanese friend asked me recently. "Well, I don't really have a *home*," said I. Having made some ten forays into Sudan, anywhere from one to twelve weeks in length; it has been a year of pilgrimage with few fixed points. "But *even the birds* have special trees they roost in," she prodded. "Where's your tree?" Perhaps I have four or five trees. Last rainy season I survived six weeks in a one-man tent (blessedly mosquito- and fly-proof) at the heart of a busy, often bemired, church compound in Panyagor, Upper Nile. From December through February this year, my nest was one of five thatched *tukhls* encircled by a

---

38. Luke 1:46–55

sorghum stock fence at Dhiaukuei Bible School. There I stayed with my teaching colleague, Abraham Dau, and a motley but endearing crew of four to six cooks, sweepers, water carriers, and hangers on, most physically or mentally impaired. Destitute all, they shared together daily from our common pot.

Other periods, traveling with Bishop Nathaniel in refugee and displacement camps, have found me sleeping on a different wood and leather cot in yet another guest *tukhl* each night. In Nairobi, too, life has been transitory. Given the short periods I normally stay, it seems a waste to rent a flat at today's exorbitant prices. Of late, I have been roosting in the home of a gracious Christian businesswoman whose tree offers temporary shelter to an extraordinary variety of friends and family who fly through. As I write, however, one "permanent" shelter is nearing completion, this at Kakuma Refugee Camp in northwestern Kenya. Designated "Abuna Marc's House,"[39] a two-room structure of mud brick, roofed in plastic and palm fronds, expresses the love and hopes of Jieng refugees.

But is not it possible to create a long-term nest inside Sudan? Part of my soul wants desperately to be woven into the fabric of communal life on *Sudanese* soil. But I vacillate. Can I create a work base (with a small library, computer, solar panel, and all the stuff of survival) given the geographical spread of my commitments and the volatility of Sudan? It has, thus far, seemed impractical. My gut is divided and sixteen months on I have no place I call "home."

There is yet another aspect of my restlessness, my "nestlessness." After a couple of months in Sudan I have found I often feel quite fragile. I am drained, even numb. For a few days at least, back in Kenya, I don't want to interact with anyone, except *perhaps* the good Lord (and even with him I'm poor company). Sometimes on the verge of tears, I need solitude, a quiet place to take inventory of the sensations I have known, the precarious existence of a land, a people, at war. For these reasons I have more recently taken days for work and reflection at a Benedictine monastery. Here the ordered life of prayer four times each day helps to compensate for the utter unpredictability of Sudan. Silence, sacrament, and song embrace the fragments of my being. It is from the Monastery of the Prince of Peace on a hill overlooking Nairobi that I now write.

Frustration

I am but one of an army of people — good-willed humanitarians and Christians alike — who try to create programs for the peoples of southern Sudan. I wonder if a third of them ever become reality, certainly none in the form they are originally envisioned. Together with Bishop Nathaniel and other ECS leaders, we *plan* to

---

39. I stayed in this house briefly in 1996. Like all of the other houses in Kakuma it had a mud floor, walls ingeniously manufactured from mud and sticks, with a blue tarpaulin roof supplied by the UNHCR.

provide at least three annual vernacular courses of two to three months each, in three locations. During the past "trial" year we have offered a six-week course at Kakuma (part of a longer six-month endeavor), another in the Diocese of Bor, and a two-month course at Dhiaukuei, in the Diocese of Rumbek. Combined, these have provided basic studies in biblical and Sudanese Christian history, a survey of the Bible, evangelism, and the theology and practice of Christian worship for some eighty-five ordained pastors and ninety-five women's leaders, teachers, and evangelists.

There is room for encouragement, hoping that something more substantial will be achieved next year. (We are planning almost continuous courses in each of three locations from July 1995 through March 1996.) Preparing for each course is expensive, time consuming . . . and precarious. Once a budget is approved and funding obtained (a two-month course inside Sudan may run between $3,000 and $5,000), supplies must be purchased, usually in Nairobi. School materials include obvious items like notebooks and stationery, reference books, blackboard paint, and chalk, all packed in locally made tin trunks. Teaching notes need to be written, translated into Jieng, typed, and photocopied en masse. Select food items are required to supplement the scanty diet of our scholars: cooking oil, tea leaves, sacks of salt and sugar, perhaps some onions, lentils, and beans. Other essentials include soap, lanterns, and kerosene, a water filter, an assortment of cooking pots, maybe a spoon and cup for each pupil. With several Sudanese colleagues away on courses, I have needed to do most of these tasks on my own.

Once assembled, supplies must be transported six hundred miles by road to Lokichoggio ("Loki") on the Sudan border, and a further three hundred or more miles into Sudan by air, hopefully courtesy of Operation Lifeline Sudan. Last July, with the sudden cancellation of flights to the Bor area, supplies purchased never arrived, leaving us limping along in Spartan simplicity. Of late the UN has been cutting back flight lists, making the transport of staff and supplies into remote locations still less predictable. Were funds available, an occasional charter would be a great help, but flights into a war zone are costly, running at least $600 an hour, easily $3,000 for a single return journey.

Last November I visited Dhiaukuei to plan for our two-month course and was assured by church leaders that sufficient food would be contributed locally to feed our sixty-plus students (daily attendance actually averaged over ninety). Arriving on December 22 I found that virtually *nothing* had been collected and regional food supplies were extremely low. I made an urgent plea to colleagues in Nairobi that, if feasible, 150 sacks of grain be sent immediately to help sustain our student body. Grain was purchased . . . and we waited. I am told that eighty sacks were sent the arduous route into Sudan, but fewer than thirty ever reached us . . . and these during *the last ten days of our course*. On return to Kenya I have been told that fifty sacks disappeared between Nairobi and Loki. I was handed a bill for nearly $6,000, the cost of the grain, most of which evaporated. The full story is yet to be told.

Throughout our two-month course the physical hunger of our students was a continual anxiety. A number of times clusters of them went for one, two, or three days with nothing to eat. Nonetheless, most conscientiously attended classes from 7:00 a.m. to 2:30 p.m. five days a week. The intense hunger for education is gratifying at least. Most needy were some twenty-six young men who had trekked southward from Aweil on foot. Having wound their way 150 miles through hazardous territory, they arrived lean and starved. Seeing them grow still thinner each week of our course, having them look to me for sustenance, was a constant torment: I pray none died on the return journey.

These are several among numerous gnawing frustrations of past months. I want to be about *my* work, I tell myself. I want to prepare teaching materials, to work on theological issues with Sudanese colleagues, to study language, research, and write. I am *not* interested — nor have I been prepared for — buying and toting trunks of notebooks or sacks of salt and sorghum, nor do I want to worry about budgets, transport, and the starvation of my students. And yet these are all part of the disorderly, anomalous fabric of work alongside communities on the frontiers of war.

Hard-heartedness

As my language improves, my circle of Jieng friends ripples ever more widely. How good it has been building ties in rural villages and cattle camps, sitting around the fire with student families by night. I learn a great deal from these resilient survivors. But in difficult times the expectations of needy people also multiply. Being perceived as a link with the affluent world beyond and one of the few foreigners who speak Jieng, I receive a continuous stream of requests. Pleas for assistance are as unending as they are heartrending. At Dhiaukuei I would receive three to five handwritten notes a day, primarily from schoolboys, but from grown church people as well. Writing in Jieng they would often open with, "In the name of the Father, and of the Son, and of the Holy Spirit . . . my Great Father in Christ, *Manguangdit*,[40] *Oichthon*[41] (or other of my Jieng appellations[42]), Mak Nikel" . . . and proceed to plead for blankets or notebooks, kerosene or medicines, pens, soap, shoes, trousers, shirts . . . urgently felt needs all. Old people, mustering all their dignified, tattered authority, would come, morning and evening, to present their

---

40. "The great bull elephant."
41. "The man who has bought a bull."
42. See the piece Marc wrote in 1999 ("On Becoming a 'Bull Elephant,'" p. 182 in this volume) for his reflections on the meaning these names had for him.

petitions, occasionally spicing them with dance, a proverb, a narrative of family history, a song.

The Jieng have the capacity of placing the weight of their entire destiny, the survival of their whole lineage, on a potential benefactor. They can be indefatigable, assertive, and resolute: subtle refusals are thoroughly ineffectual. This *can* be overwhelming, especially when work is taxing and emotions run low. Even after years relating to Jieng friends, I occasionally feel threatened, intimidated, in the face of yet another assault on my *private* work time, my perceived affluence, my person, my soul. Wanting space, I sometimes go rigid, refusing to engage in the customary verbal sparing, unwilling to launch into yet another evaluation of legitimacy. To respond in anger or abruptly turn someone away is reprehensible. In truth, what most petitioners require is to be met eye to eye, and to be engaged with vigor. They demand to be recognized. A refusal may be accepted but must be arrived at with decorum. Only gradually have I learned to respond with a modicum of humor seasoned with respect. I speak honestly of my limitations and more often give what is asked. Less frequently do I capitulate to emotional sabotage.

At times, on *this* journey alongside *this* people I want to invest my life without reservation, interminably. At others I want to retreat, to close down and escape. Sometimes it seems that virtually everything, *everything* is vulnerable. I feel as if our work, every plan we envision, every preparation I make, every lesson I teach, every relationship I nurture, even the dwellings I inhabit . . . could be swept away in hours. All the people, places, and processes I entrust my heart to could be eradicated. Will factional violence erupt tomorrow leaving hundreds dead and forcing a mass evacuation? Could a fortnight's leave find my re-entry barred? Within a decade could the consuming fires of Muslim fundamentalism ravage this land, eradicate its church, and claim the souls of children yet unborn?[43] There is an enormous tenuousness about life with Sudan.

Why hang on? I occasionally ask myself. Why not return to the United States and earn at least four times as much (even as a manual laborer) and create for myself a "secure" home. A plethora of reasons come to mind, some psychological, some historical. But at heart, there is the sense of the presence of God in this tumultuous land, among these incomparable people, in the work which absorbs me. In no other context have I been so overwhelmingly aware of the compassionate,

---

43. In the year 2000 Paul Marshall wrote: "Sudan is one of the world's worst religious persecutors. It practices forced conversions, represses those who do not subscribe to its version of Islam, has applied *shari'a* law to its entire population, enslaves its opponents, and is engaged in a war that the U.S. Congress, East African Bishops Conference, the U.S. Commission on International Religious Freedom, and many other observers have explicitly labeled as 'genocidal' " (Marshall, *Religious Freedom in the World,* 284).

sustaining, and healing presence of God. Amid infinite uncertainty and vulnerability, *here* amid a people near breaking, yes, even in *my own* frailty, there is one
who affirms, secures, and loves. This One does not take the vulnerability away.
He does not assuage precariousness, but is at the fulcrum of my uncertainties,
my anxieties, amid all the difficult relationships I so cherish. He does not offer to
remove the abyss of potential losses, but exists on that precipice. Because of this
Presence I expect I will continue. Recently I met these words, so akin to my own
perceptions, concerning the nature of God's compassion:

> Here we see what compassion means.
> It is not a bending toward the underprivileged from a privileged position;
> it is not a reaching out from on high to those who are less fortunate below;
> it is not a gesture of sympathy or pity for those who fail to make it in the
>   upward pull.
> On the contrary, compassion means going directly to those people and
>   places
> where suffering is most acute and building a home there. God's compassion
>   is total, absolute, unconditional, without reservation....
> It is the compassion of a God who does not merely act as a servant,
> but whose servanthood is a direct expression of his divinity.
>
> —Henri J. M. Nouwen[44]

This is God's compassion. It is certainly not mine. Amid my fear of rootlessness,
of futility, of my own impulse to hold so tightly onto what I have...he makes
his home. And there he tells me that I can share with him in the far, far greater
vulnerability that is the daily fare of those whom he has entrusted to me as friends.

With my home still under construction,
Marc Nikkel

Nairobi
October 10, 1995

HOME IS HOME AND BUSH IS BUSH

You may be in another country, a country that is very rich,
    but if you can't return to your homeland, you're still in the bush.
Away from your homeland anyone can treat you as if you're worthless.

---

44. Henri Nouwen, *Compassion: A Reflection on the Christian Life*. Marc was often comforted by
Henri Nouwen's writings. After hearing that Nouwen had died, Marc wrote to me in Toronto, where
Nouwen had also been living, asking if I could find and send him any obituaries or tributes that had
been written about him.

Away from your homeland you endure life as a vagrant.
Away from your homeland you encounter prejudice and misunderstanding.
Away from your homeland your integrity is ruined.
Away from your homeland people see you as useless.
Away from your homeland your kinfolk faint away,
    the respected elder as well as the child.
Away from your homeland you persevere amid disaster.
Away from your homeland you're like a baby that's been weaned too soon.
Away from your homeland you're disowned by your friend.
Away from your homeland you're devoured by a toothless animal.
Away from your homeland you're made into a docile creature.
Away from your homeland your soul knows deep sorrow.
Away from your homeland life seems useless, useless, useless, too useless.

These are the words, with a few revisions, of Bartholomayo Bol-Mawut Deng (here, "Bol"), a twenty-four-year-old "evangelist" at Kakuma Refugee Camp. In these lines he expresses, more directly than most, the heartache and estrangement of life in an alien land. Like many of his young comrades, he first left Sudan eight years ago. Nonetheless, his present life appears anything but dispirited or useless, even amid the monotony, deprivation, and stifling heat of Kakuma. Throughout Bol's refugee wanderings across Ethiopia, Sudan, and Kenya, he has proven himself a capable leader, respected for his "cool heart," resourcefulness, and integrity. The Episcopal Church in Zone 4,[45] with a Sunday attendance of some twenty-two hundred, is under his care. Within its brushwood fence at least seventeen services take place each week.

It is with Bol and his colleagues in the church's compound, Group 51, that I have been living for most of the past three months in the two-room house they have built for me. During this, my second extended stay at Kakuma, I have been teaching at our newly constructed ECS Bible School, its seven mud and thatch buildings a short walk along the dry riverbed from my abode.

Is it my growing familiarity with Sudanese in exile, or is it that their plight has worsened, that I find people more restless, less healthy in body and spirit, than I did nineteen months ago? Undeniably, there's some regression. Most of my friends, like Bol, are thinner then when I first met them. The WFP (World Food Programme) has, by stages, cut food rations and people complain of hunger continually. The nutritious *makech* — "the yellow stuff," soya mix, a gift of the USA — I once enjoyed from our common bowl, has, like much else, disappeared from the relief diet. Though a rudimentary hospital and health system exists in the

---

45. The UNHCR divides refugee camps into sections called Zones, further subdivided into Groups. The Zones are often separated according to ethnic and linguistic lines.

camp, people say medicines are utterly insufficient. Six of my friends, scattered across the camp, have had severe dysentery during the past week. In his poem Bol grieves over his existence "in the bush." The transience of years away from home is taking its toll... and dissatisfaction rises. This is not only homelessness of body, but homelessness of mind and spirit as well.

Physical homelessness

During the past two years I have been amazed by the movement of southern Sudanese. People from isolated cattle-herding communities who, for centuries, have seldom strayed beyond time-honored routes of seasonal migrations, have, within a few years, become seasoned travelers — by foot, by lorry, by bus, by *matatu*,[46] and, when possible, by air — across the frontiers of four countries and more. Individuals I have met hundreds of miles away, at camps in Uganda, in Ethiopia, or in Sudan's provinces of Equatoria or Upper Nile, are now at Kakuma.... Others are wending their way homeward, trying to reunite dispersed families or eke out a wartime living. Young refugee entrepreneurs obtain used clothes to barter in the "liberated areas," returning to Kenya with goats which will, they hope, pay for education in a Kenyan school, or a relative's treatment. Still other refugees defy the networks of food distribution contrived by foreign NGOs and, with enormous effort, convey relief goods from 100 miles inside the war zone back to northern Kenya to feed hungry kids at Kakuma. At the same time meager rations from the camp may seep 250 miles south to feed lads at a Kenyan school.

Southward travelers head for towns along the five-hundred-mile route to Nairobi, despite the illicit $2 fee (no mean amount) demanded of every undocumented alien at roadside police posts. While UN and Kenyan officials may deride this "illegal" transit, neither offers incentives sufficient to keep refugees in place. Within the souls of many people, pressure keeps rising as they cast about for better options, outside, beyond the incessant tidings of war. Increasing numbers wrestle with prospects of severing ties and "going for resettlement" in Australia, Canada, the United States, and now, we hear, South Africa. In Nairobi I meet anxious teenagers who, having obtained their documents, await departure, claiming they will return as soon as they have finished their education. They will not. For many the links with family and culture are already tenuous, the homeland continues to degenerate in factional fighting; while existence at Kakuma seems a dead end.

---

46. *Matatu* is a Kiswahili word meaning "three." *Matatus* are privately owned taxis, usually minibuses, that form the backbone of the Kenyan transit "system." They are named after the original price that was charged for a ride (many years ago!) — three shillings.

Homelessness of mind

Only ten years ago most Jieng youth in southern Sudan were being instructed, disciplined, and prepared for life, in the rarefied proving ground of cattle camp. Today, with cattle culture eradicated or diminishing, many youngsters fall between two stools, having neither the social formation of their ancestors, nor anything but shreds of formal schooling. In his poem, "Ten Years Away from My Parents" Bol writes:

> Because of the war I am like a son who has no parent.
> Because of the war our country has become a land of orphans.
> Because of the war a child is no longer instructed by his father.

In displacement camps intelligent children often wander aimlessly with little to inspire them but the throb of mortar shells. Many have come to believe that formal education, in tandem with Christian faith, is their most hopeful route into the future. Inside Sudan I meet youth who conceive of Kakuma as a haven for good education, its curriculum based on Kenyan syllabi. Many who arrive soon want something more.

The UN has contracted education to *Rader Barnen* (Swedish Save the Children), under whose administration teacher absenteeism has declined, new, "permanent" buildings are rising, and funding has not gone astray as previously. Kakuma's twenty primary schools have an enrollment of 18,233 (though 20 percent are absent on any given day). These pupils are instructed by 420 teachers, most whom are refugees.[47] Many pupils are now in their late teens and twenties, their lives wavering between the strong pull of Sudan's battlefront, and a belated education. Across Kakuma one finds these students, alone and in clusters, laboring over textbooks in daytime heat, and at night, if they are lucky enough to have a lantern. Sadly, there is but one secondary school at Kakuma with a capacity of little more than two hundred, this, when next year's primary finishers will exceed three thousand. A vision of the world expands in these young minds, but with it grows the feeling of having been left far behind in new terrain where formal education constitutes survival.

Homelessness of spirit

A decade of increasing rootlessness has also evoked probing questions of the soul. In this sphere, however, homelessness has borne extraordinary fruit as people struggle to understand the meanings of their pilgrimage. From Exodus to Diaspora

---

47. Although there are some school buildings at Kakuma, many classes meet outside, under trees. During my time in Kakuma when we passed by one clutch of pupils with their teacher my Sudanese guide asked, "Do you see that Mama under the tree? — She knows the alphabet. We teach what we know."

rootless wanderings are essential to our Christian heritage: in the wilderness of Kakuma the Bible provides its consolation. Like most of Bol's songs, the following is addressed to the God of homeless people:

> Turn your ear to us O God of peace;
> Our minds are confused with the things we suffer.
> We are roaming about in the bush enduring the life of homeless people,
>   and we keep our hearts turned toward the word once spoken
>   through the mouth of Isaiah concerning our land.
> We know that the entire world exists through the power of the word
>   and ultimately it will be removed by the word alone;
> therefore we know salvation will finally come
>   according to the word you have spoken.

The Word of God has produced all that exists, be it transitory or constant. The final word of salvation, security, and "home" will come from this same source. While his brothers give their lives in battle and big men dispute "peace" in Nairobi, a young alien, and some of his kinfolk, grasp upon the Word as their supreme hope, irrational as it may appear. Bol's physical rootlessness and longing for his homeland also give birth to hope for *eternal* security. My Western mind sometimes chafes at images of heaven, so recurrent in the songs of refugee Christians ("O Happy Day!" being a favorite survival of the missionary era). Nonetheless, it is at Kakuma that I glimpse the broader landscape of our "home above," as the Jieng say it. It is a place from which we will never have to run for fear of being killed, and where peace pours forth, a river of communion unobstructed by death. Amid fragmentation, and barrenness, eternity glows radiant. Bol invites his people to sing:

> We call upon you, O God, to visit us with peace. The world afflicts us continually. Hear the moaning of humankind, the souls crying out, looking toward eternal life. Let us grasp the Cross with two hands so your salvation will arrive as we wait. Open the windows of eternal life for us.

Among people who have neither homeland nor kinfolk the churches are places where eternity draws near. The vitality of the ECS I described in an earlier letter[48] continues to spin off new forms. Young Christians have composed over a thousand vernacular songs in this arid place, many choreographed with energetic and exacting dances. From Friday through Sunday evening the drumbeat hardly ceases as one group waves over another, dancing under trees, singing, and interceding. Each Saturday finds older people gathering from 6:00 to 10:00 a.m., their

---

48. The letter of April 15, 1994, p. 108.

prayers focused on healing, peace, and an eminent return to the homeland. Small children have built miniature churches where diminutive pastors pray and preach, imitating their elders. Continually, the Spirit performs her alchemy, transforming suffering, death, and homelessness into celebration, prayer, and kinship.

Nonetheless, I wonder if, amid the rapid evolution of soul and psyche, paired with the exertions of mere survival, the crest of this movement is not waning. For some recent converts the meaning of faith is dulled amid the tangle of new ideas and the current drive for formal education. The excitement of defeating old spiritual powers abates in the face of new conflicts of culture and values. Some turn away, disappointed by the seeming impotence of their fellow "children of God," you and I included.

My hope is that the exhilaration of recent years is not withering but being transformed, taking root, even in alien lands. I pray those vital sightings of the *eternal* homeland will not be abandoned, but inspire values of the Kingdom to be lived out in the present and future. Communal harmony, equal coexistence, and justice are as essential here as in the war zone, or in a renewed ancestral homeland. In Jieng the word *weï* describes that dynamism which is both breath and life, the immediate, physical, as well as eternal dimensions of living creatures. Bol avows his fidelity to the source of *weï*:

> I will not depart from the Lord Jesus for I have found my *weï*;
> There is nothing more satisfying than the Bible.
> If I should grasp all the meaning that is therein and contain it within
>   my *weï*
>   there is nothing I could say that would surpass it.
> Don't allow me any deficiency, O Lord, for in your Kingdom there is
>   nothing lacking.

Amid illness and destitution a young refugee affirms the all-sufficiency of his God. I am often staggered by the polarities embraced within this young church. Away from their homeland there are those who envision their eternal dwelling; in poverty they sing of plenitude; sickly and emaciated, they affirm the divine *weï* that animates their frail bodies. In perplexity, they invoke the certitude of God's Word. Nevertheless, these affirmations do not deny the reality that, as Bol declared in his poem above, forced exile amid war is tormenting and degrading.

In their Saturday morning prayers the elders, the majority women, cry out for divine mercy upon the children of Kush,[49] as they sometimes call themselves,

---

49. Kush, or Cush, is the Old Testament name which usually designates that part of Africa south of Egypt. Some English translations call this area Nubia, a later name for this same area. Other translations use the word Ethiopia: which is, again, an anachronism. The Greek word from which "Ethiopia" is derived means "burnt-face," and in ancient times the term was used to describe the

inhabitants of the land divided by rivers (Isaiah 18). They long for an end to their forced dependency on the international agencies few can comprehend or feel they can trust. They plead for genuine reconciliation and friendship among the "black peoples" of Sudan. They pray for liberation from the spiritual powers that enslave them, as well as for political and military liberation. Above all, they beg God for the miracle that will end their life at Kakuma: a just conclusion to the war and a peaceful return to their homeland.

On behalf of refugee Christians in this place, I invite you to affirm that we are, each of us, inhabitants of "another country, a country that is very rich." For the present may we, alongside them, do all in our power to make the peace of that Kingdom a tangible reality.

Still on pilgrimage,

Marc Nikkel

Nairobi
January 20, 1996

The God of the Jieng, ah, this God is HOT!

"Thanks, and thanks, and very thanks," for the many cards and letters sent to mark the Feast of the Incarnation. Though most have reached me only in the past few days, it is so good to reaffirm our far-flung ties of faith, hope, and affection. Now briefly in Nairobi, I have been in the Diocese of Bor on the east bank of the Nile since early December. With some sixty church leaders now gathering, classrooms and housing under construction, we plan to open a ten-week course on January 24.

During recent weeks I have again confronted the radical shifts in values and beliefs, aspirations, and physical culture underway among the Jieng. Southern Bor is a center from which peoples have dispersed, their tenuous webs of kinship stretching across Africa to places as diverse as Khartoum, Kakuma, and Cairo, Dallas, and London. Despite its seclusion, this Jieng heartland, still virtually stripped of cattle, continues its own remaking. Occasionally some Western friends accuse me of a missionary agenda to undermine the ancient traditions of a great Nilotic people, of my participation in the demise of religious and social institutions that have survived millennia. For myself, however, I often feel somewhat peripheral, an observer, standing in the tide pools of a surging river of reassessment and innovation. This is a process occurring largely from within Sudanese societies, not

---

residents of Africa. In modern times the term has come to mean the residents of a particular nation state, but the term did not originally refer to that part of Africa alone (see Adamo, *Africa and Africans in the Old Testament;* Yamauchi, *Africa and the Bible*).

from without. I ask how I should respond to this metamorphosis. Should I grieve, as is sometimes my impulse? Or should I take up my wooden cross and celebrate the birth of a new, self-consciously Christian, order?

Without doubt much of Upper Nile Province opts for the latter. Between December 13 and January 4, I have walked with Bishop Nathaniel and thousands of his people, on a confirmation tour of southern Bor, his first in four years. With banners flying, drums reporting through the forests, crowds bellowing, it had all the buoyancy of a medieval pageant. A wonderfully genuine, unpretentious celebration, the only note of twentieth-century technology was the diocesan video camera that floated down our trails and the solar panel that tottered on the head of a young porter, wired to the battery in his pocket. We trekked over a hundred miles on foot, conducted some twenty-three confirmation services, with attendances often over a thousand. The bishop laid hands on 5,364 people, these, we are told, but a third of those awaiting the Spirit's "empowering" (*Cok riel,* to "make strong"). Across the Nile in the region of Rumbek, the new bishop of Chuei Bet, Reuben Machir Makoi, confirmed some sixteen thousand people on his first tour in late 1995.

The sheer numbers involved and the level of their industry must exceed those required for an international tour of the archbishop of Canterbury. Our parade usually consisted of several hundred people, armed guards interspersed among them. Mostly young, good-natured, SPLA soldiers, their numbers swelled to thirty or forty when the Commissioner of Bor County accompanied us. There were fifty to a hundred porters, the majority girls and women, each group regularly relaying their loads to those of the next rural church. At these changing posts we would be welcomed, drums pounding, crosses jerking to the rhythm, crowds singing, "He has come, he has come, he's arrived; he came in the night, let's welcome him; he's arrived!" At roadsides the hoarse voices of old women belted their incantations: "*Nhialinyda! Nhialinyda!*" "Our God! Our God!" "He comes to enlighten our land! He moves slowly! He moves slowly!" To the bishop and his Divinity they would shout, "*Kudwal,* Great Lord, Greetings, O *Nhialic!*" Another matron cleared the bishop's way as she derided those who demanded sacrifices to ancestral powers: "You who devour cows, cast yourselves in the bush!" Our party received not sacrifices, but offerings of respect and love, cooked by succeeding bands of women. In our wake we left the bones of chickens, goats, and occasionally an ox, remnants of the finest feasts these rural folk could muster.

More fortunate communities had a week's notice of the bishop's coming, others as little as one night. Nonetheless, small villages were constructed at virtually every location to house him and his retinue. Often marvelously sculpted in sorghum stock and grass, these included three or four huts, each topped with a cross, a couple of *rakuba* shelters,[50] a bathing stall, a freshly mudded pit la-trine, all surrounded by expanses of fence. These were adjacent to the church, the largest and most elaborate structure in any village. Although the churches are normally rectangular, 80 to 106 feet in length, more recent "byres of God" are cruciform, their carefully mudded seats radiating in three directions. Jieng tradition likens the diminutive stature of humankind to tiny black ants (*acuuk*) when compared with the greatness of *Nhialic*, God Almighty. Known also for their single-minded industry, extraordinary strength, and swarming numbers, ants now provide a metaphor which Christians use to describe themselves as they work to build the Kingdom of God. For decades missionaries lamented the tepidity and lethargy of the Jieng church. Not so today.

Bishop Nathaniel was radiant. Though a little portly and sometimes limping, he never missed a beat, even when we walked fifteen miles and conducted a four-hour service at a go. He carried himself with pastoral warmth and confidence. His sermons were biblical, spiced with anecdotes tailored for the day. He would describe churches flourishing among the Bor diaspora in Equatoria, Kenya, and Uganda, recounting the astonishment of onlookers as throngs of Jieng Christians march by, drums booming. In southern Sudanese Arabic he recalled their excla-mations, *"Rabuna beta Denka, de Rabuna gowi!"* "The God of the Jieng, that God is potent!" sometimes translated, "Their God is HOT!" God is serious, determined, strong . . . not so unlike the Jieng church of this day. Comparable to prophets of the Exile, the bishop would encourage these fragmented, remnant communities to prepare for the eminent return of their kinfolk, the glorious reunion of parents and children from the Babylons they now inhabit.

I was often moved by the themes of Bishop Nathaniel's prayers, their focus on the nature of *Nhialic*. Despite continual requests for food and clothes, water pumps, school supplies, and medicines, he seldom offered petitions for *things*, but focused primarily on the character and authority of God. Ever present was the *Nhialic* who oversees history. The God who has delivered Israel can be expected to be with those whom he has called in the present day. The God who sent Christ in the flesh of a human being that we might be redeemed, this *Nhialic* is moving mightily in Sudan. "What you have prepared in heaven is now being fulfilled among your people here on earth." Often he would declare, "Our life is in your hands; we are utterly dependent on you. There is no other like you: you are the only one able to accomplish your work." Every prayer opened with thanksgiving, "that you have given us this time together," as if each moment in community is precious amid war's vulnerability. In stillness these huge congregations, every

---

50. A local style structure made of sticks and straw.

person familiar with death and loss, seemed intent on prayers which focused as much on the tenderness and constancy of God as on his power.

In stark contrast, it is the defeat of the *jak*, the myriad spiritual powers of Jieng heritage, that is the subject of fireside conversation. Pastors and laity recount stories of the stupidity of *jak*, their greed and deception, their pathetic retorts, their final destruction, and the conversion of those who once maintained their cults and received their sacrifices (the *tiet*). Parts of our trek through southern Bor were like a tour through an old battleground, names of heroes and villains often recounted. Twice we passed through and slept at the remarkable, sprawling church of Zion, 180 feet, length and width. Three years after its construction, I am told that I am still the only Westerner to have visited it. This is no small privilege, for it marks the site of the single most dramatic event in the history of Bor Jieng religion. It was there that such awe inspiring *jak* as Benydeng, Bar, and Miutpen, together with thousands of lesser *jak* — as well as the artifacts that represented them, leopard skins, ceremonial stools, sticks, drums, spears, and baskets — were cast into fire. There, the clans of Bor relinquished the spiritual powers that segregated them. Before that cruciform edifice, its four doors open to the nations, they declared their union in *Yechu Kritho*, son of *Nhialic*.[51]

I was startled to learn of the demise of *Lirpiou*, the most renowned *jok* of the Jieng Bor, certainly the best known to the outside world. The great spear of the cult of *Lirpiou*, the *jok* of the "cool heart," was documented by anthropologists as early as 1910. It became famous when, in 1948, it was confiscated by Condominium authorities and "imprisoned" in Khartoum for having inspired the murder of a local chief. During intervening years *Lirpiou's* absence was believed the cause of famine and floods. When, after the Peace Agreement of 1972, the spear was restored to Bor area, it was received with tremendous celebration including the sacrifice of a hundred oxen. The status of the great *jok* of Gwalla remained secure through the mid-1980s, but by 1992, as *jak* were being collected for incineration at Zion, *Lirpiou* was forced to flee, carried by several faithful adherents across the Nile to the land of Mandari. Soon, however, the Mandari were undergoing a religious movement even more zealous than that of Bor, and *Lirpiou* was threatened with death along with his keepers. Escaping back to Bor the *tiet* met a cold reception. Fearing the harm he could inflict, nobody wanted the great *jok* near them. At last the venerable spear was left in the forest, later to be retrieved by a group of soldiers and churchmen. Again *Lirpiou* was imprisoned. Several times he was humiliated and publicly "beaten." It was only in February 1995 that a service before the church at Kulnyang, the heartland of the old cult, saw the destruction of *Lirpiou*. With singing and prayers its shaft was burned. The massive iron blade

---

51. See the letter of June 9, 1994 (p. 113).

was broken into four pieces and cast into its grave, as were spears of lesser *jak,* at the bottom of a deep well.

"The God of the Jieng is HOT!" His radiance burns "powers" which have been venerated for centuries. It is difficult for a foreigner to perceive — certainly to comprehend emotionally — the significance of these events. The *jak,* for all their greed and unpredictability, expressed the identity and dynamism of tightly knit communities. Though capricious and temperamental, they were endowed with power to protect, punish, inspire, and exalt those who venerated them. Yet, for Christians, their demise is shear liberation, the dawning of a new age, its repercussions bursting forth in every realm of life. Socially, people speak of new cohesion between long separated clans. Once isolated, some are reaching out to former enemies. In his sermons Bishop Nathaniel calls for Jieng evangelism among their age old adversaries, the Murle, the Nuer, and beyond, to peoples previously unknown. Indeed, several hundred newly converted Mandari crossed the Nile to be confirmed under Nathaniel's hands. This is accompanied by an unprecedented hunger for formal education as well as interest in new crops and new techniques for fishing, cultivation, and husbandry. The wearing of clothes becomes a religious mandate in this revolutionary day.

Many discern the demise of the *jak* as a tangible victory in this double-edged war. Spiritual triumph over *"shatan"* is perceived as a foretaste of victories yet to come, not least those of the SPLA over the government of Omer el Bashir. Hope rises that the "New Sudan" might itself be healed, leaving behind the factional fratricide of recent years. Not without biblical precedent, Christians sometimes claim the prior victory. The SPLA itself is not unchanged by recent events, and indeed participates in them. As I have been moving in circles of the church I have found few soldiers exhibiting the suppressed rage and rash hostility I felt during our abduction in 1987. Some commanders are now devout churchgoers, themselves leading in prayer. There is a growing band of commissioned evangelists nurturing the souls of young, cross-toting, soldiers within the movement. Of these I will not forget sinewy Jon Akengwet. Six feet seven, he would stand before the people of God barking out the "gospel of our Lord," his M47 dangling at his side. Spiritual and military warfare mingle, but I find few hints of an impulse for "holy war" among civilians or combatants. Soldiers with whom I conversed were toughened but temperate souls who crave an end to killing. Nonetheless, they are committed to the preservation of their people, their soil, their faith.

On several days we felt the dull thud of aerial bombing in the distance and once the frantic surge of adrenaline as the Antonov bomber responsible passed repeatedly over our procession. Our journey took us through the village Pandiar, only days earlier the site of a foray by Khartoum's soldiers garrisoned at Bor. From tanks and lorries they had raided the meager stores cultivated by civilians and forced a mass evacuation. A flurry of combat left thirteen civilians wounded and three young SPLA soldiers dead. At the heart of a deserted village stood the charred walls of Pandiar's church, its depictions of angels in flight still awaiting the Christmas that never came.

Potential insecurity aside, I was grateful when the commissioner laid on a day's excursion to Malek, in 1906 the first CMS outpost in southern Sudan. Now over-grown, its giant mangoes and stately avenues of Neem trees[52] still delineate the old station at the Nile's edge. Here stood that mission trinity — school, dispen-sary, and church — all of which today's leaders would dearly love to revive. This was home base for the irascible Archdeacon Archibald Shaw (1879–1956), train-ing ground for new missionary recruits, and school for generations of Bor children destined to become southern intelligentsia. Shaw's rusted boat, the iron founda-tion of his house, and the concrete fragments of his "swimming pool," blocked off at the river's edge, still remain. It is ironic that, amid the present transformation, Jieng Christians hold the memory of "Machuor" in such affection. Virtually a patron saint, he is the one who first planted the fragile seeds of Christian faith in the land of Bor and, despite demoralizingly slow growth, would not desert them.

Having repudiated the *jak* of their forefathers, members of today's church explore another branch of their spiritual genealogy. During his day Shaw was known as "hot," potent, unswerving in his commitment. Infinitely more so is the Crucified God who today surges through these scattered, remnant communities. From within, not from without, he nurtures revolution, casting down old powers, creating new alliances, and giving hope for a future.

From the tide pools,
Marc Nikkel

Nairobi
October 16, 1996

> *A pilgrim from a distant land travels toward his home . . .*
> > *One who has tasted the honey of eternity*
> > > *knows the pilgrim will only find his home above.*
> > *Here he is restless from morn to night, ever longing for his home . . .*
>
> — adapted from an old German hymn

Dear Friends,

As I return to East Africa I am filled with gratitude. I thank God for the rich and varied journey of the past six months, for the faithful friendship and

---

52. A broad-leafed conifer introduced into Africa from Asia in the 1920s.

hospitality I have received from many of you (even if a reunion by telephone had to suffice in some cases). Following a successful four months in the Diocese of Bor I left southern Sudan on April 10, departing Nairobi nine days later. Since then there have been three months in the United States, largely given to renewing ties with family in California, punctuated with special services and conferences. In early August I again crossed the Atlantic for my first visit to Ireland, graciously facilitated by CMS, Ireland, a period which encompassed reflection around the high crosses of the early Celtic church. Six valuable weeks followed, primarily with "Link" churches and extended "family" in Scotland (Edinburgh and Alloa) and England (Saltburn, Bradford, Salisbury, and London). On October 7 I flew back to Nairobi and a fine, tree-shrouded bungalow on the edge of the city. Here, at last, I can settle down to writing a long overdue letter. In these first days back it has been, as ever, joyful and sobering, renewing ties with Sudanese companions, refugees all, on the journey.

Throughout my travels I have toted, not without difficulty, a fifty-five-inch coffin-shaped wooden box containing some fifteen Sudanese crosses.[53] Entrusted to me by friends and colleagues during my last sojourn in Bor, each long (two to three and a half feet), hand-held cross provides an evocative touchstone with those who fashioned them. How I have enjoyed seeing folk in America and Britain pass them around, smell and caress them, pondering their origins as I told their stories. Each conveys a narrative of faith and survival in the war zone, of continuity amid displacement and famine, carried in processions, exorcisms, and through flights from gunfire and cattle raids. Some are rough and rugged, others quite refined. Crafted of various woods or metals, some decorated with ivory, cow horn, or brass bullet casings (one topped with the head of a rocket-propelled grenade, RPG), they reflect the traumatic, sometimes exhilarating processes of culture change now underway. They declare tangibly — as women and men must in this era — that amid displacement and death, *God is present among his people.* These crosses have also helped me to remain inwardly rooted during months of transience, often tempted by the lure of affluence and *apparent* stability.

In Ireland it seemed I had brought this new generation of crosses to meet their forebears in the ancient high crosses of the Celtic church. How moved I was to kneel before the stone "scripture crosses," some seven yards high, standing as they have for a thousand years and more (unlike earlier pilgrims, however, I knelt only when fellow tourists had departed). From those worn images carved in relief, I tried to decipher, and then to contemplate, the progression of Bible stories, all rising to their crescendo: there, at the heart of each immense, circled

---

53. A videotape of Marc explaining the significance of these crosses is available; it is entitled *The Crosses of Dinka Christians.*

cross the Crucifixion is portrayed or, alternatively, Christ the reigning King, at the fulcrum of eternity. In the cross, heaven and earth are interwoven around our compassionate, self-offering God.

In numerous ways I found the stories of crosses and their makers, present and past, Sudanese and Celtic, mingling across the centuries. While these objects are resolutely Christian, all bear traces of the meanings and uses of the pre-Christian foci of veneration they supplant. In Ireland the crosses were the immovable center point for trekking, sailing pilgrims, ever searching for "the place of their resurrection." In Sudan they are the portable shrines of desperate, uprooted peoples longing for a homeland, immediate, tangible, and eternal. In the crosses they fashioned these great peoples, European and African, confirm the good of their existence, their loves and longing for continuity, while reaching toward eternity. These first luminous reflections on the cross of Christ by newly Christian peoples have much to teach us who are too often satisfied with the appearances of wealth and paucity of meaning.

As I reflected on the early pilgrims whose journeys the stone crosses punctuated I thought as well of my own forebears. At the head of this letter are several lines, once scrawled in German and tucked into the casket of my great grandfather: "Pilgrim in a foreign land, wandering from his home...." In the 1870s Benjamin Nikkel immigrated to America from a colony near the Dnieper River in the Ukraine. Plying his skills as a farmer he homesteaded in the state of Kansas but soon ventured further west to Colorado, only to return to Kansas. A refugee, as our Mennonite ancestors have been time and again over four hundred years, he vested his life in "looking for his home." Only recently have I realized that, just as far as my great grandfather traveled westward, so far have I "returned" eastward. Tracing the longitude due south from Benjamin's starting point near the Dnieper I come to Bor, on the Nile River in southern Sudan, the heartland of my present work. It appears, from recent years, that I continue his pilgrimage, east to west, west to east, but now embracing a southern route. Here, with displaced and refugees, kin of our kin, our passage continues, "tasting the honey of eternity" and together "longing for our home."

The scholar-pilgrims of Sudan

I have learned how Celtic saints crossed seas and ventured through alien territory establishing monastic centers of prayer and learning at such sites as Kells, Glendalough, Monasterboice, Iona, and Lindisfarne. Sadly, there will be no stones remaining for future generations to ponder our life at Panyagor and Yomciir in Upper Nile, nor will our purpose-built structures of wood and grass endure much beyond a year (recent flooding has swamped them). Nevertheless, with our determined student-evangelists traversing far distances by foot and in canoe through contested regions, carrying few provisions but their crosses, our efforts to build worshiping-learning communities in virgin territory is not so dissimilar. Having described our December 1995 confirmation tour in my letter of January 20, 1996 (p. 140), I will now sketch our pastoral training course at Yomciir, Bor Diocese, from January 24 through Easter, 1996.

No word had been radioed ahead that we were to arrive at Yomciir by charter flight from Lokichoggio, northern Kenya, on December 10. Bishop Nathaniel was concerned that large crowds would prove an easy target for aerial bombardment as had happened elsewhere. When we arrived word immediately went out that Christian leaders should come for a course to begin in mid-January. Members of nearby churches were assigned to collect materials and construct classrooms and dormitories to house a community of over two hundred. On our return three weeks later we found four very adequate buildings near completion, each measuring about five by eleven yards. Such voluntary effort distinguishes our work from that of other organizations which, being perceived as the innovation of wealthy aliens, is less rooted in local initiative, and so relies heavily on payment-in-kind to start and maintain their projects. During this era at least there is a grassroots craving for Christian education.

As ever, there had been considerable uncertainty as we prepared to leave Kenya to conduct our course. For a period in late 1995 I was declared persona non grata for propagating "anti-Jieng policies" (a charge no one has yet explained), but, with Bishop Nathaniel's return from a lengthy confirmation tour, this was quickly resolved and my freedom of travel restored. Abruptly, the Khartoum government then prohibited all aircraft from entering Sudanese air space with the threat of being shot down. We waited at Kakuma in northern Kenya until this was withdrawn ten days later. Naturally, we could not fly on UN flights because we were transporting several trunks of Bibles, Christian books, and supplies for the church, all contraband due to UN agreements with Khartoum. Thankfully, a friend provided US$2,300 to fund a charter flight to carry six passengers and supplies into Yomciir. Given the limitations (1.1 tons) of a Caravan airplane we could take little in the way of food supplies for our community, but we negotiated with an agency to transport a ton and a half on their dry season convoy. Remarkably, sacks of sugar, cooking oil and tea, Bibles and drinking cups, arrived just as teaching commenced. To supplement the limited food supplies contributed by local churches we bartered peanuts, dried fish, sorghum, and maize for blankets and much sought after polyester cloth.

During a previous course one of our archdeacons had rigidly restricted attendance to forty ordained — and so all male — clergy, but our course in Yomciir was to be open to women leaders and younger evangelists and teachers alike.[54] While few of our sixteen women had formal education and most were sporadically drawn away for practical duties, their presence was invaluable. Offering so lengthy a course amid war's uncertainties meant there was a continual ebb and flow among our students. While ninety were enrolled, only half of these actually attended the entire period. Pastors from northern Bor were in the process of resettling their people and, with security and feeding tenuous, they arrived halfway through our studies.

Crises often arose. One day in March all our young women and girls, their labor essential to food preparation (grinding grain by hand for several hours each morning, gathering firewood, cooking), were commandeered to carry supplies to a needy garrison some two days away by foot. Our students resorted to eating unground grain, which inevitably erupted in diarrhea, halting teaching for three days. Then there were the sporadic days of aerial bombardment, which, in late February, prompted all non-Sudanese, apart from myself, to evacuate for the next five weeks. Each time the distant roar of an Antonov[55] was heard, attention slackened in the classroom, faces grew rigid, and ears cocked heavenward. As planes approached we would bungle ourselves out, into "bomb shelters," large open holes functioning as protection from shrapnel. Strange how the soul responds to such vulnerability, subject, it seems, to the whim of a pilot high overhead: to turn, to drop, not to drop his payload. Is it random fate or providence? During such moments before eternity, *kairos* surpasses *chronos*.[56] "God is strong!" "It's passing to the east, he's gone; no, no, he's circling, he's coming back!" "Jesus is powerful; save us," gasped those with whom I huddle in a pit. Thankfully, after days of bombing, the only local casualty was one goat, which, some said, was a sacrifice for those of us who remained alive.

In the first week of our course we were privileged to receive Bishop David Stancliffe of the Diocese of Salisbury, his wife, Sarah, and their two intrepid companions.[57] I will not forget the scene in our humble classroom, packed wall to grass wall with church leaders, most seated on mats, listening attentively to the eloquent, articulate bishop through the haze of the translated word. As head of the Liturgical Commission for the Church of England, David spoke, over three days,

---

54. Since this time the Episcopal Church of the Sudan has opened the door to the ordination of women.

55. Soviet-made Antonov bombers were used repeatedly against civilian targets in the war. It is, of course, a terrible irony that for a time the SPLA were supplied with Soviet weapons through Ethiopia and that Soviet weaponry was also being used by the Sudanese army.

56. These two terms, *kairos* and *chronos*, are both Greek words meaning "time," *kairos* often thought to have the nuance of "season," or "opportune time" and *chronos* thought to have the nuance of "moment by moment," measured time, although the terms are often simply synonyms.

57. On this relationship see the brief essay by David Stancliffe, "The Salisbury-Sudan Link."

on the theology, symbolism, history, and practice of the eucharist, culminating in our shared communion. Here, again, complex, ancient traditions mingled, one refined, elegant, articulate; the other *equally so,* but undergoing the convulsions of self-analysis, dialogue, and disquieting revolution in encounter with Christ . . . and with Western values. Precise, mutual comprehension could not be expected, but the determined efforts of fellow Christians, Jieng and British, to know each other in the broken Bread of dark sorghum cakes and the Blood of red *kirkedé* (a locally grown red tea) was profound and worthy.

During weeks that followed we unpacked some of the bishop's meanings. My slow, meandering course was a study of sacrifice, the cross, and communion, a rite strangely neglected among people for whom blood sacrifice has, for millennia, been the pivotal symbol of communal harmony, reconciliation, and healing.[58] Our reflections were vivid and contemporary, from Abel to Abraham, from Noah to the Passover, from the blood of the Lamb to that of Christ, the Temple to Christ's Body. Ours was also a dialogue with Nilotic sacrificial rites and the divinities to whom they are offered.[59] There were numerous historical and theological eddies along the way, often revealing the distance we have yet to go before the rites of Christian faith are as encompassing as those of the highly integrated, gradually evolved systems they supersede. This was the longest of six courses, others being offered by Bishop Nathaniel and a succession of visitors.

I had hoped our studies could persevere through Easter, April 7, despite low food supplies, bombing, and the urgent need of students to return home to cultivate. In late March we halted lessons for four days so pastors could build and thatch a fine new church for Yomciir, our hallowing place for Holy Week. On Palm Sunday we met at the airstrip, crosses in hand, well *before* sunrise, again for fear our white-robed procession might be spotted from the air. On Maundy Thursday our service began with foot-washing, everyone participating, Bishop Nathaniel washing the feet of the humblest evangelists. Extravagantly, we slaughtered two goats for our agape meal-cum-communion service. Laterally I was asked, to my surprise, if some of our number might not go out to bury Mama Monika, her corpse lying on the mud floor under the mosquito net at the back of the church. I had not realized that she had died just as we began our three-hour service. She was an elder, one of several who had walked eighty miles to join us four days earlier. On arrival she had became ill and dehydrated, and died at the heart of Holy Week. As our service ended we heard the hymns of those who mourned.

---

58. The "neglect" of the eucharist to which Marc refers may be explained in part by the lack of available elements during wartime and in part by the word-centered evangelical tradition of the first Anglican missionaries to the Sudan.

59. The recently published prayer book of the Anglican Church of Kenya (*Our Modern Services*) also emphasizes the connection between traditional sacrifices and the sacrificial death of Christ (for a discussion see LeMarquand, "A Faithful Descendent").

Good Friday held a somber, gentle, drama of betrayal and crucifixion, but hardly a hint of violence or blood. These were actors who had never seen a passion Play but had intimate experience of the carnage of war. It was in awe and honor and love that they refused to enact brutality against their Lord. The reverence for sacrificial blood prohibited portrayal of the piercing of Christ's sacred flesh. So wonderful, immediate and fearful was the mystery of this day that there was no place for play with passion.

The crescendo of our week began beneath the full moon of Holy Saturday. By lantern light we gathered, filling our vast, new barn of a church. In death, we, with the disciples, longed for life. We read twelve "Mighty Acts of God," from the Creation to Exodus to Zephaniah 3, each interspersed with Psalms, prayers, meditations, and *three* hymns(!). I was again amazed by the broad repertoire of Bible stories narrated in song as thirty-six vernacular pieces perfectly complimented our readings. This newly literate people who, in ninety years, have never possessed a vernacular Old Testament, have themselves put many stories to music. At 4:00 a.m., excitement mounting, dozens of us surged out to vest and ignite one small candle from new fire. And what did we hear? At that moment a baby was delivered into the night and released its first cry. Our pilgrimage had come full circle, an infant delivered on resurrection morning. Sleepily, joyfully, we proceeded through our eleven-hour service with baptism, confirmation, and the ordination of fourteen clergy, all culminating in the breaking of bread and sharing of the cup, tasting once more of "the honey of eternity."

Faithfully,

Marc Nikkel

Nairobi
Ash Wednesday, February 12, 1997

> *We no longer weep at gravesides.*
> *We have cried for the dead too often during recent years.*
>   *You want to know what makes us weep?*
> *We cry when we think how the gospel of Christ came into our land and our lives.*
> *We weep when we think that our land is being taken by force*
>   *and our faith being replaced by Islam.*
> *This makes tears rise from the dry places inside us.*
>
> — Rev. Mark Atem, ECS Pastor, Kakuma

Arriving back from a six-month leave last October, I longed to be with friends at Kakuma Refugee Camp once again. Within two weeks after arrival in Nairobi I drove the five hundred miles northward through that marvelously marbled swath of Kenyan peoples and terrain, the foliage, geography, languages, and cultures ever changing en route. Kakuma is but sixty miles from the Sudan border, sprawling its discontented huts of mud and plastic sheets across the merciless Turkana desert. Those who have read my letters know that with each stay at Kakuma — all totaling some ten months now — I have been consistently moved by the resilience, creativity and tenacity of Sudanese refugees. Kakuma had become for me a place of spiritual pilgrimage. Since my twelve-day stay last October, however, followed by two more recent visits, such idealism is withering. As physical life degenerates, despair pervades the lives of many people. As I encounter increasing malnutrition and death, I wonder at the impotence of our response.

Abraham Dau Warabek died on October 18, having lain unconscious in Kakuma's ill-equipped hospital for a month. His *karama* — the memorial gathering that occurs three days after death — took place on my first full day at Kakuma. Beneath a *rakuba* of poles and blankets among the huts that Dau built, several hundred mourners gathered to share a meal, pray, and invoke his memory. Among them were his wife and two children, his brother's widows and their children, dependent all. At forty-three years Abraham was one of the church's best-educated laymen. Having been an enthusiastic member of the church's youth during the 1960s, he later put himself through a degree in education and a diploma in theology in Cairo. For five years he had served in the SPLA but, at Bishop Nathaniel's request, had been released to serve the church full time. As a teacher he used his extremely lean frame of six feet eight inches, to good effect. Extending his reach with a pointer Dau would tap out his every syllable on the blackboard. For three months in early 1995 he had been my confidante and teaching companion in Bahr el Ghazal. Hopeful that he would play a central role in the translation of the Jieng Old Testament, we had placed him in a two-year diploma course in linguistics. That was not to be.

Sorrow surrounding Abraham's death was intensified by the illness of a number of friends. Inside the church compound in Zone 4 where I have my small mud brick house, I found all five fellow residents, young men between seventeen and twenty-eight years old, thin, ill, too poor in body or mind to attend school. David Ayuen, twenty-one, who normally serves as my resilient helper-in-residence, lay on a hospital bed for six weeks, diagnosed with the plodding anemia so common among Kakuma's youth. I visited him daily with small cartons of "long-life" milk available in the market (if you have the money). Through the night I could hear Michael Anai coughing heavily, bedridden for three weeks. A lover of song, he was ever copying Kakuma's new vernacular compositions in his careful scrawl. Severed from his family in Bahr el Ghazal for ten years now, he was depressed, having heard that his mother had died leaving no one to care for his siblings. Six foot six Samuel Galuak had been a soldier, but opted to obtain a primary education. Weighing not more than 110 pounds, he, like many of his mates, suffered from bloody diarrhea. Small, normally radiant Ador, seventeen, was now listless, emaciated. I was told by one of the refugee doctors that five young men had died in the hospital during the week of my stay. Common, curable diseases — anemia, malaria, chronic headaches, amebic dysentery, any range of parasites, exacerbated by malnutrition — seem to affect virtually everyone, and people complain relentlessly of the inadequacy of medical supplies.

Jacob Mameer died on the night of Abraham's *karama.* The anguish of his loss swallowed up the sorrow that preceded it. Mameer was one of several of the church's commissioned evangelists whose health had slowly degenerated over the past two years, recently diagnosed with "jaundice." Wednesday morning found us under the scorching sun in a rock-strewn refugee graveyard, dark shadowed forms hovering over deep pits. Gravediggers had been hard at work in the sterile earth. That morning four clusters of mourners prepared to bury their kin: three Sudanese males, one Ethiopian woman. As Mameer's fellow evangelists sweated and hacked, further shaping the grave, women sat silently around the body in sparse shade. Here, death is uncompromising: a rigid, deteriorating corpse wrapped in a skimpy sheet and tied, neck to big toes with a cord. Once wedged into a slot deep in the earth the body was covered with rows of sticks, then with green branches, and the soil replaced, broken earth marked with a simple cross.

As we prayed I gazed at each so familiar downturned face, now virtually unrecognizable, drawn, expressionless, silent. No tears were shed; no sobbing. With illness so pervasive and death so immediate, each one knows that their next ailment could just as rapidly usher them back to dust. For the next three days, people gathered to mourn, their numbers swelling and subsiding, like their songs and prayers, in the compound where Mameer had lived. During his years in Ethiopia he had served first as a soldier, then faithfully as a church teacher and evangelist, training Sudanese children during their pilgrimage. Quiet, observant, he had tried desperately to take a wife two years ago, but with lack of resources was rebuffed. In the mind of his companions the tragedy is that, at thirty years, Mameer died leaving no child to survive him.

The Jieng of Kakuma describe their myriad wasting illnesses as "lack of blood." When someone is weak, no longer able to function, it is said, "she has no blood," meaning, "she is near death." Mameer had no blood. The lament is heard, "Our people are finished: their blood is gone." For a people, not unlike the ancient Hebrews, among whom sacrifice has always been the central rite, blood is the embodiment of well-being and vitality.[60] The ritual shedding of the blood of an

---

60. On "blood" in African and biblical traditions see LeMarquand, *An Issue of Relevance,* chapter 4.

ox could bring about reconciliation and healing, whether in the sphere of human beings or the divine. Never was blood to be shed without purpose. When there was famine, a calf could be bled to obtain life-giving blood to be cooked, food for the infirm. In recent decades young men, especially, could be relied upon to offer blood donations for the injured, for those who had lost blood in the hospital. In the relentless "war of liberation" it is grievously acknowledged that blood is being shed daily, avowedly to good purpose. But here, at Kakuma, the loss of blood is a foreboding, incomprehensible thing. It is not only the old and infirm who are losing their blood, but many young men who should be the source of the future. Never in known Jieng history has this happened, that the blood of the youthful, the unmarried, those on whom hope rests, should drain away, dissipate. In desperate attempts to replenish life's crimson juices some grasp on red-colored foods — orange squash, tomatoes, liver, grape drink — to sustain their dying... if the money can be found. The vulgar substitute for life's vital force comes down to money.

Since the UN population count at Kakuma in August 1996, the rations for residents have been radically cut. Where once there was a varied diet including beans, soya, lentils, and sorghum, offerings have been stripped to three items: white flour, a small cup of vegetable oil, and raw maize, only the last of which is known to rural Sudanese diets. A small ration is expected to last fourteen days, but for many does not exceed eight or ten, particularly when people barter their flour for the bits of meat or vegetable their bodies crave. I consistently meet individuals, not least among the youth, who have gone for three and four days without food. Little wonder some cannot study, and so easily succumb to disease. Surveys by WFP experts have done nothing to increase rations.

One night last week I sat under the dark, star-strewn sky and listened as a neighboring mother scolded, then slapped, her inconsolable child. He refused to eat the bland gruel before him and screamed frantically for the food his senses still remembered. Atem, the pastor in Zone 4, told of how he refrains from going to his own family compound during the daytime because he cannot bear to hear his children pleading for the milk he cannot give them. No surpluses exist in Kakuma today, and church offerings amount to no more than a few cents. Parents of hungry children, pastors of distraught flocks, hungry all.

Disease and death now erode the human spirit. Depression arises in ways I have not met previously among Jieng, even in war and famine zones. As despair increases symbols of faith lose their glimmer. Malnutrition is culling the saints. If it is an indicator, church attendance has dropped considerably, some say because people's bottoms are too withered to sit for two hours. Two years ago the largest ECS church in Zone 3 regularly had Sunday congregations of three thousand to forty-five hundred, but attendance now drops to a thousand or eight hundred. Where the youth gathered en masse for prayers, morning and night, huge numbers now flock to pulsing week-end dances in a bid to retain remnants of their culture. Some church leaders condemn the gatherings for the old hostilities their taunting songs sometimes provoke. Have hopes placed in Christ's cross been too weighty, too concrete? Was it wrong to expect that deliverance — both spiritual and tangible — should come quickly to the followers of Christ? Was it naïve to anticipate that the suffering of a rapidly growing church might be alleviated through solidarity with the worldwide church? There's no money to replace blood.

At times I wonder if I have been so enamored with the resilience and faith of this people that I have not taken their degradation seriously. Have I betrayed my friends in my infatuation with their capacity to survive? Is it possible that my admiration of them has done disservice in not addressing more bluntly the horror that daily envelops them? Have I become a voyeur, spellbound by the torment of my friends? In my writings, have I described only symptoms, neglecting the base inhumanity of this war: nothing less than an effort to denude a land of its peoples, and eradicate them, their cultures, histories, and identities. Have I refrained from describing the sense of abandonment that eats at the hearts of my comrades and so closely accompanies their expiration?

The RPG (Rocket-Propelled Grenade) cross

Certainly, I believe the thoughts and words of Sudanese Christians are eloquent and potent in themselves. It is these I struggle to convey; not least those surrounding the symbols of faith they create. In my last letter I wrote of crosses I carried around during visits last summer in the United States and Britain. The most provocative of those was an ebony cross topped with the five-inch silver alloy, the spiraled head of an RPG, and, at its base, a large-gauge brass bullet shell. On Northern Irish television it even became the focus of an evening news spot. What meaning was in the mind of its maker, we would ask, as we examined it? Was it a mingling of forces, spiritual and military? Was it a blessing and empowering of the weapons of war? Was it merely decorative? Or were the RPG head and shell themselves a form of cross, a sign of suffering and death intertwined with Christ's? Last summer I could not provide a definitive response. However, during the past two months in southern Sudan, December 10 through February 3, I met the man who conceived and commissioned the cross, evangelist James Lual Achol, forty-two years of age. He told me how he had found the bullet shell at Bor garrison in 1989 and the RPG head after a battle at Yomciir in 1990, the cross itself being fashioned in 1992. I translate the words of James Lual:

Jesus came into the world as a man of righteousness, but he was persecuted and suffered and put to death on a cross. He brought the good news but was crucified with the spikes that nailed him down. In the same way, the gospel has come to our land in Southern Sudan, and we suffer for his Word, that which we've accepted. Our children are raided and made into slaves because of it. We are put to death because of it. Our cattle have all been raided because of it. We suffer starvation and are scattered across the earth because of it. All those who receive the gospel will suffer... and so do we. In this day the RPG is used as a tool of killing against our people as certainly as spikes were used to crucify Jesus on the cross. Still, we carry within us the hope that we will ultimately have victory through the cross of Christ. It is the cross that will judge between us and the aggressors who seek to kill us. I want people of the West to see the cross brought to them from Sudan because it is the cross they once brought to us. I want them to see that we are people like them, and this is the suffering it has brought us. See this cross. We have given up our old divinities, and virtually everything we possess, and we have taken up the cross alone. Pray for us that we will remain crucified upon the cross, that we will remain faithful. We are forever stuck to the cross.

This letter, which describes so much of our "return to dust," was written at the beginning of Lent, our communal journey toward Christ's cross and resurrection. During these weeks hold all who suffer for the cross, and all their myriad forms of sorrow, within your prayer. Think of those who no longer possess the capacity to weep at gravesides... as well as those things for which tears still flow. Pray for a restoration of blood in withering bodies, and an apprehension of the blood that reconciles fragmented tribes and races and religions. Pray for resurrection.

Faithfully,
Marc Nikkel

All Saints' Day, November 1, 1997[61]

Peace exists across all the earth
   but the peace of Sudan is being clawed to shreds by birds.
This is how such great numbers of our people die.
   They expire, bereft of a just law to oversee the land.
Black people exist in the very habitation of evil.

---

61. Marc made revisions to this letter in January 1998.

The deceiver is evil, and the person who doesn't grasp the law is like
    the *jok,*
    the one who doesn't know the truth that animates another human being.
If we are killed to the last person, and every one of us is gone,
    can you accept that, you who abide with us upon the earth,
        if we no longer exist in this world?
Isn't it God who has created us?
    We are speaking we women: Who knows what is good?
        Is it God who has this knowledge, or is it we human beings?
Who was present when God created the earth?
    Raise up your hands, you who hear me!
        Or have you yourselves died, all of you?

You Peace, are you deaf, or are you blind, or are you mad?
    You, the wives of those who are still living! We are speaking to you!
        Peace is the life of those who have not encountered death.
The birds have their leaders, but the leader of the Black people does not
    exist.
    Our leader, death, he is the one who abides with us.
I am weeping, lamenting over my people who have perished,
    ah, how wonderful they were!
My children have all been slaughtered.
    They pass away with no one to help them.
        They are abandoned, without any kinspeople.
            They have no one to stand judge over the forces that oppress them.
America has gone to the moon, but leaves suffering people below
    with no one to cultivate peace upon the earth.
You have succeeded in placing people on the moon,
    but you are miserly about the peace of Black people.
People are killing themselves out of sheer arrogance
    so their own homeland is raided and laid waste!
        Let us cry out, "*oayo! oayo!*" to Jesus.
        Our brothers, the Arabs, are killing us!

Those who have life, those who have wisdom; You women, have you heard?
    You must pray fervently for us! Pray for those who kill their own brothers.
        Pray for those who are sick, and those whose legs have been cut off,
            and for the aged, and for the fetus still unborn.
We are dying because of the laws our brothers are trying to impose on us!
    They have killed our pastors with the bullet.

Jesus Christ, hear me, hear me, me, me.

I am a feeble person, and I am being killed by one who is powerful.

...Oh, good people of Jesus![62]

These words were read to me in Jieng last week, cutting and clear, by Mary Achol. As she finished applause rose from the dozen women seated around us in Kakuma's mud and thatch Mothers' Union office. Composed at the end of a hard-hitting week of prayer and fasting, October 19 to the October 26, they express Achol's confrontation with me, and more specifically with women around the world, "the wives of men still living." Her words are rich in paradox, pleading the utter powerlessness of herself and her kin. She inspires them to self-assertion. Declaring that "Black people" have no leader but death, Achol herself leads them into spiritual warfare. Demanding advocates to speak in their defense, she herself takes up their case like a sharp-witted lawyer. Describing a people surrounded by evil, she speaks on the righteous authority of the Creator she knows so intimately. Respectful of the achievements of wealthy technocrats who have reached the moon, she exhorts them to have compassion on those they have left behind. Tormented by the recent killings of church leaders, her words are pregnant with life. In a manner typical of this era, vulnerability intertwines with the rigorous self-assertion of a tough Nilotic people. Their numbers averaging some 250, ECS Christians gathered daily from 6:30 a.m. to 2:30 p.m., fasting through the day (no small sacrifice on Kakuma's rations), alternating their prayers between the camp's seven open-air ECS churches. Through this and a succession of related acrobatics of the spirit organized largely by women, refugees have been fortifying themselves in the face of murder and near starvation.

The months since my last letter in February have included much travel, with a tour in the United States and Britain, in the company of Bishop Nathaniel Garang and evangelist Bartholomayo Bol-Mawut. Returning to East Africa, I spent much of June through August on pastoral training courses at Kakuma and across the Sudan border at Naruse. In September, I was invited back to Washington, D.C., where, at a conference entitled "Religion, Nationalism, and Peace in Sudan," convened by the U.S. Institute for Peace, I presented a paper on "Christian Identity in Sudan."[63] Following on was a brief address before a hearing of a congressional subcommittee on religious persecution in Sudan. These, and a stream of similar events, reveal a higher degree of American interest in Sudan than I have known during the past sixteen years. Again in East Africa since early

---

62. Written by Mary Achol Deng, Mothers' Union Leader, at Kakuma Refugee Camp, October 26, 1997.

63. Marc's paper at this conference can be found at *www.usip.org/religionpeace/rehr/sudanconf/panel2.html.*

October, I just returned from Kakuma, where CMS colleague Paul Savage and I are preparing a week-long ecumenical event for some 250 Sudanese youth leaders, November 24–30.

Some of you have requested an update on health and nutrition at Kakuma. In offering such observations I underscore that I am not a health professional, but a teacher and priest. Although several nutritional analyses have been made (a WFP study underway last week), rations have varied little (in fact events in Kenya forced a traumatic two-week halt to all food supplies during September — more about this below) UNICEF and WFP officials in the camp disagree, the former wanting to increase rations, the latter wanting to reduce them, pointing to quantities of USAID wheat flour on sale in Kenyan markets. (Certainly many refugees sell out their flour, alien to the traditional diet, in a search for more appetizing alternatives. Because few can afford either the oil, yeast, firewood, or equipment to make bread, they use flour to create a pasty parallel to mashed potatoes. Many "minors" tell me this is the only food they eat in a day.) While anemia exists, I have not met the debilitating lethargy or chronic stomach problems of a year ago. Thankfully, the caked and rotten maize flour that caused widespread diarrhea was withdrawn. Officials promise that the outdoor kitchens built to provide nutritional soya mix porridge for some twenty thousand primary school children will be fully operational by January. Several well-qualified new NGO staff, including an American doctor who oversees health care, have recently arrived and are intent on improvements. Tragically, in this day of budget cutbacks, the poor nutrition and health care that typifies Kakuma during some phases exist with equal severity in refugee camps dotted across the globe.

Cholera and the cross

In April Kakuma was hit by an epidemic of cholera, the result of poor hygiene due in part to contaminated water containers. While official reports state that some twenty people died, several NGO staff and educated refugees vow that over a hundred expired during a five-week period. Diagnosis of the disease and measures to stem its spread were slow in coming, with at least four deaths daily over several weeks. As camp officials struggled to put health measures in place, refugees became increasingly frightened, and Kakuma's ECS women assumed spiritual authority.

The women report how, one day in May, they banded together in a force of some 520 to lay siege against the powers of death. Carrying their hand-held crosses, they marched around Kakuma's main hospital compound where some 108 people were understood to lie ill with cholera. Praying and singing they converged at the heart of the complex. There, with the permission of hospital staff, they planted a long, wooden cross in the earth and called on God to restore life to the dying. This, the cross of Christ, they likened to the bronze serpent erected by Moses in the desert, which brought healing to all the afflicted who looked on it (Numbers 21:8–9; John 3:14–15). Indeed, as they narrate events, divine grace was imparted, the plague of cholera ceased from that day, and all 108 returned to health.

This was the first in a series of marches initiated by ECS women in which they seek to supplement apparently impotent hospital care with initiatives of the spirit and transcend their sense of helplessness through united action. Because these events are conducted in the Jieng language, non-Sudanese NGO staff have sometimes felt threatened by them, interpreting them as aggressive, politically styled demonstrations. Undeniably, resolute masses of marching women, singing buoyantly, crosses thrusting in rhythm, have a military flavor. For them, however, their processions are literal battles of the spirit in which they are supplanting the powers of death and oppression, as a composition they sang reveals:

> We are carrying burdens that oppress us; Great Lord of peace help us!
> We bear loads that lead us astray (from your way): Great Lord of peace
>   help us!
> We accuse the enemy in your presence.
> Great Lord who has power, come near and help us, Christ help us upon
>   the earth.
> O Protector against evil, our Helper O Father. Christ help us!
> The suffering you suffered shows us how to live upon the earth.
> Come near and help us, Christ our Helper, our Father upon the earth!

The assertive words of Mary Achol and these "military" marches may make us uneasy. They also help us grasp the seriousness of symbols that recall forty years of continuing war.

Encircling the camp with "weeping prayers"

Fear flared again in August with a series of killings in which the churches, as it seemed to many, were prime targets. On the night of the August 24 a young member of the Murle Presbyterian Church was shot dead in Zone 1. At 8:30 on the following moonless night two armed men crossed the dry riverbed to the largest ECS compound in Zone 3. One carried a gun and the other a torch. At the gate (a sheet of zinc roofing), they put a bullet through the stomach of twenty-two-year-old Daniel Yor. In the black chaos three shots rang out. Only with dawn's first light, however, did wailing erupt, when the body of Rural Dean John Majok Tuil was found where he had bled to death the night before. Yor, one of our finest young evangelists, was rushed to the hospital at Lopiding, given transfusions and survived, but remains depressive and weak, a paraplegic for the rest of his life. Majok was responsible for his brother's orphaned children and leaves twenty dependents.

Then during the first half of September political unrest in the Kenyan port of Mombasa severed food supplies and rations to Kakuma, igniting tensions as refugees neared starvation. Confronted with insecurity and hunger, several hundred people sold their meager belongings and left Kakuma in a vain effort to return to Sudan. False rumors circulated among the local Turkana resulting in attacks on the refugees and the looting of their last possessions. On September 4, 5, and 8 consecutively, three refugee men were shot dead in the camp. Word spread that an armed band of fifteen was responsible, some of whom had been arrested by Kenyan police. As Achol's words reveal, she is one of many who believe that the Khartoum government sponsored these efforts to destabilize Sudanese refugee life at Kakuma (as has occurred with the Khartoum-funded violence of the Lord's Resistance Army in northern Uganda[64] and more recently, the carnage at Lebone Displacement Camp inside Sudan, which left thirty-four dead). While refugee leaders, Turkana chiefs, UN officials, and the Kenyan police engaged in urgent discussions to restore security, the Mothers' Union, led by Mary Achol, determined to storm the gates of heaven.

At 6:00 a.m. on September 10, 171 determined women (and one man), all fasting (for there was "no fire in the kitchens") put on "sackcloth" (their most ragged old clothes), wrapped themselves in dark rags, and gathered in Zone 1, at the southernmost point of the camp. They determined to act with one heart crying out for God's salvation, offering their petitions, first, for an end to the killings, secondly, for an improvement in health care in the camp, and, finally, for the restoration of food rations. After initial prayers they divided into three groups, one walking along the *khor,* the dry riverbed bordering the west side of the camp, another following the *khor* which forms Kakuma's eastern parameter, and the third, walking down the central road, all to converge at the camp's northern tip, some five miles away. For four days, September 10–13, from 6:00 a.m. until 1:00 p.m., they encompassed the camp with their "weeping prayers." Among the songs they sang, crosses jerking, was one familiar from years as refugees in Ethiopia (1986 to 1991). Deriving from Isaiah 18, it is from this piece that Achol took her first line:

We ask you, O Creator who created us, Who has created us? Isn't it you who created us? We call upon you, God of all peoples: Who has created

---

64. Founded in 1986 by former prostitute Alice Auma (known widely as "Lakwena") as the "Holy Spirit Mobile Forces," the Lord's Resistance Army is a guerrilla group based in northern Uganda which is attempting replace the Ugandan government with one based on a rather peculiar interpretation of the Ten Commandments. The army consists mostly of children who have been forcibly abducted. The movement is widely believed to be funded by the Sudan government.

us? Isn't it you who created us? You have said that the land of Sudan will be clawed to shreds by birds, flapping their wings.

(Refrain):
Look upon us, O Creator who made us. God of all peoples, we are yearning for our land that we may pray to you in freedom.

Hear the prayer of our souls in the wilderness. (R)

Hear the prayers of our bones in the wilderness. Hear our prayer as we call out to you. (R)

Hear the cry of our hearts in the wilderness. (R)

On September 11 the women took their lamentations before the double iron gates and razor-wired fences of the UN compound, there casting themselves on the ground, rolling in the dirt (knowing, as they recall, that some thought they were mad). The gates drawn tight by the guards, they implored God with a song of refugees:

Are we going to stay here until we are old? Will we never see our land again? Never seeing our home? God hear our prayers and have mercy upon us.

UN officials were, as the women perceived them, initially bewildered and disturbed by their loud songs and lamentations. At last three leaders, Mary Achol, Rebekah Lueth, and Rebekah Ayen, were invited into the compound to explain their intentions. They told NGO staff how deeply troubled they were, wondering why their people were being killed. "We have fled from war, believing we would be protected in a refugee camp. We have no way to obtain food in this desert but through the provision of the UN. Now we are being killed and are near starvation. Since the UN does not help us, we cast ourselves on God." Officials assured the women that negotiations were underway: the Kenyan government would restore security, and food rations would again flow into Kakuma. Finally, on September 14 the women took their lamentations to Kakuma's burgeoning cemetery. Kneeling among the heaps of gravestones, they pleaded that no more of their people be taken to the realm of the dead. Again, some thought they were mad.

These are the resolute cries of the saints of Kakuma as they besiege the Kingdom of God, the dark forces of evil, the land of the dead, and the UN compound. It is little wonder that NGO officials, labored with quotas, schedules, and mounds of paper, have little time for these epic events. If the sometimes strident words of the women make us uneasy, that is their objective. If their conceptions of well-being seem eccentric, certainly their marches and their tears are efficacious in dimensions beyond our comprehension. Confronting death and hunger, they grasp onto life. Certainly they are not mad.

Faithfully, with all the Saints, living and departed,

Marc

Pentecost, May 31, 1998

> *... We are not sojourners pillaging a foreign country;*
> *we are the real owners of the land.*
> *The soil which has taken our blood will heal our wounds;*
> *the land will come to our rescue.*
> *Is there a soil which does not know its owner?*
> *The country resembles us....*
> *Our own land which God gave us, the black land,*
> *and planted us in it, so that we ripened becoming like it.*
> *If we are mistaken about our soil tell us, O God, that we may withdraw.*
> *Look back upon us, O land, you are not owned by foreigners;*
> *we will not forsake you....*

—lines from a song of liberation composed by
Mary Alueel Garang in 1988

This is no longer a land fit for human habitation.
The earth has been utterly destroyed.

—an elderly woman in Mariam, Western Aweil, Bahr el Ghazal

This is my home, the home of my father and my grandfather. Today old men and girls and women and young people, we hate ourselves in this place. We hate ourselves because our possessions, our cattle, our food stores are repeatedly destroyed by Arabs. We are enslaved. Take us, all of us, take us to your place so that we can live. We loathe ourselves.

—Yaai Deng Yaai from Mariam, Western Aweil, Bahr el Ghazal

What power of spirit sustains the remnant, I have asked myself, in this place where less than half the population still inhabit their homeland? I have wondered what constitutes the tenacious identity of the *Muonyjiang* (Jieng) of northwestern Bahr el Ghazal — the Ngok, the Rek, the Malual, and Tuic — whose ancestral lands form the beleaguered frontier between north and south.

It is they who have borne the brunt of forced abductions of women and children (literal *enslavement* as many describe it), the wanton slaughter of their men folk, the annual raids of the Miseriyya[65] and Baggara, intent on decimating a population

---

65. The largely Muslim and pastoralist ethnic group known as the Miseriyya, a subgroup of the Baggara, is believed to be largely responsible for the continuing government-sponsored violence in

("we want the land and not the people," is a phrase reverberating southward). The desolation of this year, 1998, exacerbated by four years of severe drought, cannot be surpassed but for 1988 when massive raids denuded the land and forced tens of thousands to flee northward. As I write, the *Jur* (the *alien*, the "Arab" as they are called) still comb the land.[66] On horseback and camel they come, fortified now by armored trucks, brandishing automatic weapons, funded and armed by the Khartoum government, turning hard-won human labor into rubble. I realize now how I have distanced myself as I have skimmed past reports of the carnage. Could these Nilotes be like others I know so well? Haven't language and culture long since been diluted, tainted with their northward movements? Have they not become a harder, less pliant expression of humanity, toughened and sterile before the unrelenting press of militant Islam? I had shielded myself from the prospect of the annihilation of a great and all too human people, those in whose charred homesteads I have spent the past three weeks.

It had been sixteen years since I last set foot in northern Bahr el Ghazal, and never in the area of Aweil, the land of the Malual, once one of the most densely populated regions in southern Sudan. On April 21, I boarded a charter flight with two pastors and Bishop Nathaniel Garang on his first pastoral visit as "caretaker bishop" of the Episcopal Diocese of Wau. At the rural settlement of Adoor he would, within the week, confirm over a thousand people and ordain seventeen deacons and four pastors in this young Episcopal church. On April 27 my companions returned to Kenya as I set off on a two-week tour of regions recently laid waste.

Before entering on this journey, however, let me survey the five months since my last letter. On All Saints' Day 1997, I described the terror and determination that motivated our Episcopal women to encompass Kakuma Refugee Camp with their "weeping prayers." Amid those events there blossomed, during the last week of November, an ecumenical "Youth Event," probably the most significant inter-ethnic celebration in Kakuma's history. With the vigorous vision and dogged organization of CMS colleague Paul Savage, an experienced youth leader, some 230 young Sudanese men and women from the camp's seven denominations, and virtually every ethnic group, united in song, prayer, and dance, around biblical teaching and plentiful food, to affirm their common identity in Christ. During

---

the western Sudan region of Darfur. For further information see the United Nation Security Council report of May 10, 2005: *www.iss.co.za/AF/profiles/Sudan/darfur/unrep10may05.pdf.*

66. *Jur* is a Jieng term meaning "stranger, foreigner." It should not be confused with "Jur" (or "Juur"), the people group mentioned in the letter of June 1987. The context in which the term is being used in the present letter implies the Arabized nomadic raiders from the north such as the Baggara, armed by the Sudanese government to wage war against the south. In this sense "Jur" means not only "stranger" but "enemy." On traditional Jieng views concerning non-Jieng people see Nikkel, "The Outcast, the Stranger and the Enemy in Dinka Tradition."

one intense week barriers of distrust gave way to unprecedented expressions of solidarity, setting a standard for future gatherings of Sudan's young leaders.

As the dust settled, December saw our three times yearly ECS Pastoral Training Course again underway, punctuated by what is now the annual "Christmas Carol," a day of vernacular song, dance, drama, and feasting (two bulls devoured) to which ECS youth invite delegates from every community in the camp. By January new guesthouses were under construction as the ECS at Kakuma prepared to receive the first official delegation from the Episcopal Church, USA.

Of these the forerunner was the Rev. Karin Lindsay, the first episcopally ordained woman our Mothers' Union had encountered. ("Ah, we thought the collar was pure gold, something no women could ever wear, but now we realize women can be pastors too!") Karin is a small woman, mother of five, a grandmother, who asked Bishop Nathaniel if she might spend a three-month sabbatical from her Virginia parish in Sudan. She was acquainted with grief as a widow and mother, a former hospice nurse and woman priest, and so an exceptional chemistry arose between Karin and her marginalized Sudanese sisters. With a combined attendance of some two hundred at Kakuma and later in Upper Nile Province, Karin facilitated the first workshops ever offered especially for ECS women.

In late February five more guests joined Bishop Nathaniel, Karin, and me for an intense two weeks: by road to Kakuma, then a charter flight deep into the Diocese of Bor, and finally the arduous road journey to New Cush and Ngatinga Displacement Camps. Everywhere the welcome was exuberant and needs on the frontier of war daunting. One of two emissaries from the Episcopal Church Center in New York was Richard Parkins, director of Episcopal Migration Ministries. Heartily embraced by the youth of Kakuma's Zone 6 church, for the first time Richard actually experienced living in mud and thatch on par with the refugees he had served for so many years. These were significant encounters in which our visitors walked, ate, breathed, and celebrated, as intimately as possible (yes, got sick, were stung, even slept, bed bugs included) alongside their kinfolk of faith. With our last guest having left by March 31, I returned to Kakuma for our April Pastoral Training Course, followed by our journey to Bahr el Ghazal.

During the three and a half hour flight from Lokichoggio, Kenya, to Madhol in Bahr el Ghazal Province, we surveyed from afar the hazy gray-tan barrenness of dry-season Sudan and for an hour traced the ribbons of the Nile, darting like silver water snakes through the dull green swamplands. I was startled to realize that the distance is more than twice that to Bor and, at $5,300, twice the cost to charter a small aircraft. Transport costs, whether for relief food, personnel, or school materials, are exorbitant. Midway into our flight the pilot tuned to BBC World Service on the cabin radio and we were sobered to hear of the 350,000

people (later revised to 600,000) who face imminent starvation across the land
for which we were destined.

The land, the land, the soil, the country (*baai, piny, pan, tiop*). These are
resonant words for *Muonyjiang*, so intimate is the link between land, people,
cattle, and *Nhialic*, the supreme God who has created, unites, and sustains them
all in harmony. It is *Nhialic* who endowed the first ancestors with the land that
is so integral to this people's continuity. It is he who invigorates the soil to bear
life, to nurture, sustain, and heal his creatures. "The big black land, the land
that looks like us," says a song composed by a woman far from home. Again
she asks: "Doesn't the soil have ears to hear nor eyes to see? Soil is greater
than friendship, greater than offspring, greater than riches. . . . " A people without
their ancestral homelands — like the refugees of Kakuma or those inhabiting the
shantytowns of Khartoum — have been cut from their moorings. To sense the
tangible and symbolic meanings of "homeland" is to begin to grasp the gnawing,
sickening void felt by those who have been forced, utterly destitute, from their
soil. Before this journey I had not seen with my own eyes the horror of the Sudan
government's systematic effort to weaken a people's grasp on their homeland, to
uproot, disenfranchise, impoverish, and dehumanize — undergirded by sporadic
sweeps of genocide and enslavement.

A more cautious traveler would not have undertaken such a tour on a cheap
Chinese bicycle (with an apparent planned obsolescence of three months) through
a war-ravaged famine zone, in late dry season. My small carton of food, a water
filter, and a pocketful of Sudanese dinar notwithstanding, sustenance and water
were a daily challenge for my emaciated hosts and me. Nonetheless, we peddled
westward through thick thorn forests and across convoluted dry swamplands without the security of a spare inner tube or patch kit, the major market at Warawaar
having been burned to the ground by an angry Arab trader during the first week
of our visit. (How then does one repair a flat tire? By tying a length of nylon string
around each new puncture, making the tube yet smaller and more contorted with
each repair.) Gingerly we rolled along sometimes repumping deflated tires every
half hour.

With three superb companions, Episcopal pastors Angelo Yuet, Jeremiah Tong,
and young Stephen Mayuen (the latter two, skilled bush mechanics), we set off on
April 28 heading from the church at Adoor to the military settlement at Pariak.
As I conversed with Commander Malong I noticed a haggard, half-clad woman
under a tree, a widow with her four emaciated children. Their home burned, they
had walked for a week, eating nothing. I would encounter both her story and her
dull, unresponsive gaze repeatedly in the days that followed. We cycled westward
overnighting under the stars at Akuemkou, home to a small school and open-air
church at the base of an enormous parasitic *kuel* tree. Following the near dry bed

of the Lol River we arrived at the settlement of Geer, its forests opening to a flat plain, the trees of the government garrison town of Aweil visible on the horizon. For a full day we trekked on foot in blistering heat, surveying the charred rubble of former homesteads, listening as an anguished people recounted their losses. In April military lorries bristling with soldiers rolled out of Aweil forcing a mass evacuation: "anyone remaining behind was killed." Hurriedly people had buried their possessions, their sorghum rolled into the earth in massive storage baskets. A week later they returned to find not an uncharred grain of sorghum nor a sleeping mat remaining. Most livestock having been looted in previous years, the last remaining animals had been driven away or shot.

Through thorn forests and stands of palm trees we cycled westward to Mariam, one of three regions ravaged during March and April. Nine of Mariam's villages had been destroyed while further west, at Ayaat, six were leveled, leaving nineteen people dead, but few abducted. The worst carnage of those days occurred on April 6 northwest of Nyamlell at Akuangaruol, where fifty-nine people were killed, forty carried into bondage, and 3,792 head of cattle looted. Now, under a tree near Mariam we found some twenty bitter and exhausted women with a few children, still smooth skinned and decently dressed from the life they had fled three days earlier at Nyamlell. These were the first we met of thousands displaced by the fighting that raged in those days, each with narratives of the carnage as government troops ravaged the town and its environs. There were descriptions of entire families who had been herded at gunpoint into their cattle byres, then incinerated. Thirty died in one *luak* said a woman. We heard of the pregnant woman who had been shot, her belly slashed and the fetus removed and hacked to bits. Women and children fell alongside men. As they spoke the women cracked their last remaining groundnuts.

Continually, a people stunned by their destitution listed the things, especially the food stocks, they had lost. Then they enumerated the wild seeds, leaves, and fruits to which they now resorted for sustenance. Dawn to dusk gaunt women and girls pick, scrape, and sweep the ground, gleaning the tiny seeds of grass they winnow and cook as *akutdo*. "Bird food!" scoffed one man, as he described how this food-of-last-resort makes one sick and dizzy. Nonetheless, even *akutdo* would no longer be available with the advent of the rains. Equally, the wild figs, the leaves known as *akuor*, and the wild fruit, *goroth*, would soon be finished. "Look at these children," I was exhorted. "If you come back in two months they will all be dead."

"A devastated land," a tormented land "no longer fit for human habitation." Perhaps. But it is also a land of profound spiritual resonance, home to a people of extraordinary humanity, dimensions that I cannot omit from this narrative. As we skirted around homesteads, I saw the shrines, comprised of carved posts or molded clay, witness to the unseen powers who are venerated in rich diversity: ancestral divinities like Deng, Garang, and Abuk, and more malign *jak* like Nyan-cham, Machardit, and Makoldit. Here the *Bany Biith*, the most respected spiritual intermediaries, continue in high esteem, most invoking and offering sacrifices to *Nhialic* alone. Whether among Christians or traditionalists, diviners, or military commanders, I found a refreshing openness to discuss the world of the spirit, and it was with several *Bany Biith*[67] that I enjoyed moving discourse on theology and history. The people who are slaughtered, abducted, and displaced are not, as some have said, primarily Christians: *all* are the object of eradication. Nonethe-less, some Christians asserted that their homesteads had not been destroyed to the degree of those who had not yet embraced the singular authority of *Nhialic* of the church.

During the colonial era this vast region of Bahr el Ghazal was designated a "sphere" for Roman Catholic missions, small Protestant enclaves emerging only in the towns, if at all. Catholic missionaries focused on formal education, rarely undertook primary evangelism, and had little success in recruiting *Muonyjiang* to the celibate priesthood, a deficiency that has remained acute since foreign missionaries were expelled in 1964. As we traveled I sought to meet the mostly young catechists who now maintain rural Catholic congregations. Uniformly they lamented that they had never been visited by a Catholic priest and their rural flocks had never received the sacraments (an assertion I cannot substantiate, though I found myself embraced as a surrogate "Father"). With the Catholic Church as the historic Christian presence in the region claimed, even if nominally, by virtually every educated person, those who have come to propagate a new denomination have not been readily received.

It is one of the miraculous anomalies of this war that the young men of the Red Army (*Jiech Amer* as they are known in Arabic) should emerge as pioneer evangelists. In 1987 as many as thirty thousand boys across southern Sudan left their homes under SPLA mandate, walking eastward, ostensibly to attend schools in Ethiopian refugee camps.[68] Severed from family and cultural roots, virtually all who survived were baptized as Christians within two years, the largest numbers into thriving Episcopal refugee churches. Among these were boys from Bahr el Ghazal who, as independently minded, militarized young Christians, returned to their home areas in the 1990s to proclaim a radicalized gospel. As an SPLA commander said, "For us the Catholic Fathers were honorable old men, people with years of education: it was very strange when these "small boys" appeared calling themselves *abunas*." Of the twenty-one young men ordained on April 26,

---

67. This singular of the term is *beny bith*; it refers to a ritual priest and literally means "master of the fishing spear," the spear being the totem object endowed with sacred power.

68. Some estimates are as high as forty thousand.

eleven were products of the *Jiech Amer,* their education now presenting a major challenge. Central to the call to conversion they preach has been the repudiation of indigenous spiritual powers and destruction of shrines. This in sharp contrast to the Catholic Church which has, in recent decades, coexisted cordially with the diviners. Despite heated accusations against them and repeated arrests (one young man was imprisoned nine times), the Red Army evangelists persevered in propagating their faith (often derided as the "church of Bor").

During the past two years tensions have cooled, shrines are no longer forcibly burned, and Catholic-Episcopal-SPLA relations are increasingly cordial. Certainly all people — be they Christian or traditionalist — drink from the common cup of suffering and death. As the *Jur* sweep the land, killing, burning houses and cattle byres, churches are prime targets, with some twenty-three houses of worship torched in recent months. As witness to the perseverance of these communities, I offer the names of churches, their denomination, possible numbers who gather, and dates of destruction, as best I could record them:

Tiomthit, ECS (200), first destroyed in 1996 (rebuilt and destroyed January 10, 1998)

Majongdengdit, ECS (200), destroyed sometime in April 1996

Manyilakook, ECS (700) & RC, both destroyed April 4

Langich, ECS (250), destroyed April 5

Akuanglang, ECS (200), destroyed April 5

Akuangmachar ECS (250) destroyed April 5

Agoor, RC, destroyed April 5

Majongalel, ECS (350), destroyed April 5

Akuangaruol, ECS, destroyed April 6

Nyinameth, ECS (300), destroyed April 20

Wunagiir, RC, destroyed April 20

Achero, RC, destroyed April 21

Agonmachar, RC, destroyed April 23

Marialbaai, RC, destroyed April 23

Mayomadhal, ECS (250), destroyed April 23

Sungabat, RC, destroyed April 24

Penhatak, RC (450), destroyed April 24

Wunaruol, ECS (300), destroyed April 24

Machol, RC, destroyed April 28

Mabioranyang, ECS, destroyed May 2

Majangbaai, ECS (700) & RC, both destroyed April 1996 (ECS rebuilt, burned again May 2, 1998)

Though constructed of palm wood, poles, mud, and thatch, these are not insubstantial buildings. The product of considerable industry, each is a center of communal solidarity and hope, an expression of the struggle for survival and the dialogue of soul underway in a traumatized land.

As I hitched my way back to Lokichoggio on May 11, my hopes rose when a WFP official told me that present deliveries of relief food were to be increased within days, becoming the largest airlift of food ever undertaken by the UN's Operation Lifeline Sudan. Five Buffalo aircraft would soon be doing multiple daily rotations with most of the food destined for Bahr el Ghazal. Back in Nairobi two days later, we learned that government military activity in western Bahr el Ghazal had intensified, placing all deliveries — and all human life — in jeopardy.

Years of scorched earth warfare are taking their toll. "We can no longer live in this land," implored one man. "Bring trucks, and we'll board them, old people, and women and children. We will all go to the safe place you have for us where there is enough to eat. One day we will return." I was sickened as I felt, firsthand, the forces that cause a people to want to leave their ancestral homeland, to "hate" themselves. I was also chastened. These are people of profound humanity struggling with all the tools at their disposal to cling to their heritage, to preserve the land that "has taken our blood and will heal our wounds." This land, endowed by *Nhialic*, is intended for renewal. The eviction and extermination of its inhabitants is an insult and a diminishing of us all.

Faithfully,

Marc Nikkel

Part Five

"My Times Are in His Hands"

Letters of Reconciliation and Longing for Home,
1998–2000

In July 1998 Marc wrote a letter to some friends explaining that he had had some health problems. After a "brisk walk" in late June, he had experienced some exhaustion and stomach pain. Thinking he was having a bout of malaria or flu he took some anti-malarial medicine and attempted to wait it out. A trip to a Nairobi clinic led to the suggestion that he had an infection and he was put on antibiotics, then later on anti-tuberculin drugs. Then an ultrasound reading revealed an "obstruction" in the bowel, and more tests revealed a case of bilhartzia.[1] Although he obtained some drugs to deal with these parasites Marc's stomach pain did not subside and he was forced to cancel a scheduled trip to Naruse, just over the border in Sudan. At that point, still thinking that the bilhartzia was the major issue, Marc had hopes that he would be up and around soon. The pain persisted into August, though, and Marc was eventually admitted to Nairobi General Hospital for tests. Stomach cancer was discovered and surgery performed. He was quickly transferred to the Royal Marsden Hospital in London where he was given a very poor prognosis, doctors saying that he might have as little as two weeks to live.

By God's grace, Marc was given not two weeks, but two years. Although these two years were punctuated by cancelled trips and events and bouts of pain, surgery, and recovery, they were also years of amazing productivity. Marc was able to make trips back to Africa, to teach, preach, and write. Most of all, perhaps, he was able to receive from his Sudanese family. As they prayed for him, whether at a distance, or laying hands on his belly in his little hut in the Kakuma Refugee camp, Marc was a willing recipient of the faithful intercessions of the Sudanese Christian community. The African community stormed heaven on Marc's behalf, and for two years his life of witness continued among them. In fact, the last two years of Marc's earthly pilgrimage, a story of life in the midst of death, seemed almost uncannily to parallel the situation of the Sudanese community that he loved. As Marc himself put it in his letter of June 9, 1999,

---

1. Also known as schistosomiosis, bilhartzia is a disease caused by water-borne parasites and is common in Africa.

*For years we lived amid the vulnerability of exotic diseases, the uncertainty of
ground attacks; repeatedly we have been bombed from the air. When I was first
told that my body was laden with cancer it seemed a natural progression: all
that had gone before was of a piece with my illness and what then appeared
my imminent death. Our suffering is one. Our death is one. And in Christ our
suffering and death, whatever form they take, are laden with meaning. As I
sought to embrace and confirm the significance of my condition, it all seemed of a
fabric with the life and ministry that preceded it. On hearing of my illness, several
Sudan colleagues observed that "anyone who draws near our people, seeking to
help them, will himself experience our suffering and death."*

Marc's life became a mirror of the Sudanese situation in so many ways: as it had for the
suffering community in Sudan, the image of the cross and resurrection of Jesus became
a focus of his reflections; as they had sought God's wholeness in the midst of brokenness,
so Marc reached out to his friends to ask for forgiveness and reconciliation and healing;
as they had implored God to provide some explanation of their pain, so Marc struggled
to understand the meaning of death and the purpose of his life. In the end he concludes
that "nothing is wasted . . . all is harvest." There are tears in these letters, but there is also
much joy. As Marc sought to die a good death, he continued to build his relationships,
perhaps becoming more aware than we were that our familial ties in the Lord Jesus last
eternally, even if they become severed for a season. And he began to realize that all
of his pain and uncertainty are somehow taken up, as he says in his final letter, in the
balance between "sobriety, whimsy, and sheer delight" knowing that his "times are in
God's hands."

Venn House, U.K.
September 26, 1998

> *My times are in his hands. (Psalm 31:6)*

My dear family in Christ,[2]

It is now just over one month since I left Nairobi. Though we are separated by
many miles, know that you are in my thoughts every day. You are in my thoughts
during the day and in my dreams at night. My heart is seldom far from you. How
I give thanks to God for all that we have experienced together during the past

---

2. Although this letter was forwarded to quite a number of Marc's friends, it was originally
addressed to a group of Sudanese friends: Bishop Nathaniel Garang, Bishop Reuben Macir Makoi,
Archdeacon Peter Bol Arok, Archdeacon John Kelei, Archdeacon Abraham Mayom Athian, the Rev.
Akurdit Ngong, the Rev. John Machar Thon, the Rev. Nathaniel Bol Nyok, the Rev. Santino Rang,
the Rev. Mark Atem, the Rev. Matthayo Garang, Evangelist Bartholomayo Bol, May Alueel Garang,
Abraham Thioong, Evangelist Joseph Aleo, James Ajuot.

five years, in Kenya and at home in Sudan. I carry within myself all the memories of these years and I thank God for what he has given us in our labors, in success and failure, in joy and sorrow, in our continuing hope for the future. Most of all I give thanks for your individual lives, for the privilege we have had of growing as fellow workers, and the diverse and excellent gifts God has given each of you to build up his people.

My illness

As you will remember, I underwent an operation in Nairobi Hospital on August 18. At that time Dr. Robin Magere found that the organs of my stomach were being surrounded by the disease called cancer. He said the disease had grown in many places, and he was unable to locate where it had originated. Once the wounds on my stomach were healed he and the other doctors wanted me to seek the broadest cancer treatment that was possible, and they sent me to the Royal Marsden Hospital in London. Here I spent two difficult weeks in the hospital. When, on September 4, an operation was attempted to help my urine flow smoothly, it was not successful because there was too much cancer growth blocking the way. The doctors were very disappointed, and the senior doctor in charge of my case said that I might not have more than two weeks to live.

Nonetheless, three weeks have passed, and, by God's grace, my body continues to work fairly well. I now have to take five kinds of medicine each day. The most powerful medicine is held in a small plastic bag that is attached to a small pumping machine on my side. I must wear the machine twenty-four hours a day. It is pumping the chemotherapy medicine directly into my body through a small plastic line. The tube enters my chest, goes through an artery, and ends inside my heart. The medical people do not say that this medicine can kill the cancer. They only say that it might make it stop growing, or make it grow more slowly, or cause it to wither and become smaller. They say it is probably not a "cure" for my cancer, but at least gives me a little more time to live, and live with less pain.

Because chemotherapy is like a poison, it can cause me to feel sick and weak. It causes sores on my hands and mouth and sometimes makes my hands tremble. Difficulty with my urinary system has made my legs and ankles swell up, but I still try to exercise every day. Because of the effects of the chemotherapy I take other medicines at morning and night to keep the pain from becoming too strong. These medicines sometimes make me feel sleepy, or unclear, especially early in the morning, but after a while they wear off and I am able to write and do other work. I am not quite like *Thon Akon* or *Manguangdit*[3] used to be. My

---

3. On Marc's ox names see his essay of 1999, "On Becoming a 'Bull Elephant'" p. 182 in this volume.

life is slower now, and I must do everything one step at a time, thoughtfully and carefully.

Friends, visitors, and the theology of healing

Before God, in my spirit and my friendships, this has been a wonderful time of learning and growth. In the way that God blesses Sudan amid great suffering, so I find he is blessing me in my sickness. When I was in Nairobi it was wonderful to have friends come to be with me in hospital. Here in the United Kingdom I receive many cards, e-mails, and letters from around the world telling me that people are praying for me each day. This week I received letters from Sudanese communities Bishop Nathaniel and I visited in America. Others came from Archbishop George Carey, and many have come from Anglican bishops around the world, as well as other church leaders. Some have been able to visit personally. I am not alone! Three times we have gathered with twenty or so people for holy communion around my bed. How good it has been sharing our history and our prayer, and always thinking of you, in Kenya and Sudan, being here with us as well.

When Bishop Daniel Deng was traveling from America he came to England to see me, but his U.K. immigration documents were no longer valid. Officials kept him at the airport for five hours until he persuaded them to give him a forty-eight-hour visa to come to the hospital to be with me. We had a deep time of prayer. In America, when Bishop Daniel heard that I had a "bad cancer," he said, "What bad cancer? If there is a bad cancer, then, by the power of God we will make it into a good cancer!"

Others who have come to visit include Rev. Joseph and Karin Ayok, Rosemary Ajja and El Haj with their children, John Amuor and Rachel Adak. In addition, my sister, Marvis, and her husband, Sam, were able to come from America and stay with me for two weeks. During their stay three other friends from North America also came — Nancy Frank for one week, Bill Lowrey and William Reimer, for four days.

Yesterday Bishop Benjamin Mangar[4] took the long train and taxi ride to Venn House where I am now living. With him were Christian women of Bahr el Ghazal: Akoi Dau, Atong Baak, Kana Ameer Dhou, Naomi Akon, and Esther Benjamin. Because of their employment in London it is difficult for Sudanese to find the time to travel, so only John Amuor has been able to come from among our Bor people. Of course, many of the staff of CMS, London, visit regularly, including Canon Ken Okeke, Rev. Kevin Huggett, Diana Witts, and Lady Gill Brentford.

Among those who come there are many who pray to God for complete and immediate healing from every trace of cancer. Remembering the story of Hezekiah

---

4. Benjamin Mangar Manur was consecrated to be bishop of the Diocese of Yirol in 1988.

in the Old Testament,[5] they call on God for a miracle without any hesitation. If God is creator and sustainer and life giver, they believe, he has power to cleanse cancer from Marc's body. I thank God for this great faith and prayer, and the hope we share with you together. From what I have heard, prayers have sometimes been organized by the Sudanese community in Nairobi and Kakuma on my behalf. How thankful I am for this. I welcome you to pray for the medicines that I am taking, for the fullest possible power of chemotherapy, and for God's power to keep my urine passing smoothly from my body (this is one of the doctors' biggest concerns that could lead to my death).

While we pray for healing, I am also concerned to be fully prepared should God call me to himself. So far as possible I want to be set right with all people. For this reason, my sisters and brothers, I ask forgiveness where I have failed you. If there is anyone among you who feels any grievance against me, if there is anyone who has an unresolved problem with anything I have done or said, please write to me about it. If there is any area that needs healing, let us confess to one another and be fully reconciled.[6] I would be very thankful to hear from you.

Travel plans

As you see, I must take each day as it comes. It is not possible to make long-range plans or hold any plan too tightly. Last week I was able to fly up to Scotland with my sister and brother-in-law to be with Robin and Marianne Anker-Petersen. Those were wonderful days with Christians from two of my Link Churches gathering on Saturday for eucharist and prayer.

However, my greatest hope now is to travel to California to see my father, Reuben Nikkel. He is old and quite weak, and his mind is no longer clear, but it is important that I am with him and other family members and friends who live near the place of my birth. At present I am planning to travel in the company of Dr. Robin Fisher, who can help me if there are medical problems on the way. As it is now scheduled, we will leave on October 5 and return by October 22. When we return I would travel up to Scotland to stay with Robin and Marianne Anker-Petersen. They are like my second family and have committed themselves to care for me if my sickness should increase.

What I pray for you

As I write many of your faces come to mind. I miss you as individuals, and I miss the great places where we met for celebration and worship. I miss Kakuma, and Panyagor, and Yomciir, and Dhiaukuei, and Naruse, and Lebone, and Adoor, and

---

5. For the story of Hezekiah's healing see 2 Kings 20:1–11 and 2 Chronicles 32:24.
6. See James 5:16.

the many other places where we have lived and worked together. When I think of you in these many places I pray above all for *unity*. I pray that by the Spirit of God you may learn to work together with greater trust, harmony, and openness. Each one of you, men and women, young and old, need each other. I pray your rich gifts may be openly honored and shared among yourselves for the benefit of all.

Secondly, I pray for *stronger structures of administration and management*. In recent years the world has seen the miracle of evangelism unprecedented in Sudan. With the powerful evangelistic leadership of Bishop Nathaniel Garang the ECS has proceeded amid terrible destruction, becoming one of the most vital, creative churches in the world. This is something that no one could have imagined. Now, in these present years, a new stage has begun. This is the time for greater organization and consolidation, not only of spiritual gifts but tangible gifts as well. It is time to lay new structures of administration and leadership to harness the great resources God has given, first within our own Sudanese people and, secondly, from the many, many new friends we have developed around the world who want to provide assistance.

This letter has become longer than I originally expected. Perhaps it shows how much I think of you, and miss you, and long for news of you. You must know that throughout these past six weeks, I have found that God is very near me. Whether I am sick or strong, whether I am in pain or free from pain, God is at the center of my experience. He is closer than my own breath, closer than the beat of my heart.

However, if there are times when I weep at night on my bed, I weep not because God is distant, but because I miss you. This is the greatest pain I have felt since I left Africa. I think of you at night and I long for your words, your prayers, your songs, your touch, and your physical presence. It is my Sudanese family that I miss most of all. The thought of not being able to see you again, that is the greatest sorrow I feel. I thank God that I have some of your crosses here with me. They speak of your faith and survival. They remind me of the meeting place between earth and heaven, between death and resurrection, between our endings and our beginnings. But most of all I long to see you again.

Love,
Marc

Venn House, Kent, England
October 29, 1998

To Friends on Three Continents,

This comes as an update on this, the most recent phase of my pilgrimage, body and soul. For three weeks I have been in the company and care of my good friend of sixteen years, Robin Fisher, M.D. Were it not for Robin's support, this last journey would not have been possible. In the process our mutual love has deepened and proved another superlative gift of these precarious months. On arrival back in Birmingham Robin and his wife, Anna, have thrown themselves into preparations to return to Sudan, she for linguistic research, and he to offer his services in medicine.

Friends at the Episcopal Church Center in New York arranged a wonderful reception for the week of October 5, with an invitation to preach at the Wednesday service and a meeting with the presiding bishop. Our first day was as rich as it could be. On Tuesday, however, it was clear I was becoming increasingly anemic, caused by the malfunction of my swollen kidneys. A doctor's appointment consumed Tuesday morning. The only opening for a blood transfusion was Wednesday at Mount Sinai Hospital. Events at the Church Center were slipping into the haze of medical expediency.

On admission I was taken to the bowels of this great teaching hospital and engulfed by a bewildering array of doctors, feeling rather like a medical hostage. During the next five days my beleaguered body received not two but seven units of blood, and a great deal else. All this on Mount Sinai, the biblical symbolism wafting around my bed. We were unable to leave until Monday, October 12. The flight itself proved difficult. Neither Robin nor I had taken seriously the time changes and the quantities of drugs I needed for the arduous high-altitude journey. Chest pains proved debilitating, and I was a trembling geriatric, short of breath, by the time we arrived.

Once back in the loving embrace of my sister and brother-in-law my health stabilized remarkably, and my strength and agility have improved daily since. Undeniably, this is also a result of the decision I have made, with the support of doctors in London, New York, and California, to terminate chemotherapy. The side effects — mouth sores, lack of taste, cracked and bleeding extremities, digestive malfunctions, degenerating skin and hair texture, a depressive, disorientated state — were proving too much, with no observable benefits. While continuing these poisonous drugs may minimally extend the length of my life, it seemed wise to proceed with a range of painkillers, seeking to facilitate the best quality of life, whatever its duration.

Know, however, that I restrain none of my friends from prayer for miraculous healing through the power of the Spirit of Christ. Increasingly I receive narratives of healing and recovery from cancer, all of which underscore the intimate links between this disease and one's spiritual and psychological resources. Doctors have, to date, appeared quite bewildered by my case. Having put a halt to chemo, my life is, more explicitly than ever, in the hands of our God and that vast worldwide community who hold me daily in prayer. To you and our Lord I commend my continuing life and pilgrimage.

While small-town Reedley was home for my first eighteen years, I have not lived there for three decades. Nonetheless, people know me ("former hostage," "the Mennonite who became an Episcopal priest"). I had no idea how many knew me. Dozens of my former high school peers from the class of '68 wanted to catch up. Having mentioned to my sister that I would like to consider constructing a homemade pine coffin with some friends — a sign of communal faith and solidarity — I found that five of my former school chums had taken the initiative and, to my astonishment, had a coffin completed for my arrival. It still awaits an occupant. Some of you were aware of my longing to see my father, Reuben. Given my status as "terminally ill," and Dad's substantial loss of memory at age eighty-six, time spent physically in each other's presence has been a priority.

During our first days in California, Robin and I felt that, given our difficult westward flights, we were not up for a repeat: I would remain in Reedley to fill out what time remains in word and drawing. However, as days progressed, and Robin found himself in the undertow of small-town America culture shock, we were forced to reassess. It became clear that my "community" are gathered nearer the Rift Valley than the San Joaquin Valley, and more concentrated in the United Kingdom than across the United States. Despite the challenges we opted to return to the U.K. Leaving the home of my birth on Saturday, October 24, we arrived back in London on Sunday. Our flight was blessedly uneventful. By Friday I will be off to the home of my friends Robin and Marianne.

But what of my journey of soul during these days? Some of the inner intensity of past months has calmed. This is a relief. A sense of love pervades the many friendships each day of these months. I can be a bit crotchety and blunt with folk who say stupid things to this "terminal patient," but I find most relationships undergirded with a new dimension of acceptance. These are days of constant dialogue with my body, this 230-pound abode of flesh that has served me so well through these forty-eight years of independent living. For too long I despised it. Only in adulthood have I claimed it with joy as a gift of God to be cherished. Strange, that it is now, during a period when I had gained a sort of loving satisfaction with my body, that it seems to have given in to destructive forces hitherto undreamed of. I struggle with how to regard it when it no longer acts on command, when it is anemic, or thoroughly out of control. Never before have I experienced this kind of physical vulnerability, and it is difficult for me. My body is limited, and it is sobering to count its limitations. How I can love and embrace this embattled and withering gift of God is a question on which I daily reflect.

Yesterday I went to see my doctor. A good, positive encounter, he was quite surprised by my improved blood readings. He found no obvious sign of the advance of cancer, and several times remarked on how good I looked. Certainly, I am aware of stomach pain, and the fact that my upper body is becoming thinner while my lower extremities remain swollen. I mentioned my dream of returning to Africa to work out my farewells with friends from whom I was severed so abruptly. His response, "I see no reason why you shouldn't make the journey." What wonderful encouragement for one who weeps little any more, except for my longing to see my kin and clan among the Jieng one last time. This too, is a dream I commit to you for prayer, one more stage on this pilgrimage.

Remember each day that "all, in the end, is harvest." Nothing of my years is wasted, nor yours. Not one scrap, not the dust and ashes of broken friendships, once thought long buried. Every aspect of our lives has its meaning and purpose, and some, as I find almost daily in recent weeks, are resurrected. Nothing wasted, but all enfolded in love. All, in the end, is Harvest.

With thanksgiving and deep affection,

Marc Nikkel

Back on African Soil, Loresho, Nairobi
November 22, 1998

Greetings, Dear Friends,

It is a radiant Sunday morning in Nairobi, Kenya, the light glistening off an array of greens. Dr. Pat Nickson and I arrived Saturday morning after a fine and uneventful flight. My strength, breathing, and all other bodily functions have been doing fine throughout, though I attached myself to the oxygen umbilical dangling from overhead during the entire eight-hour flight.

We were met at the airport by Andy and Sue Wheeler and my good friend Ajuot, who will be with me during the weeks ahead. We returned home to pots of flowers throughout the house and a fridge stocked with food, thanks to my gracious landlady. I plunged into bed, waking three hours later to find Bill Lowrey had made his way to my house — another joyous reunion. Bill will stay with me for the last three days of his Khartoum-Nairobi sojourn, working long, unbroken hours on the Nuer-Jieng peace process.[7] Pat travels on

---

7. What became known as the "People to People" Peace Process began in 1994 at the instigation of the New Sudan Council of Churches as a way to address the deteriorating relationship between two Nilotic groups who have been ancient enemies, the Nuer and the Jieng. Tragic raids on Jieng cattle in 1991 led to further conflict in 1993 and finally to an all-out war between the two groups in the dry season of 1993–94. "Estimates on the cost of the conflict indicated that more than 1300 people had been killed, 75,000 cattle had been raided, 3000 homes burned and 1300 tons of grain destroyed. More than 100,000 people had been displaced" (Werner et al., *Day of Devastation*, 659). A series of peace

to Kisumu[8] for meetings today, and next week to the WCC meetings in Harare.[9]

Today, Sunday, we will attend two Jieng services, arriving early at Uthero to greet people at the beginning of the service and departing early to meet the bishop and a still larger congregation across town at Ngumo. How I pray I will find appropriate words to speak my heart both to individuals and groups, knowing my statements now carry a new sort of weight in the mind of my hearers. I invite you to pray for my wisdom and sensitivity each step of the way.

My health remains a joyful mystery of God. It is sometimes difficult for me to recall how sick I was five days ago, let alone two months ago. As everyone tells me with surprise, I look great — and I feel good.

Must close as we prepare a small communion service,

Marc

Nairobi
December 9, 1998

Advent Greetings,

One more stage on this globe-embracing pilgrimage of farewells completed ... and I am feeling better of body than when I began. I flew from Kakuma to Nairobi yesterday. Bishop Nathaniel and four colleagues are following in my car to arrive this evening. Kakuma was a billow of dust and celebration, with some four thousand souls marching out to welcome me, banners waving, song abounding, at my arrival on Wednesday. On Sunday, December 6, the head count for our united service came to 6,855, many gathering under the acacia trees simply to hear words of greeting from this dead man walking.

"The man who died has risen again," was a phrase often repeated with giddy laughter as people exalted in the power of their prayers extending halfway around the world and confounding the death predictions of medical professionals. More than any time previously, I am claimed as the possession of the Jieng of the ECS, for it is their faithful prayers, heartfelt and determined, day and night, offered by

---

conferences, in Akobo, in July–September 1994, in Lokichoggio, Kenya, in June 1998, and finally in Wunlit in February–March 1999 has resulted in substantial restoration of the relationship between these two peoples. For more information see *http://www.southsudanfriends.org/wunlit/* and the article "Passing the Peace" by William Lowrey in Wheeler's *Land of Promise*. Marc mentions something of his role in the Wunlit conference in his letter of June 9, 1999 (p. 194), and his role in a continuing part of this process called the "East Bank Nilotic People to People Peace & Reconciliation Conference" in his letters of January and April 2000 (pp. 196, 198).

8. Kisumu is a major city in western Kenya.

9. The Eighth Assembly of the World Council of Churches met in Harare, Zimbabwe, December 3–14, 1998.

children, women, elders, in small groups and large, that raised me up. Indeed, word had arrived from Nairobi some weeks back that I was already dead.

A number recounted how they had crammed themselves into my mud brick house in Zone 4, laying hands on my bed, praying that I would return to sleep there once again. And so I have. On Friday, I rose at 6:00 a.m., groggy and disheveled, from my bed to find Kakuma's Zone 4 women gathering after their daily pre-dawn prayers and demanding that I stand at the heart of their circle as they grasped hands in prayers of thanksgiving for my recovery. Passionately, they petitioned the "God of widows and orphans, the God of the weak, the suffering, and dying."

As I walked down the potholed roads of Kakuma old men came out to embrace and bless me, an unprecedented phenomenon from these usually reserved but observant elders. The kids, more buoyantly than ever, shouting, "Mak, Mak, Mak...Mak, Mak" (sounding, for all the world, like frogs in the rain, as one colleague put it) came running to shake my hand from every compound I passed. I cannot deny that some folk perceived about me the glow of the numinous, as they reached out to touch me, like the hem of a garment or an apostle's kerchief.[10] The engine of prayer, lubricated by the tears and fears of refugees, had produced a tangible sign of divine grace.

I found myself suddenly transformed in these days into a symbol of resurrection for the marginalized of Kakuma Refugee Camp. I was a sign of God's efficacious new life, of his response to the petitions of the most sidelined, among whom raw, unexplained death and rotting corpses are a daily reality. My little efforts at "development" (such a potent word at Kakuma), the educational projects I had fostered, would not be terminated by a shadowy death beyond distant oceans. If I offered any qualification about my return based on the progress of my illness, the response was inevitably, "Nothing can hurt you. Your work is not finished. God will bring you back." It is hard not to be uplifted, perhaps blindly encouraged by such unswerving affirmation of life. And so I have been.

As I prepared to go to Kakuma several friends encouraged me to let the refugee community focus their prayers for me with all their energies. Let them muster their spiritual resources to the full toward miraculous healing. And so they did, laying hands on my cancer-ridden lower belly each night — young soldiers, clergy, determined students, prophetic women — grasping the flesh of my abdomen with visionary prayer. One has the sense that those who suffer most, those broken and near death, are the very ones most potent in the realm of the spirit: "By his wounds we are healed" (Isaiah 53:5). Certainly such perceptions were integral to the past six days.

---

10. For these biblical allusions see Mark 5:24–34 and Acts 19:12.

Four days ago I found, to my chagrin, that I had not counted my morphine painkillers accurately and lacked two days of pills while at Kakuma. Stretching my meager stock to cover my days, I anticipated I had more bubble-packed tablets awaiting me in Nairobi. False. Thus, for the past two days, I have gone without any painkillers which is altogether rather remarkable at this stage of my illness (but utterly unremarkable to those who embraced me so fervently at Kakuma).

With this I wish you every blessing in your Advent pilgrimage, and your own reception of our incomparable Guest.

Faithfully,

Marc Nikkel

On Becoming a "Bull Elephant"[11]

Reconciling the bland, often painful and introverted qualities of my life growing up in middle America's San Joaquin Valley in California with my experiences in Africa over the past three decades has come but slowly. At times there is a hazy blur between the two, leaving me to wonder, "Which world am I in?" "Which am I *really* a part of?" "To which am I most greatly indebted in the formation of the person I am today?" Naturally, my resolution must necessarily be some synthesis of the two, one set of influences informing and shaping the other over thirty years.

I remember well one sweltering day in 1982. I had been living with my Jieng Aliab[12] friends in one of the cattle camps they share with the Mandari in Sudan's Equatoria Province. Our bed was the soft ashes of the dung fire and my sole food was fresh milk direct from the teats. I had driven out from the rural college where I taught, some sixty rugged, convoluted miles, left my little blue Suzuki at Tali Police Post, and walked another ten or fifteen miles to locate my *gol*, my "adoptive" Aliab kinfolk in their ever moving dry season cattle camp.[13] Now I was trekking still further northward toward the main Aliab village of Awerial, through the forests and savannah lands that form the bumper between the territory of the western Mandari and that of the Aliab to their north. My friend Ija and I had been walking for five hours in the sweltering Equatorian heat and I was feeling a little dizzy.

Our dirt path took us through a ragged forest region utterly bereft of another soul. In my stupor of thirst and exhaustion I noticed large plugs along the way,

---

11. This short essay was written in 1999.

12. The Aliab are one of the subgroups of the Jieng people.

13. *Gol* in *Thuongjieng* literally designates the dung fire around which cattle are tethered and people often congregate. The term also designates the average number of cattle, perhaps twenty-five or thirty, that belong under one family's ownership, as well as the community of people, the subclan or family to whom the cattle belong and who congregate at the dung fire.

the color of rich dark brown earth, scattered intermittently, for miles. They were perfectly formed, some broken but most intact. Dreamily, in the back of my numbed mind I thought of medium-sized red clay flowerpots, thrown out, broken, the hard soil that remained perfectly retaining the shape of their container. This shape, texture, and size were familiar from my childhood home with the avid gardening of my mom. But as we plodded on a moment of lucidity suddenly came over my dazed mind and I asked myself whatever clay flowerpots might be doing deep in the forests of southern Sudan. Which world am I in? I've never seen a flowerpot in Sudan, certainly not in this utterly uninhabited land, and it is unlikely one might exist anywhere in a three-hundred-mile circle. With no answer coming quickly I finally turned to my companion, Ija, a herdsman fresh out of cattle camp, to ask what these brown soil plugs might be. His simple, clear-as-day response was definitive: *"weer akon!"* meaning, quite simply, "elephant shit!"

Of course! What was more obvious? What incredible naïveté. But then, I'd never been in elephant country before, not that I'd known, certainly not where entire herds left their potting soil behind. It had simply been beyond my numbed reason to think of anything beyond my own California frame of reference: flowerpots at the uninhabited heart of southern Sudan.

Given my upbringing the true concept of "elephant" has proved a far greater challenge for my psyche to comprehend. First there is the need to develop some realistic notion of what an elephant *is*, and then — ever so much more difficult — to believe that there might be something positive if and when I myself should be abusively likened to one. I will try to describe a process that has occurred only over several years of gradual, reflective assimilation in my adult life.

When I was a teenager in grade school and high school we used the names of animals to assault one another. Kids of every society do it, drawing on the imagery, associations, and stereotypes their people cultivate. As a teenager I was fat. No, I was distressingly obese. By the time I was fourteen I had a forty-four-inch waist and my profile from mouth to chest made a straight line. I had no neck. I could not play sports with other boys, nor did I want to. With my layers of fat rolled protectively around my midriff, I was a physical and social oddity in our tightly knit little "Christian" high school. I was called names: "He's as big as an elephant!" came the chant. "You fat bull elephant! Look at his loose skin jiggle. He's not a boy. He's a Jell-O mountain! You jelly elephant!"

My own use of name-calling was, however, among the most acerbic, the most destructive. Today I am overcome with guilt and embarrassment when I recall the names I would ruthlessly fashion for others with some physical flaw; those I hoped were my inferiors. Out of my own pain and poverty I would manufacture epithets for the obese girl who many thought to be my twin sister for her massive girth. I ridiculed her as the "fat cow," all the while drawing pictures of her rotund body waltzing along the margins of my notebooks. These memories mortify me now.

The Jieng with whom I have spent my adult years have purged any negative associations from my conception of cattle, cows, calves, steers, bulls...and certainly from bull elephants. After even a brief stay in cattle camp witnessing the symbiotic relationship between human beings and their cherished cattle, the harmony and mutual respect, the utter interdependence with which they live, one might celebrate the *love* between human beings and their bovine kinfolk. It does not take long for one to be completely purged of any negative associations with the beasts. Undeniably I have imbibed some of the profound respect the Jieng have for their cattle and internalized the affection and limitless attention a young herdsman lavishes on his biggest, beefiest, and thus most handsome, of steers. Indeed, his "name ox" becomes his alter ego, a reflection of himself, to whom he composes songs, and whose muscular bulk and wobbling fat reflect his own strength and virility. Bull, steer, cow, bullock, heifer, and, yes, bull elephant: each is worthy of unqualified respect among the Jieng.

I doubt that as American kids we could really conceive of elephants as real living creatures. Certainly we never imagined them flowing elegantly in vast herds like royalty in full authority over their limitless savannah kingdom. As kids we would see them solitary, lonely, shackled, from afar, behind fences, through high, specially built doorways in sterile zoos, always pathetically outsized in their ill-fitting enclosures. They were pictured on African travel posters or, more likely, in children's storybooks. Soft, plump little Dumbo flying with his enormous ears (you ride on his back as he flew at Disneyland). Or Dr. Seuss's pathetic Horton, the simple-minded, if faithful elephant who waits eternally for an abandoned egg to hatch in a nest at the top of a tree. However, what I remember with greatest anguish from my early years are the derisive phrases: "He's as big as an elephant"; "You fat, clumsy elephant!" No, the loose flabby skin around my arms, neck and thighs was not unlike an elephant's haunch, rippling humiliatingly with each ponderous step.

Africa has transformed and challenged such demeaning images. Walking the slopes of Mount Kenya or the forests of Sudan, I have confronted the unbridled power of these majestic creatures. There I have seen enormous limbs torn from the tree tops and massive sashes of limp bark stripped from high overhead, the marks of a herd of playful pachyderm passing through. Occasionally entire forests are stripped, pulled up by the root, annihilated. Just as intensely one senses the anxiety of those who struggle to maintain their gardens against these massive predators, straining against their government's protective prohibitions. Still more awe-inspiring is the site of a herd of elephants moving en masse through the glorious plains at the foot of Mount Kilimanjaro. There one senses their cohesiveness, their intelligence, and the grand elegance of their individual and united movements. Ah, these were revelations of a kind of bestial dignity and beauty never conceived of in childhood!

And then that I, nearing middle age, still a light-skinned alien to this great continent should, with all spontaneity, be endowed with the prestigious appellation: "bull elephant," and this by sons and daughters of the land. On the Nile's east bank at Bor are people familiar with elephants, though much more in the past than in the gun- and war-ridden present. When they bestow this name there is no derision; rather it is an epithet of dignity, respect, and honor. Here was a miracle of transformation, that an elephant's finest attributes should be associated with my large frame, my loose flesh swaggering through the villages of southern Sudan, in the secluded cattle camps of Upper Nile Province, along the dirt roads of Kakuma and Lebone Camps for the disenfranchised. Everywhere, in each of these locations I hear, *"Thondit Akon!"* "Great bull elephant!" as kids greet me from the roadsides. Radically transformed, these are words of love and adoption.

The Jieng have always claimed those they desire as their own by naming them, sometimes giving them numerous names. They adopt the respectable newcomer by endowing him or her with a name. In colonial times the Jieng knew no district commissioner or missionary by his personal European name, but by the names with which the Nilotes endowed them. Once given, these names spread across the land, eclipsing any others. His identity, his mythology among the Jieng was shaped by his name. The Jieng embrace, name, and brand the one they choose, adopting him or her irrefutably into their lineage, their mythology, their social narrative. It was not of my own choice that I have been given names among the Jieng. I have neither sought nor refused them, but they have come and multiplied. None are demeaning. All are honorable, a world away from the derision of adolescence in middle America.

I received my first name early in my associations with the Jieng Aliab. It occurred in 1982 in a Jieng cattle camp on the edge of Mandariland. Through the negotiations of my friend Ija, I had purchased a couple of sheep and a very small, motley white bull. Immediately I became *"Oichthon!"*: "The one who has bought a bull!" In granting this gently prestigious name, a young herdsman confirmed that I had crossed the threshold into Jieng life: I was a *cattle owner*. Noteworthy was the fact that the name giver was endowed with six fingers on each hand and six toes on each foot, certainly a sign of divinity. His was a simple affirmation, a small point of prestige, for doesn't virtually everyone in this society have his own bull? But now an alien had entered the habitation of the Jieng Aliab: I was a bull-owner, my name endowed by an especially efficacious "man of divinity."

Eighteen years later, over a wide swathe of Mandari and Aliab territories I am known by this name alone: *Oichthon,* "the one who bought a bull."

Years later, Jieng students at the college where I taught confided in me the various names by which they covertly referred to our teaching staff. Our vice-principal, with his massive display of facial ivory and enormous grin, was known as *Malechbuot,* "the man of a hundred teeth." Our principal, Benaiah, with his small round, bald head was, *Manhomakopf,* "the man with a small round calabash head."

The name given me was of another order altogether, lacking the whimsical tone of these two. Was it that I had lived in cattle camp and been assimilated, even if in so limited a degree, into Jieng society? The name by which our Jieng students referred to me in private was *Manguangdit* — "Great Bull Elephant." *Ma* is the male prefix. *Nguak* refers to the turn of a great bull's horns, thrusting upward, with the points thrusting forward. Horns such as these are aggressive, to be respected and avoided by other cattle. *Dit* means "great" or "large" or "old, venerable." I was, as my students perceived me, a great bull with forward thrusting horns to which other cattle — my fellow staff at the college — demure. The name continues in some quarters, the more appropriate, perhaps, as I have grown older.

And other names followed. In 1995 we labored against great odds to create a dry season Bible school at the new settlement of Dhiaukuei (meaning "the cry of the eagle") in rural Bahr el Ghazal Province (meaning the "River of Gazelles"). Those were difficult, even traumatic months, trying to feed some ninety hungry students academically, spiritually, and, especially, physically in the midst of great barrenness. Arriving emaciated and lethargic, one determined group of twenty-five young men had walked over a hundred miles through the war zone from northwestern Bahr el Ghazal to attend our course. We pulled our little school together, struggling merely to survive one day at a time.

To call students for classes I had brought a cheap brass school bell, probably Chinese in origin, the best Nairobi school suppliers had to offer. Without question I was the most vigorous bell ringer among our several tutors. When my classes began I rang with the greatest vigor by far. Three times the clapper came detached and went sailing out across our open-air classroom. Three times it was repaired. The name that arose was, perhaps obviously, "The bull that breaks the clapper from its bell": *Madthuangtuur.*

And so I was. However, my English translation has rather a pedantic, prissy sound in contrast to the full bodied, aggressive meaning it carries in the Jieng language. The mind of a native speaker, on hearing this name, immediately glows with the imagery and romance, the competition and pride of a Jieng cattle camp bristling with vitality. There is no frantic American schoolteacher here, standing under a tangle of trees calling students to assemble. What comes to mind is an enormous bull, rippling with muscle, the leader of its herd. On its massive neck it bears its own home-smelted bell, thirty pounds or more of solid iron, a symbol of this lead bull's incomparable prestige. With each majestic step it takes the bell swings clanging loudly, deftly, slowly — bong . . . bong . . . bong . . . bong — commanding the attention of the entire herd. It is this massive and powerful beast which, out of sheer exhalation, swings its great neck so vigorously that the clapper breaks from the bell: an act of sheer visceral energy. The bull that breaks its bell is a powerful beast indeed! Such names suggest a kind of power, energy, and leadership I have never associated with myself. Is it the Jieng love for powerful images of masculine virility, or do these names actually describe facets of myself I am fearful to discern?

In my naïve and sheltered American childhood I must sometimes have belittled the majesty of Africa as many Western children do. Yet it is Africa, at its verdant, unpredictable depths that has, over the years, reclaimed and renamed me. "Bull Elephant" and "Great Bull Elephant" suggest how distinctive is my large frame, my broad hips and thick calves, my ample flesh and soft skin, all of these so alien to the smooth, sinuous bodies of my Nilotic counterparts. Their impregnable pitch-black skin, toughened by unprotected decades in a severe climate, their gait perfectly matched to the greatness of the land, and I, in stark contrast, am an oddity. As in childhood an oddity . . . but here I am beloved.

A pencil portrait scrawled by a refugee boy reveals my enormous calves and thighs as he saw them. Certainty this is the human counterpart of Bull Elephant! In the bleak world of the near starving, he sees in my flesh the fecundity of the land he has left behind, or perhaps some other exotic world of fatness — America, Canada, Australia — where he hopes one day to find refuge and fortune. His image could humiliate me, but for the affection in his gaze. Bull Elephant is white and soft and fleshy, and his skin ripples as he walks. And as this mass of flesh moves it does so as kinsman. I am friend and relative and through the dignity of the animals of Africa, I am humanized.

In the energy and dynamism of names such as those bestowed on me the Jieng seek not only my health, security, and wealth, but their own as well. In exalting me as Bull Elephant, as *Manguangdit* and *Madthuangtuur,* they seek my strength and security . . . and with mine, all that I might try to care for as my own. My names are an investment not in me alone, but in the hopes of the entire community. I am *their* bull elephant.

It is, then, a travesty, when Bull Elephant becomes radically sick. Today I am told my belly is filled with cancer. Its fatness is not benign. I look down to see my legs and feet swollen, bound round with supporting hosiery. The legs I once took pride in for their capacity to walk thirty miles a day are today as bloated as a victim of elephantiasis. Ankles, shins, and thighs are bloated and uncomely, an embarrassment, oozing water from within. Bull Elephant is sick these days, and not a little embarrassed to reveal himself. When my friends gather to pray for this sick and withering bull elephant they invoke the good he has done, his resilience, his capacity to rise again, and the hope that he will again do well by them.

Tragic, then, that, just as Bull Elephant has claimed this affirmation of his ever-too-large body — the very mass of fat and bone, the organs of his belly, his mark through life — he should fall so low, the swaggering majesty of Bull Elephant undercut, lain flat to rot on the overpopulated savannah lands of North America.

Marc

The Royal Marsden Hospital, London
April 15, 1999

And again I affirm, "My times are in your hands" (Psalm 31:15)

Greetings to beloved Friends across the globe,

Yes, as always, with profound thanks for your prayerful solidarity. My journey continues, now back in London. From my hospital bed at the Royal Marsden Cancer Hospital, I begin to write the letter I have hoped I would not need to write. "My journey must be canceled." As I say those words to myself, images of a number of friends pass through my mind, friends I have longed to see during the weeks ahead... in Indianapolis, Pittsburgh, New Haven, New York, Rochester, southwestern Virginia, California. A number had planned to drive in from far distances, joyful at prospects of meeting after years apart. What a feast it was to be, with relationships renewed, deepened. But, dear ones, not now. Our times are in his hands. Not now. I am so sorry.

After six days in Nairobi Hospital I was released last Saturday, delighted to return to my forest-shrouded "cabin," to the quiet and the bird song. By Monday, however, it became clear that my system was still not functioning properly, and I was vomiting anything I ate or drank. It seemed I had two options: either return to Nairobi Hospital, or take up the first leg of my journey and go to the U.K. for immediate medical care (with a broader spectrum of tests and procedures available). On Tuesday my beloved Sudan friends, Andy and Sue Wheeler, determined that Sue should travel with me (after thoroughly rearranging a tight schedule). Flying through the night we arrived in London yesterday at 5:15 a.m., a good, uneventful flight.

By 1:00 p.m. I was ensconced in my bed at the Royal Marsden in London. By 5:00 p.m. I had seen two oncologists and a surgeon, the latter offering to perform surgery this morning (!), Thursday the 15th. X-rays reveal that I definitely have an obstructed bowel. I may end up with a colostomy, wonder of wonders! My friends in Scotland, Robin and Marianne, have offered to receive me if and when I recover . . . and so life takes a new twist . . . ever "in his hands."

Know that I think and pray for you daily, those who receive this message, grateful for the bonds of compassion and prayer we share across the miles. We are part of each other, your journey is mine, and mine, yours, in the wonder of intercession.

"Into your hands I commend my Spirit"[14] are words that have taken on a new meaning this Easter season, very intimate, near to the center of my being. I commend my Self not only to God, but also to those who stand with me in prayer. I close with words of St. Anselm that have tumbled through my mind amid the sober joy of Easter.

A Song of Christ's Goodness

Jesus, as a mother you gather your people to you,
you are gentle with us as a mother with her children.

Often you weep over our sins and our pride,
tenderly you draw us from hatred and judgment.

You comfort us in sorrow and bind up our wounds,
in sickness you nurse us and with pure milk you feed us.

Jesus, by your dying we are born to new life,
by your anguish and labor we come forth in joy.

Despair turns to hope through your sweet goodness,
through your gentleness, we find comfort in fear.

Your warmth gives life to the dead,
your touch makes sinners righteous.

Lord Jesus, in your mercy, heal us,
in your love and tenderness, remake us.

In your compassion, bring grace and forgiveness,
for the beauty of heaven, may your love prepare us.

— Anselm of Canterbury

Love,
Marc

---

14. Luke 23:46; Psalm 31:5

Two hours later...

It is 12:30 p.m. Having had a dozen tests and scans, spoken with a flurry of doctors, and got all dressed down in my operating room best...surgery is delayed. At the last moment it was found that my blood is not clotting adequately due to a drug I have been on. It is now clear that I will have a colostomy installed to bypass my cancerous bowels...but this operation will have to wait a few more days. What a sobering education in the vulnerability, weakness, and transience of this, our fleshy packaging...and the wondrous resilience of the spirit.

Cheers,

Marc

The Royal Marsden Hospital
Friday, April 23, 1999

Keep your bags packed.

Greetings Friends,

This message comes as an early sign of life out of days of numb, drug- and pain-induced hibernation. It has been quite a roller coaster of sensations — or utter lack of them — often overwhelming any capacity for communication I once thought I had. Nonetheless, this comes as an expression of affection and longing and gratefulness for your companionship on the journey. Having entrusted my computer to security during the operation, I have only now been able to retrieve it, and so am putting it to use with this, my first e-mail.

I went into surgery this past Tuesday, the 20th, and only now am I surfacing with some clarity of mind (though I still can't read more than two paragraphs without getting lost). I am pleased to announce that, on coming to consciousness, I found that a colostomy had not been installed. Tumors had begun to choke off digestion at the meeting place between the small intestine and large intestine (why do I forever have the impulse to say, "the New Testament and the Old Testament"?). The ends were joined for hopeful smooth sailing...for some time at least, and the anticipation that the Spirit of God and the poison of chemotherapy will together suppress the tumors.

Never have I been so doped up and tubed down as during the past week, what with eight tubes feeding, draining or rehydrating my house of flesh. Feeling rather like Gulliver, staked out to the earth, I am overjoyed as each one was severed or dislodged. Doctors estimate that I will have a dozen more days in hospital, by which time I hope to be on a diet slightly broader than the ice and water to which I've been limited during the past two weeks.

Through it all I have been grateful for the care of a dozen friends and more, who have come to offer support (though I confess I rarely have much presence of mind in the time of their appearing). Still more am I thankful to our ever-present Lord, binding us and the fragments of our lives all together.

As I was writing, one of the staff nurses came in, announcing that Dr. Cunningham is doing rounds and will come into my room shortly with his entourage. Indeed, he showed up, a dapper Scotsman, to say that recent biopsies revealed that the cancer in my abdomen has its primary in the intestine and is a form the treatment of which has had particular advances in recent years. He would, therefore, like to put me on another combination of chemotherapies, administered in the hospital in two-day slots over a six-week period. He advised that I may well loose my hair, but that I would be free to travel out for extended periods, possibly for six months at a time, before undergoing another series. As he parted, he encouraged me to "keep my bags packed," all quite encouraging to my peripatetic spirit.

As I write, the Sudan conference I was to attend in Indianapolis is getting underway, and my heart races from London hospital bed to the cathedral in Indi, so much wishing I could participate in this and the two conferences following it. The good doctor's words give some hope that some segments of that travel schedule (and reunions with many of you) will be feasible in the weeks ahead. As ever, this comes with thanksgiving for our miraculous community, gift of our relentlessly gracious God.

Faithfully,
Marc Nikkel

The Feast of Columba, Missionary
June 9, 1999 (my forty-ninth birthday)

> My good angel, messenger of God, protect my body and my soul;
> Protect me from the evil spirit, and above all else, from sin.
> I pray you, saints, men and women, to protect me;
> obtain for me from Jesus a good and happy death.

> — A "night prayer" for a good death, from Breton

> Death of anointing and repentance,
> Death of joy and of peace;
> Death of grace and forgiveness,
> Death of heaven and life with Christ

> — Prayer for a happy death translated from the Gaelic

*If there is a bad cancer then we will pray that God will make it into a good
cancer!*   — Bishop Daniel Deng Bul in London, September 1998

The person who died has risen from the dead!
— Exclamation often repeated on seeing Marc
at Kakuma Refugee Camp, December 1998

It is nine months since I was told my abdomen was full of cancer and that I
probably had but two or three weeks to live. As I recall, when I received that
news my soul shifted gear, and I wondered just how far my ailing body would allow
me to go in preparing for the "good and happy death" the old Celts prayed for.
My body's sudden frailty threw spiritual priorities to the fore, and every moment,
every movement, took on new meanings. With my soul having put down roots
on three continents I realized it would be as difficult deciding where to prepare
to die as it had been deciding where to live and work. With the support of
many friends, my first "pilgrimage" unfolded, back to the United States. And
then another, impossible as it had seemed, "farewell" visit to East Africa. And
another . . . until life has come to seem nearly normal again. Undeniably, these
months on the precipice have emerged as the most valuable of my forty-nine
years, never to be relinquished. My inner life and myriad relationships have been
greatly enriched, as have my ties with Sudan. Since I have not written one of
these "missionary letters" for a year now, it seems good to sum up some of what
I have gleaned during these tenuous months.

As I write I am in "my room" at Blackruthven House, brilliant spring sunlight
splashing across my worktable and up the walls. This fine eighteenth-century
manor house is home to friends from early Sudan days, Robin and Marianne
Anker-Petersen (the A-Ps) and their two daughters. This is "the Bield at Blackruthven," *bield* being an old Scottish word for a shelter, a place of healing, of
nurture and restoration. The farm verges on the tiny village of "the well of Mary"
so reaffirming this as a place of Tibbermore, another Scots name meaning refreshment for the soul of the sojourner. And so it has become. Last September,
as my options seemed to narrow, the A-Ps invited me to come and take shelter
under their ample roof as I negotiated (or so we thought) the last stages of my
life. What a fine chemistry of care and commitment arose between us and a few
other friends. During long December and January nights gathered in my room by
candlelight around the "Sudan altar" with its ebony crucifix, praying and laying
on hands.

Since I first encountered the crosses, music, and integrative theology of Celtic
Christianity over a decade ago, I have been struck by its complementarity with
expressions arising from the Jieng church in Sudan. St. Patrick's Breastplate could
so easily have burst from an African soul. If I could not return to live in East

Africa, I thought, then at least dwelling in environs where the Celtic heritage is being reflectively revitalized stimulates facets of faith that move me most.

Since my first days in Sudan eighteen years ago I have been continually astounded by the resilience of its people in the face of oppression and death. I have lost intimate friends to Sudan's civil war. For years we lived amid the vulnerability of exotic diseases, the uncertainty of ground attacks; repeatedly we have been bombed from the air. When I was first told that my body was laden with cancer it seemed a natural progression: all that had gone before was of a piece with my illness and what then appeared my imminent death. Our suffering is one. Our death is one. And in Christ our suffering and death, whatever form they take, are laden with meaning. As I sought to embrace and confirm the significance of my condition, it all seemed of a fabric with the life and ministry that preceded it. On hearing of my illness, several Sudan colleagues observed that "anyone who draws near our people, seeking to help them, will himself experience our suffering and death."

And yet, in contrast to most Western friends, my Sudanese family defied any mention of a negative prognosis. When Bishop Daniel Deng was returning to Khartoum in September he determined to visit me in my London hospital room. His response to the doctor's diagnosis: "If this is a bad cancer, then we will pray to God and he will make it into a good cancer!" And pray he did. Nine months later it appears that Bishop Daniel's prayers were efficacious. Contrary to his earlier declarations, my oncologist now says that the tumors in my abdomen are among the most responsive to recently developed chemotherapies (so explaining their sudden remission last October). If a "good cancer" exists mine must be one. Equally defiant was every Sudanese I met during three weeks between Nairobi and Kakuma. With any mention of my illness came the rebuke, "Nothing will kill you! You are God's man and he will protect you!" This kind of unfaltering certainty does wonders in the soul of the afflicted!

Colleagues in Nairobi had arranged for me to have six days at Kakuma. Nothing could have prepared me for the reception that awaited me, banners waving, drums and choirs in procession, as several thousand people, mostly young people, came marching down the camp's main road to welcome me. Everywhere I was told how women, children, and men had been praying for me morning and night. In my own mud brick house in Zone 4 neighbors had crowded in to lay hands on my bed, beseeching God to heal me, so that I would return to sleep there once again. Spontaneously, groups of women would grasp hands, encircle me, and offer prayers of thanksgiving for my recovery. Upon seeing me for the first time some shouted, "The man who died has risen from the dead!" Walking Kakuma's dusty roads children and old people came out to shake hands, thanking God for my miraculous recovery, as they saw it. Among these people, so acquainted with death, citizens of a land of death, there is no place for a "good and happy death." God is quintessentially a God of life.

I returned to Scotland in December to undergo another month of self-administered chemotherapy, nestling in the warmth of Blackruthven. In Kenya and Sudan preparations were then underway toward the "Jieng-Nuer West Bank Peace Conference" scheduled for early February. My friend and colleague Bill Lowrey, serving as facilitator, asked if, health permitting, I would return as scribe for what would probably be the most promising grassroots peace initiative of the war. With doctors' consent I set off on this, a third pilgrimage. My Jieng language held me in good stead as I attempted to record on solar-powered computer every word spoken during nine days of deliberations. This was indigenous leadership — Jieng and Nuer chiefs, women, spiritual leaders — at their finest, drawing from their wisdom, their social networks, heritage, folklore, and ritual to address issues essential to the survival of their peoples. Every resource was wielded toward concerns of reconciliation and peaceful coexistence. In contrast to the repetitious, costly, and pretentious posturing of warlords and politicians, these deliberations held the authenticity and integrity of the suffering, the rooted, the common people. Before anyone entered the meeting house blood sacrifice set the tone, its social symbolism woven through each day's addresses, affirming (if anyone doubted) the spiritual realities underlying all that transpired: Divinity would oversee every word spoken by these leaders, encompassing marriage and progeny, the traffic in cattle wealth, grazing land and water rights, indeed, the entire created order. For me this "third pilgrimage" was one of the most significant events of my Sudan years.

After the conference, followed by a week preparing related documents, I had planned to stay in Kenya through Easter Week, but began having problems with digestion on Palm Sunday (the chemotherapy I had expected to self-administer having been repeatedly delayed). Two weeks later it was clear, with increasing pain and vomiting, that I was in serious difficulty, tumors having caused an intestinal blockage. By April 20, I was back in London and under the knife at the Royal Marsden Hospital. As I complete this letter, having spent much of May recuperating in Scotland, I am now back in London beginning six weeks of intermittent chemotherapy. This is an intensified regimen involving forty-eight hours of treatment every two weeks. Remarkably, my sympathetic oncologist still encourages me to "keep my bags packed," suggesting that by July I should be free for six months of work and travel as is necessary. Amid the lethargy of a body and mind weighed down by drugs, I wonder what I will be able to produce among the many writing projects now before me.

Precarious as recent months appeared, they have yielded unforeseen and blessed fruits. Yes, there have been periods of anxiety, of futility, occasionally of anger. There are times I declare to myself, "This is my pain; this is my death, my sense of void and no one else's. This is my lot now. Let me know it and endure it, and cherish it as my own. Let me make of it the best death I am able!" Verging on death, I reassess the significance of my life, the directions it has taken...and consider options for the future now unfolding. At other times I relish the sense of the miraculous, the intimacy of the Divine, of the wing of my "good angel" flickering across my bedroom ceiling. As I prepare to die, every breath, every hour, become gifts, unveiling new prospects for life, each one a brush with that encompassing blanket of love. Unexpected. And now, there is little I conceive as endings. So much converges toward "a good and happy life." This week I celebrate my forty-ninth birthday, no small marker as another pilgrimage begins.

Faithfully,
Marc Nikkel

Winnipeg, Canada
November 13, 1999

From the vast, flat, gray chill of Manitoba sheltered in the cozy wood frame home of Ingrid and William, long time friends from East Africa.

Greetings Friends,

This was the tour I have twice been forced to cancel over the past fourteen months. How grateful I am to have pulled through, not omitting a piece of it. There were three celebrative nights in New Haven, surrounded by the hubbub of an honorary doctorate, me serving as a symbol of the church worldwide, well beyond the heady circle of Berkeley Divinity School. (My special appreciation goes to the Rev. Sarah Buxton-Smith who took up the rigorous task of nominating me and seeing the process through.)[15] There were six nights in New York City, meeting colleagues at the Episcopal Church Center, among other offices, and tramping those familiar, exhilarating streets; a week in Rochester, New York, with the supportive people of St. Paul's (here my profound thanks to Nancy Frank, who arranged the tenuous schedule for this tour); four nights at Virginia Theological Seminary, preaching, offering lectures, reminiscing with former Sudan students; six nights in the Diocese of Southwestern Virginia, visiting churches, renewing ties, in Lynchburg, Waynesboro, Blacksburg, and Lexington, for the first time realizing what an old hand I have become, with eighteen years "canonically resident" in the diocese, outlasting most other clergy; and five nights ensconced in Indianapolis's elegant old Columbia Club, guest of the generous folk of Christ Church Episcopal Cathedral.

---

15. Berkeley is the Episcopal Church seminary at Yale University.

After some twenty-four sermons and presentations, most of the latter focusing on Sudan's People-to-People Peace Process in which I shared, the more "official" segment of this tour is complete. Throughout, friendships have been deepened both for myself and for Sudan, and a variety of projects carried forward, their completion now in sight. Everywhere I have been embraced as a living sign of the efficacy of intercession, welcomed by prayerful companions on the journey of the past fifteen months of sustained life. As an unexpected gift, autumn colors were at their peak, orange and yellow, gold and red, cloaking mountain ranges, shrouding the motorways from New Haven to Lexington.

I have made it this far . . . but it seems that my energies are running low (or the tumors are again getting the better of me). Between those good times speaking and preaching, I have had to lay low, especially more recently. As I experience increasing stomach and chest pain, accompanied by lethargy, I wonder if it might not be wise to draw my December 2 departure a bit earlier. Still before me is a reunion with my family in California (utterly unthinkable a year ago), a visit that might be abbreviated by a few days.

As ever, I treasure your prayer, your companionship, whether near or far apart. On return to London it seems likely that my doctors at the Royal Marsden will want to put me back on chemotherapy. Unpleasant as that prospect is, it may provide an additional window for the work I would like to accomplish.

Know this comes with much thanksgiving for you, your lives, your solidarity.

Faithfully,

Marc Nikkel

Ross Hall Hospital
January 20, 2000

Hi Dear Ones,

A blessed New Year to all, on a sunny day from my hospital bed in Glasgow. Several of you have asked for an update through this phase. This I offer, with full permission for a painless deletion should my words prove too many. Here goes.

I returned to the U.K. on December 2 and enjoyed ten days among friends with hospital appointments in London. I was able to link up with an excellent doctor and nursing community at Ross Hall Hospital in Glasgow, from where I am now writing. My dream is to return to London by March and, following a CT scan and appointments, be off to Nairobi by the 11th, and into Sudan by mid-month to participate in the "Pan-Nilotic People-to-People Peace Negotiations."[16]

---

16. This conference was delayed several times, but was eventually held in Liliir in the Upper Nile region of Sudan in May 2000. The official name of the event became "East Bank Nilotic People to People Peace & Reconciliation Conference."

On this front your prayers are welcome toward the complex logistical preparations now underway aimed at bringing three hundred delegates together from six major ethnic groups. Undeniably, security in the midst of dry season will be of concern, with the possibility of government attacks by land or by air.

In the realm of my treatment, the cycle is familiar: days in the hospital followed by days of hazy lethargy at home, followed by a fairly stable and productive week, then back to the hospital to begin it all again. Your prayers for a full remission are welcome, as I continue to affirm that "my times are in his hands."

For me life at Blackruthven has been a profound joy of the spirit since we have been reunited at New Year. It is remarkable how deeply I have responded to visual symbols; they give me such exhilaration. With my small altar, ebony crucifix, and candles on one side of my bedroom I easily move into prayer through the day. As well, I have shifted table and chair so I now have a view across to the spreading Copper Beech, the Monkey Puzzle Tree, and the grasslands and pastures beyond. The morning light on old buildings, ancient trees, and rolling, snow-dusted hills is a joy. My room continues to develop: along with a couple of prints to hang, I hope to get the Sudan crosses up soon.

The normal working cycle at Blackruthven sees folk gathering in our chapel for prayer at 9:00 a.m., which I usually join in. Unless there are guests when evening prayers are laid on, Robin and Marianne come by my room by 9:00 p.m. for prayer with laying hands on my belly. Good times, always, for each of us.

An addition to this ailing phase of life has been an alb, arrived from seamstresses in Newcastle two weeks ago. These ladies normally make liturgical garb for clergy. Sixteen months ago I was quite weak and my legs badly swollen; clothes didn't fit and even changing trousers was traumatic. I envisioned creating a big, very warm robe, hooded against the chill of Scotland, ample enough to cover my uncomely legs and feet. Having searched unsuccessfully in the largest fabric shops of London, my first stop in Fresno, California (!?) unearthed a plush brown material with a discreet black pattern, precisely what I was after. I bought six yards, recalling they had required but four. Well, nearly all of it got used to create an ample, hooded slipover alb in the style of Franciscan monks, black rope belt, broad sleeves and all. I'm delighted as are others . . . though a little reluctant to venture out in public, I look so much like a genuine monk. It feels warm and huggable: one more way you can think of me, ensconced alongside my big work table in a terra-cotta room hung thick with icons and the crosses of Sudan. Pardon my too many words. I remain with you on the journey, ever hopeful in the resurrection life of our Lord, always thankful for your prayer and solidarity.

Love,

Marc

Loresho, Nairobi
the length of April 2000

Greetings dear friends, at the beginning of Holy Week,

With this note I wish you a profound sense of the Risen Christ throughout the days ahead. Palm Sunday, yesterday, marked five weeks that I have been back on African soil. It is difficult to express what a profoundly joyful period this has been, both in relationships with my Sudanese kinfolk and in terms of my own inner journey. Each day is filled with gratitude for the privilege of living in this flourishing green environment, free (for a time?) from needles and hospital beds.

In my small clapboard, tile-roofed cabin on a hill outside Nairobi, two good Sudanese friends are with me. Bartholomayo (Bol), age twenty-nine, is completing an intensive college prep course across town (desperately hoping he will be able find funding for a university degree). Ajuot, twenty-two, is in secondary school, with us for the holidays, wrestling with difficult issues, the theft of all his properties back at Kakuma and the perverse complexities of Jieng bride price payments (in which I will have a stake). As we gather at home each evening, there are hours of conversation followed by evening prayers with the stream of intercessions that flow so easily from the chemistry of our souls. Bol and Ajuot conclude by laying hands on my belly and offering the most focused of Jieng prayers.

Nor have I remained close to home, apart from recent days. There was a swift drive up to Kitali (500 miles round trip) to visit a number of Sudanese students in various secondary schools and theological colleges. Returning to Nairobi I was soon off again for three exhilarating days among the good folk of Kakuma Refugee Camp (1,020 miles round trip). No longer do I make the fourteen-hour drive, portions of which are on exceedingly rugged roads, in one day. Rather we (there is always a carful) sleep over at Kitali's "elegant" Alakara Hotel. Kakuma always amazes me for all the vital creativity being sustained in such a dusty, scorched, and often sickly environment. It happened that we were in Kakuma for what the English lectionary calls Mothering Sunday, a celebration little known among Sudanese. In our Zone 4 church we let fly, me surveying the marvelous, life-giving tenacity of Sudanese women, comparing them with Hannah and Mary. What fun, prodding the men, mostly young veterans of war, to consider what honor they might offer their indefatigable mothers. During Holy week in Nairobi I will have the pleasure of preaching in several Sudanese congregations.

The Nilotic People-to-People Peace Conference seems, after numerous postponements, finally to be on course for May 8–14. With some four hundred delegates from five major ethnic groups — Shilluk, Anuak,[17] Murle, Nuer, and

---

17. Anuak villages are situated along the banks of the rivers of southeastern Sudan and western Ethiopia. Unlike the other Nilotic groups involved in this conference, economically the Anuak are

Jieng — and laborious translation conducted in six languages on complex topics, it is somewhat difficult to imagine just how it will be packed into six days. I will serve as scribe throughout, having received firm assurances of a working solar electrical system to power my computer deep in the bush. Please keep this very significant event in your prayers.

"Gratitude" is, I suppose, the single most descriptive word I could scrawl above this phase of life, and life renewed, as we enter Holy Week. Many of those resonant Celtic images of the pervasive presence of God, within, without, before, behind, above, below, seem to find fulfillment in this phase of life, more than any preceding it. I affirm again how thankful I am for your solidarity and prayer. On most evenings, as Bol, Ajuot, and I pray, we consider the marvelous web of people of whom we are a part.

Love,

Marc Nikkel

Reedley, California
August 14, 2000

I greet you warmly (very warmly!) and with much affection,

Some have been asking just where on earth Marc has got to. I am pleased to say that, for the past five weeks I have been nestled with my family in the perpetual sunshine and warmth (95–105 degrees Fahrenheit!) of the San Joaquin Valley (at last I realize why Scotland seems so cold and wet). Marvis and Sam have been taking wonderful care of me through the last stages of recuperation from surgery, and with some of God's good soul work of recent years I find myself "at home" in Reedley, the town of my birth, in ways I never dreamed possible in my adult life.

I had emergency abdominal surgery in Glasgow on June 3, from which I woke with a very finicky ileostomy, what initially seemed a relentless Niagara Falls, rich in acidic bile, gushing out about three inches to the left of my navel. No other adjustment in life (apart perhaps from birth itself) has proved so demoralizing, such a deep level of humiliation, as this little gusher, impervious to my colossal efforts to cap it with a plastic bag. Ten weeks on, my last yard of functioning intestine (all the rest being well and truly infested with cancer) has decided to settle down, producing a more solid and negotiable sort of sludge. Though the constant demands of this finicky addition to my increasingly cut-and-paste sort

---

largely based on farming. The Anuak are believed to be closely related to the Shilluk, who live north of them, and their language is related to their neighbors to the south, the Acholi.

of body are tiresome, we are now coexisting fairly amiably and I am free to enjoy, if taken slowly, almost any kind of food I desire.

My doctor released me from hospital with the extraordinary hope of flying to the United States on July 2. Sadly, the rise of a severe fever a day later saw me back in hospital for two more days. Though delayed and wobbly as a drunken goose, I maintained sufficient determination to drag myself onto a flight for Denver on July 6. Wondrously, I enjoyed two glorious days of reunions with dozens of beloved friends (a little prep for heaven?) at the General Convention of the Episcopal Church. This gathering was followed by the most traumatizing, smelly, and soggy flights of my life, Denver to LA to Fresno, in the company of a radically misbehaving ileostomy. On arrival I collapsed in the embrace of my sister and was promptly dumped in the shower.

Having made it to California I suddenly realized I was quite tired. No, I will not travel for a couple of engagements on the East Coast before flying back to the U.K. (indeed I doubt I will ever fly again). Here, in the home of my birth, in the fine bedroom my dad and I prepared for me thirty-four years ago, I have laid low, very low. I have had some fruitful days, writing between six and ten hours a day. At last five long-pending articles, all related to mission and church in Sudan, are nearly ready for publication.

As I have regained strength I have delighted in walking for an hour or two through the fields that surround our home in the cool of each evening. Peaches, plums, nectarines, and melons galore are in full harvest and our tables are laden with the largest and sweetest tree-ripened selection (how I wish I could send a basketful to each of you!) Ileostomy or no, I am imbibing to the full.

Having thought I would never regain energy in the wake of this last operation, I can now say that I have come to a degree of stability, despite the feeling that I am carrying a boulder in my belly. I find myself a little hunched and thinner, not certain if I have two weeks or two months or more to hobble along on this dear old earth. I am deeply thankful to our God that I have passed through the bout of weighty depression that followed my last surgery and have come to more amiable terms with my ileostomy.

My oncologist at the Royal Marsden would probably like to put me back on another round of chemotherapy, but I remain uncertain. God has given me two marvelous years (August 18 marks the anniversary of the discovery of cancer). I welcome your prayers that I will make the best use of each day, each hour yet allotted to me, that I will make the right decision regarding whether or not to return to chemo, and that my meditations on life, death, and eternity might have the right balance of sobriety, whimsy, and sheer delight.

As ever, my times are in his hands. Love to you all,

Marc

Epilogue

Marc Randall Nikkel died on Sunday morning, September 3, 2000, at his family home in Reedley, California. On the night before he died his sister Marvis and his brother-in-law Sam were at his bedside:

> Little did we know that in only twelve hours he would no longer be with us, but would be changing his residence forever.... As we came near Marc's bed, Sam led in a most precious time of reflection, focusing on 1 Corinthians 11:23–26. It was so meaningful to us that...this might be the last communion we might have with Marc. The next morning he left us at 5:25 a.m. What a celebration it will be when all of us will be participating in the Greatest Eucharist ever, with Christ leading it with all his children.

Marc was buried in the pine coffin made by his childhood friends, and wrapped in the patchwork quilt, the quilt that reminded him of his heritage, the same quilt he carried on his trek through the bush when he was kidnapped by the Sudanese People's Liberation Army. A Jieng cross lay on his casket at the funeral. He was mourned on three continents. The archbishop of Canterbury said, "In the death of Marc Nikkel we lost an outstanding scholar of Africa and the Sudanese Church, and also a model of self-offering and mutual commitment that should mark our communion and the Christian church around the world." The e-mail from Marvis and Sam on September 4 stated, "He is no longer a Pilgrim, but home...."

The situation in the Sudan has changed since Marc's death. On January 9, 2005, a peace treaty was signed between the government of Sudan and the Sudanese People's Liberation Movement, ending two decades of one of the worst conflicts of the late twentieth century, a war in which between two and three million people died. Enormous amounts of foreign aid will be needed for reconstruction. Six million displaced people will begin to rebuild homes, communities, schools, hospitals, churches, and, if possible, cultures. It is not yet clear if the peace will last, but it does appear at the moment that both sides are tired of fighting. Sadly, the peace treaty does not include the now troubled region of Darfur in the west of the country, where hundreds of thousands of new refugees have been created.

The Episcopal Church of the Sudan is going through its own turmoil. The amazing growth of the last decade and a half has left the church with large numbers of Christians but a dearth of trained leaders. The added confusion and disorder of war has made the always complex task of equipping men and women for leadership in the church into an almost impossible undertaking. In such a situation dissension seems inevitable and, indeed, the church, particularly in the Jieng areas, is experiencing a certain amount of internal conflict.

But the God who has suffered with his people through the horrors of war, will not leave them now. As Bishop Garang persistently reminded the people of his diocese "God has not deserted you." The God whose self-giving love is revealed to us in the cross of Jesus is also the God who brings life from the dead by the power of the Spirit. We can pray with confidence that, by the power of that Spirit, God will continue to bring new life to the beloved people of the Sudan.

Bibliography

Works by Marc Nikkel

"Archibald Shaw 'Machuor': The Only White Man with the Heart of the Jieng." In *Gateway to the Heart of Africa: Missionary Pioneers in Sudan*, edited by Francesco Pierli, Maria Teresa Ratti, and Andrew C. Wheeler. Nairobi: Paulines, 1998, 102–25.

"'Children of Our Fathers' Divinities' or 'Children of Red Foreigners'? Themes in Missionary History and the Rise of an Indigenous Church among the Jieng Bor of Southern Sudan." In *Land of Promise: Church Growth in a Sudan at War*, edited by Andrew C. Wheeler. Nairobi: Paulines, 1998, 61–78.

"Christian Identity in Sudan." Paper delivered to the conference "Religion, Nationalism, and Peace in Sudan." U.S. Institute for Peace. *www.usip.org/religionpeace/rehr/sudanconf/panel 2.html*.

"Contemporary Religious Change among the Dinka." *Journal of Religion in Africa* 22, no. 1 (1992): 78–94.

"The Cross as a Symbol of Regeneration in Jieng Bor Society." In *Land of Promise: Church Growth in a Sudan at War*, edited by Andrew C. Wheeler. Nairobi: Paulines, 1998, 86–114.

"The Cross of Bor Dinka Christians: A Working Christology in the Face of Displacement and Death." *Studies in World Christianity* 1, no. 2 (1995): 160–85.

The Crosses of Dinka Christians. Video. Fox Video Production, 512 Autumn Springs, Suite D, Franklin, TN 37067; *www.foxvp.com*.

"Daniel Sorur Farim Deng: 'Comboni's Adoptive Son.'" In *Announcing the Light: Sudanese Witnesses to the Gospel*, edited by Andrew C. Wheeler. Nairobi: Paulines, 2000, 43–45.

Dinka Christianity: The Origins and Development of Christianity among the Dinka of Sudan with Special Reference to the Songs of Dinka Christians. Faith in Sudan 11. Nairobi: Paulines, 2001. (Published version of "The Origins and Development of Christianity among the Dinka of Sudan, with Special Reference to the Songs of Dinka Christians." Ph.D. dissertation. University of Edinburgh, 1993.)

"ECS Worship and Music: Isolation and Innovation." In *But God Is Not Defeated! Celebrating the Centenary of The Episcopal Church of the Sudan, 1899–1999*, edited by Samuel E. Kayanga and Andrew C. Wheeler. Nairobi: Paulines, 1999, 137–48.

"The First Sudanese Bishop: Daniel Deng Atong." In *But God Is Not Defeated! Celebrating the Centenary of The Episcopal Church of the Sudan, 1899–1999*, edited by Samuel E. Kayanga and Andrew C. Wheeler. Nairobi: Paulines, 1999, 178–94.

"'Hostages of the Situation in Sudan,' 1987: Christian Missionaries in Wartime." *Anglican and Episcopal History* 71, no. 2 (2002): 187–222.

"Jieng 'Songs of Suffering' and the Nature of God." *Anglican and Episcopal History* 71, no. 2 (2002): 223–40.

"'Look Back Upon Us.' The Dynamism of Faith among the Jieng." In *But God Is Not Defeated! Celebrating the Centenary of The Episcopal Church of the Sudan, 1899–1999,* edited by Samuel E. Kayanga and Andrew C. Wheeler. Nairobi: Paulines, 1999, 149–58.

"The Outcast, the Stranger and the Enemy in Dinka Tradition Contrasted with Attitudes of Contemporary Dinka Christians." Unpublished master's thesis. General Theological Seminary, 1988.

"Salim Charles Wilson: 'Black Evangelist of the North.'" In *Announcing the Light: Sudanese Witnesses to the Gospel,* edited by Andrew C. Wheeler. Nairobi: Paulines, 2000, 46–49.

"Songs of Hope and Lamentation from Sudan's Unaccompanied Minors." *Sewanee Theological Review* 40 (1997): 486–98.

Other Works Cited

Abuyi, Sapana A. "'From the Margins to the Centre': Jonathan Mamuru and the Evangelists of the Jur." In *Announcing the Light: Sudanese Witnesses to the Gospel,* edited by Andrew C. Wheeler. Nairobi: Paulines, 2000, 122–47.

Adamo, David Tuesday. *Africa and Africans in the Old Testament.* San Francisco: International Scholars Publications, 1998.

Alier, Abel. *Southern Sudan: Too Many Agreements Dishonoured.* Sudan Studies Series 13. Exeter, U.K.: Ithaca Press, 1990; Khartoum: Abel Alier, 2003.

Anglican Church of Kenya. *Our Modern Services.* Nairobi: Uzima, 2002.

Arenson, Jonathan. "Bringing Christ to the Murle: A Culturally Sensitive Approach." In *Land of Promise: Church Growth in a Sudan at War,* edited by Andrew C. Wheeler. Nairobi: Paulines, 1998, 115–28.

———. "Conversion among the Uduk: Continuity versus Discontinuity." In *Land of Promise: Church Growth in a Sudan at War,* edited by Andrew C. Wheeler. Nairobi: Paulines, 1998, 79–85.

Bediako, Kwame. *Christianity in Africa: The Renewal of a Non-Western Religion.* Maryknoll, N.Y.: Orbis, 1995.

Bok, Francis, and Edward Tivnan. *Escape from Slavery: The True Story of My Ten Years in Captivity — and My Journey to Freedom in America.* New York: St. Martin's, 2003.

Caramazza, Giuseppe. "Comboni Brothers: For Integral Human Development." In *Gateway to the Heart of Africa: Missionary Pioneers in Sudan,* edited by Francesco Pierli, Maria Teresa Ratti, and Andrew C. Wheeler. Nairobi: Paulines, 1998, 59–71.

Dinka-Bor Hymnal. Episcopal Church of the Sudan, 1998.

Evans-Pritchard, E. E. *The Nuer: A Description of the Modes of Livelihood and Political Institutions of a Nilotic People.* Oxford: Oxford University Press, 1940.

———. *Nuer Religion.* Oxford: Clarendon, 1956.

———. *Witchcraft, Oracles and Magic among the Azande.* Oxford: Clarendon, 1967 (1937).

Fraser, Eileen. *The Doctor Comes to Lui: A Story of Beginnings in the Sudan.* Cape Town: Frontline Fellowship, 2000 (1938).

Glendon, Mary Ann. "Sudan's Unpunished Atrocities." *New York Times*, December 8, 1998, A-31.

Jackson, H. C. *Pastor on the Nile: A Memoir of Bishop Ll. H. Gwynne.* London: SPCK, 1960.

Kayanga, Samuel. "Archbishop Elinana J. Ngalamu." In *But God Is Not Defeated! Celebrating the Centenary of The Episcopal Church of the Sudan, 1899–1999,* edited by Samuel E. Kayanga and Andrew C. Wheeler. Nairobi: Paulines, 1999, 181–82.

———. "CMS in the Nuba Mountains." In *But God Is Not Defeated! Celebrating the Centenary of The Episcopal Church of the Sudan, 1899–1999,* edited by Samuel E. Kayanga and Andrew C. Wheeler. Nairobi: Paulines, 1999, 80–82.

———. " 'Faith, Integrity and Freedom': Elinana Jabi Ngalamu (1917–1992)." In *Announcing the Light: Sudanese Witnesses to the Gospel,* edited by Andrew C. Wheeler. Nairobi: Paulines, 2000, 230–52.

———. "Miracles in the Episcopal Church of the Sudan: The Testimony of the Bishop Henry Riak." In *But God Is Not Defeated! Celebrating the Centenary of The Episcopal Church of the Sudan, 1899–1999,* edited by Samuel E. Kayanga and Andrew C. Wheeler. Nairobi: Paulines, 1999, 135–36.

Kayanga, Samuel E., and Abe Enosa. "The Miracle of Reconciliation in the ECS Juba, 1 November 1992." In *But God Is Not Defeated! Celebrating the Centenary of The Episcopal Church of the Sudan, 1899–1999,* edited by Samuel E. Kayanga and Andrew C. Wheeler. Nairobi: Paulines, 1999, 159–64.

Kayanga, Samuel E., and Andrew C. Wheeler, editors. *But God Is Not Defeated! Celebrating the Centenary of The Episcopal Church of the Sudan, 1899–1999.* Nairobi: Paulines, 1999.

LeMarquand, Grant. "Appropriation of the Cross among the Jieng People of Southern Sudan." *Journal of Inculturation Theology* 5, no. 2 (2003): 176–98.

———. "Bibles, Crosses, Songs, Guns and Oil: Sudanese "Readings" of the Bible in the midst of Civil War." *African Narrative Readings of the Bible: Essays in Honour of Prof John Mbiti.* Ed. Justin Ukpong. Forthcoming.

———. "A Faithful Descendent: *Our Modern Services Anglican Church of Kenya 2002.*" In *The Book of Common Prayer Worldwide.* Ed. Charles Hefling and Cynthia Shaddick. Oxford: Oxford University Press, forthcoming.

———. *An Issue of Relevance: A Comparative Study of the Story of the Bleeding Woman (Mk 5:25–34; Mt 9:20–22; Lk 8:43–48) in North Atlantic and African Contexts.* Bible and Theology in Africa 5. New York: Peter Lang, 2004.

Lowrey, William. " 'Passing the Peace': The Role of Religion in Peacemaking among the Nuer in Sudan." In *Land of Promise: Church Growth in a Sudan at War,* edited by Andrew C. Wheeler. Nairobi: Paulines, 1998, 129–49.

Malou Ater, John. "The Dinka Priesthood." Unpublished master's thesis. Near East School of Theology (Beirut), 1976.

———. *Out of Confusion.* Nairobi: African Christian Press, 1973.

Marshall, Paul, editor. *Religious Freedom in the World: A Global Report on Freedom and Persecution.* Nashville: Broadman & Holman, 2000.

Marshall, Paul, with Lela Gilbert. *Their Blood Cries Out: The Untold Story of Persecution against Christians in the Modern World*. Dallas: Word, 1997.

Martin, Randolf. "Sudan's Perfect War." *Foreign Affairs* (March–April 2002): 111–25.

Mbiti, John S. *African Religions and Philosophy*. 2nd rev. ed. Oxford: Heinemann, 1990.

Nazer, Mende, and Damien Lewis. *Slave: My True Story*. New York: Public Affairs, 2004.

Nhial, Abraham, and DiAnn Mills. *Lost Boy No More: A True Story of Survival and Salvation*. Nashville: Broadman & Holman, 2004.

Nouwen, Henri. *Compassion: A Reflection on the Christian Life*. New York: Image, 1983.

Partee, Charles. *Adventure in Africa: The Story of Don McClure: from Khartoum to Addis Ababa in Five Decades*. Lanham, Md.: University Press of America, 2000.

Pierli, Francesco. "Daniel Comboni: An Unquenchable Passion for Africa." *Gateway to the Heart of Africa: Missionary Pioneers in Sudan*, edited by Francesco Pierli, Maria Teresa Ratti, and Andrew C. Wheeler. Nairobi: Paulines, 1998, 26–58.

Pierli, Francesco, Maria Teresa Ratti, and Andrew C. Wheeler, editors. *Gateway to the Heart of Africa: Missionary Pioneers in Sudan*, edited by Francesco Pierli, Maria Teresa Ratti, and Andrew C. Wheeler. Faith in Sudan 5. Nairobi: Paulines, 1998.

Ratti, Maria Teresa. "Comboni Sisters: Missionary Women in the Evangelization of the Sudan." In *Gateway to the Heart of Africa: Missionary Pioneers in Sudan*, edited by Francesco Pierli, Maria Teresa Ratti, and Andrew C. Wheeler. Nairobi: Paulines, 1998, 72–85.

Rone, Jemera, et al. *Civilian Devastation: Abuses by All Parties in the War in Southern Sudan*. New York: Human Rights Watch/Africa, 1994.

Salopek, Paul. "Shattered Sudan: Drilling for Oil, Hoping for Peace." *National Geographic* 203, no. 2 (2003): 30–59.

Sharland, Roger W. "Kenneth Grant Fraser: Mission, Evangelism and Development among the Moru." In *Gateway to the Heart of Africa: Missionary Pioneers in Sudan*, edited by Francesco Pierli, Maria Teresa Ratti, and Andrew C. Wheeler. Nairobi: Paulines, 1998, 146–60.

Stancliffe, David. "The Salisbury-Sudan Link." In *But God Is Not Defeated! Celebrating the Centenary of The Episcopal Church of the Sudan, 1899–1999*, edited by Samuel E. Kayanga and Andrew C. Wheeler. Nairobi: Paulines, 1999, 195–97.

Taylor, John V. *The Primal Vision: Christian Presence amid African Religion*. London: SCM, 1963.

Tingwa, Peter Obadayo. *The History of the Moru Church in Sudan*. Nairobi: Sudan Literature Center, n.d.

United Nations Security Council. Report of May 10, 2005. *www.iss.co.za/AF/profiles/Sudan/darfur/unrep10may05.pdf*.

Walls, Andrew F. *The Cross-Cultural Process in Christian History: Studies in the Transmission and Appropriation of Faith*. Maryknoll, N.Y.: Orbis, 2002.

———. *The Missionary Movement in Christian History: Studies in the Transmission of Faith*. Maryknoll, N.Y.: Orbis, 1996.

Werner, Roland, William Anderson, and Andrew C. Wheeler. *Day of Devastation, Day of Contentment: The History of the Sudanese Church across 2000 Years.* Faith in Sudan 10. Nairobi: Paulines, 2000.

Wheeler, Andrew C. "Church Growth in Southern Sudan 1983–1996: A Survey of Present Understanding." In *Land of Promise: Church Growth in a Sudan at War,* edited by Andrew C. Wheeler. Nairobi: Paulines, 1998, 11–38.

———. "The Church Missionary Society." In *But God Is Not Defeated! Celebrating the Centenary of The Episcopal Church of the Sudan, 1899–1999,* edited by Samuel E. Kayanga and Andrew C. Wheeler. Nairobi: Paulines, 1999, 51–52.

———. "Introduction — Church Growth: But How Deep Are the Roots?" In *Land of Promise: Church Growth in a Sudan at War,* edited by Andrew C. Wheeler. Nairobi: Paulines, 1998, 7–10.

———. " 'Life in the Village of God': Training for Ministry in the Episcopal Church, 1947–1999." In *But God Is Not Defeated! Celebrating the Centenary of The Episcopal Church of the Sudan, 1899–1999,* edited by Samuel E. Kayanga and Andrew C. Wheeler. Nairobi: Paulines, 1999, 99–116.

Wheeler, Andrew C., editor. *Announcing the Light: Sudanese Witnesses to the Gospel.* Faith in Sudan 6. Nairobi: Paulines, 2000.

———, editor. *Land of Promise: Church Growth in a Sudan at War.* Faith in Sudan 1. Nairobi: Paulines, 1998.

Wheeler, Andrew C., and Gordon Tikiba. "The Missionary Bishops." In *But God Is Not Defeated! Celebrating the Centenary of The Episcopal Church of the Sudan, 1899–1999,* edited by Samuel E. Kayanga and Andrew C. Wheeler. Nairobi: Paulines, 1999, 83–93.

Yamauchi, Edwin M. *Africa and the Bible.* Grand Rapids, Mich.: Baker, 2004.

Yukusuk, Paul. "Archbishop Benjamin Wani Yukusuk." In *But God Is Not Defeated! Celebrating the Centenary of The Episcopal Church of the Sudan, 1899–1999,* edited by Samuel E. Kayanga and Andrew C. Wheeler. Nairobi: Paulines, 1999, 183–84.